WITHDRAWN
L. R. COLLEGE LIBRARY

T5-BBY-795

954.0317
L49r

142767

DATE DUE			

The Rani of Jhansi

The Rani of Jhansi in battle. An example of contemporary poster art.

The Rani of Jhansi

A Study in Female Heroism in India

Joyce Lebra-Chapman

CARL A. RUDISILL LIBRARY
LENOIR RHYNE COLLEGE

University of Hawaii Press
HONOLULU

© 1986 University of Hawaii Press
All Rights Reserved
Manufactured in the United States of America

Library of Congress Cataloging-in-Publication Data

Lebra-Chapman, Joyce, 1925–
The Rani of Jhansi.

Bibliography: p.
Includes index.
1. Lakshmi Bai, Rani of Jhansi, d. 1858. 2. India—History—Sepoy Rebellion, 1857–1858. 3. Heroines—India. 4. Legends—India—History and criticism. 5. Revolutionists—India—Biography. I. Title.
DS475.2.L34L43 1986 954.03'17'0924 85-20677
ISBN 0-8248-0984-X

954.0317
L49r
142767
Nov. 1987

For Gurbakhsh,

Billo and Ajay, and the people of Jhansi

Contents

Preface

The Rani of Jhansi is a household name in India, her story the subject of primary school readers and comic books. And yet, few Westerners other than those with a serious interest in India are aware that a little more than a century ago a young woman, the widow of the maharaja of Jhansi, fought for her state in Central India and died valorously in battle against soldiers of the East India Company.

While working on a book on the Indian National Army I learned of the women's unit called the Rani of Jhansi Regiment. This unit, named by Subhas Chandra Bose, aroused my interest and prompted me to turn from World War II and the struggle for independence waged by the INA back to the rebellion of 1857 and in particular to look at the role played by this extraordinary woman, Rani Lakshmibai of Jhansi.

A story lives through its narrators and listeners. British sources provide one side of the Rani's story, but the image of this woman has largely been shaped by the celebration of her spirit and valor in poetry, ballad, folktale, and drama throughout India. This popular, indigenous tradition is an important source for understanding the Rani's life and especially her legend. Her epic struggle against a superior power has made her a compelling legend and gained her a kind of immortality in popular Indian culture. The layerings of her image inform the collective memory of the nation; her story continues to be told by the poets of Bundelkhand. Her history as recorded by the English is therefore not enough.

Lakshmibai became the raw material of noble aspirations and idealistic visions. It also became apparent to me that her legend, told during the last half of the nineteenth and early twentieth centuries, fed into the stream of growing nationalism. She became a potent political symbol, a symbol that is being reinterpreted in fresh ways even today.

Convinced that the Rani would capture the imagination of Western readers even as Joan of Arc did, I embarked on the present study. I visited Jhansi, Kalpi, Gwalior, Lucknow, and Kanpur, saw the forts where she fought and died, and taped the poetry and songs still sung by poets in Jhansi and Gwalior. I consulted the National Archives and Nehru Memorial Museum Library in New Delhi and the India Office Library and British Museum in London. I used the Ames Library collection on South Asia at the University of Minnesota. I sought the counsel and assistance of Indian scholars and archivists, in particular historians in Gwalior and Jhansi. And I listened to recollections by residents of Gwalior and Jhansi of tales told them by parents and grandparents, tales that form the oral legend of Lakshmibai.

I became intrigued by the process by which a historical figure is transformed into a legend. What is the genesis of such a process and through what stages does it pass? How and why is it that the story of this particular woman has been transmitted across so many generations of Indians through ballad, song, and folktale, through plastic, visual, and performing arts, to more modern evocations in cinema? What was the political impact of the image and metaphor of the Rani during the period of developing nationalism? What sources of Hindu civilization were tapped or activated to produce so powerful an impact, so potent a myth?

The Rani, like Joan of Arc, supersedes the available Western taxonomy of female archetypes; both were beyond the categories of wife, mother, temptress, and witch. But unlike Joan, whose legendary status brought her sainthood, the Rani could ride goddesslike to immortality. The Hindu image of female heroism afforded a richer matrix within which the Rani legend could incubate. Her exploits and valorous semblance proclaimed the Rani's bravery and spirit in the classical Hindu idiom. Thus she was able to surpass the Western lexicon of female heroism and to become the most famous of all Asian heroines.

This book is an attempt to discover why she became transmuted into a legend that is lodged permanently in the hearts of Indians. It is also an attempt to make her as real to Westerners as she is to Indians. What follows, then, is necessarily part history and part mythology, part fact and part reflections of the fact, concerned both with popular mythmaking and with political manipulation in the interests of a national movement.

It would be impossible to acknowledge adequately the advice, suggestions, assistance, and encouragement I received in the course of researching this volume over a period of four or five years in several countries. I would nevertheless like to mention a few individuals whose contributions were invaluable.

In Delhi: Ajay and Billo Jain, S. N. Prasad, the late Jaya Appasamy, Ravinder Kumar, Dr. Panigrahi, V. C. Joshi, Bimla Prasad, and Hari Dev Sharma

In Jhansi: Col. G. S. Dhillon of Shivpuri, B. D. Gupta, P. K. Samadhiya, B. K. Misra, Rekha Singh, Shri Avadesh, Peggy Cantem, Mr. and Mrs. Ralph Seefeldt, Margaret Vigeland and Iona Hepner, J. L. Kanchan, Romesh Chaube, and Chhaki Lal Verma

In Gwalior: Hari Har Nivas Dvivedi and Rituraj Dvivedi, Arthur Hughes, and Jaya Ram Jakhenia

In Nagpur: Dr. and Mrs. E. G. Tambe and Vasant Varkhedkar

In Datia: Basudev Goswamy

In Calcutta: Sisir and Krishna Bose

In Kanpur: Prem and Lakshmi Sahgal

In London: Martin Moir and Andrew Cook of the India Office Library and K. A. Ballhatchet of the School of Oriental and African Studies

In Cambridge: the late Eric Stokes

In Minneapolis: Henry Scholberg, Ames Library

In Boulder: Robert Lester, Chandran Kaimal, Ronald Bernier, and Paul Levitt

In Durham, North Carolina: Jack Cell

In Melbourne: Ian Copland

For financial support during the spring of 1983 I am grateful to the U.S. Sub-Commission on Education and Culture for an Indo-American Fellowship; also to P. R. Mehendiratta and Mr. Suri and the staff of the American Institute for Indian Studies in New Delhi for logistic support.

For translation of much of two volumes of B. D. Mahor's work on Lakshmibai and the events of 1857, I am indebted to Niti Mahanti of New Delhi. B. D. Gupta of Jhansi kindly provided translations of portions of works by Hardikar, Parasnis, and Vrindan Lal Verma. Translations of poetry were almost entirely provided by Col. G. S. Dhillon, himself an Urdu poet of note. In some of the translations he was assisted by Rekha Singh of Jhansi and P. P. Soti and Mohan Aterkar of Gwalior. For translations of the poems and songs performed for me by the women of the Nagpur Rashtra Sevika Samiti I am also indebted to Pramila Medhe. Billo Jain translated portions of V. Varkhedkar's novel on Tatya Tope and also furnished a translation of the song sung by the Sepoys in 1957, recorded from the voice of B. D. Mahor.

For help in unraveling the mysteries and marvels of the word processor I am grateful to Nancy Mann and Ray Cuzzort.

The convention adopted by the author for transliterating Indian names beginning with the initial sound *sh* is to use *Sh* rather than *S* with diacritical markings, therefore, Shiva, Shakti, and so on. The modern spelling of Indian names is used except in quotations, where the original spelling is preserved.

Responsibility for errors of fact or interpretation, of course, rests with the author alone.

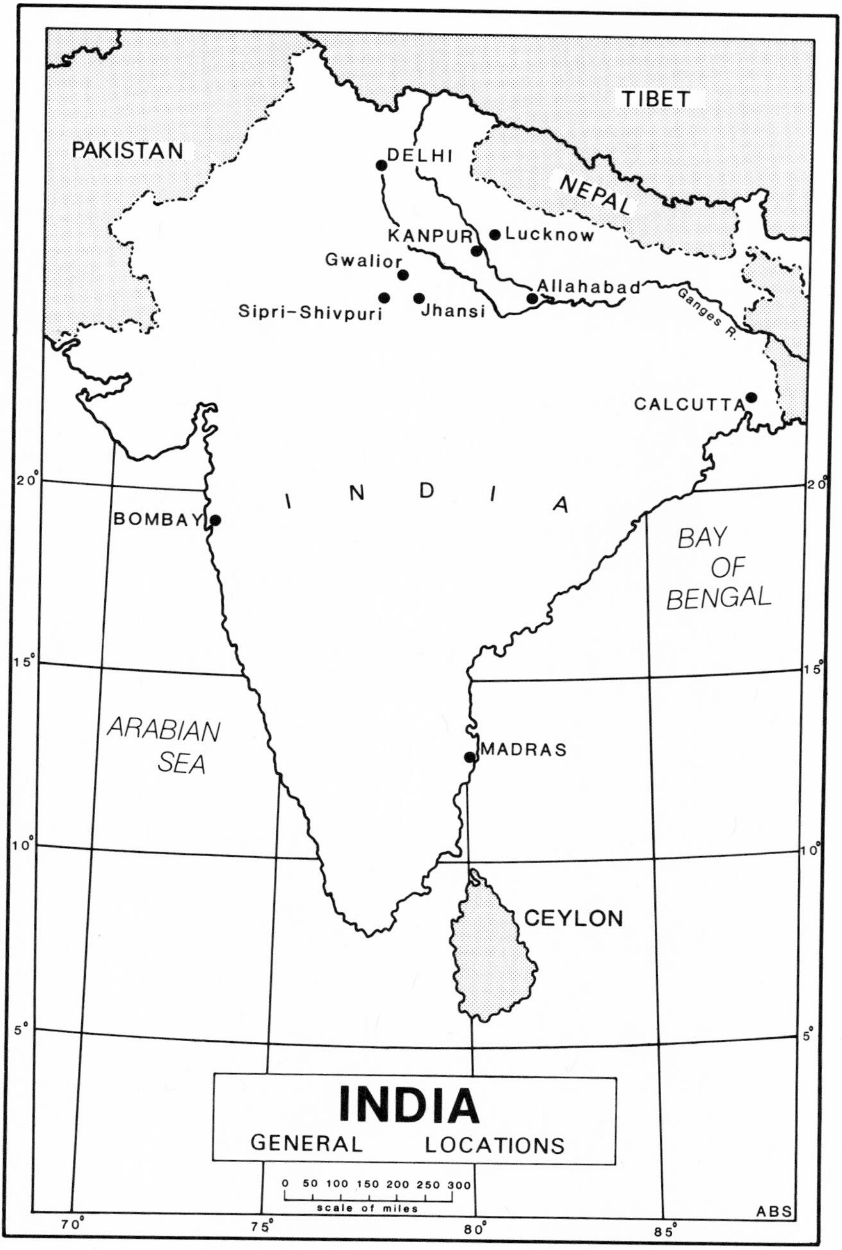

Map by Brent Schmocker

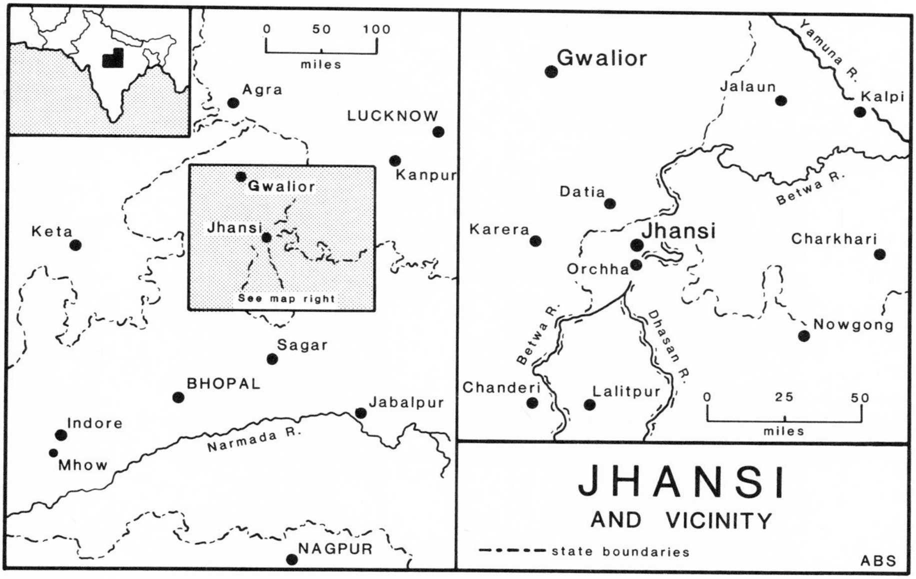

Map by Brent Schmocker

Introduction

Once or twice in a millennium a hero or heroine transcends history and passes into legend. Why? In the case of the Rani it was because she served a yearning for absolute goodness and bravery and a need for a national symbol. It is surprising that so little has been written about her. Joan of Arc, with whom she has often been compared, has inspired over twelve thousand volumes in French alone, not to mention a long list in English, and is said to be the most written-about individual of the fifteenth century. A few novels, plays, and biographies of the Rani have been written in Indian languages, but the better part of Indian sources on the Rani are unpublished. They consist of ballads, poetry, folktales, and stories in a tradition perpetuated orally by the people of Bundelkhand and retold whenever poets gather.

This popular outpouring from the folk culture is perhaps more important for reconstructing the life and legend of the Rani than are the scant written sources extant in Indian languages. Her legend, which broadens its appeal through relying on familiar formulas, informs us importantly about Indian images of female heroism. In Indian history and culture, legend is often more important than fact, since legends proliferate spontaneously through their close connection with folk or rustic culture and their lack of dependence on literary traditions. Mythification is a potent force and feature of Indian civilization and is a significant part of the legacy of the Rani.

The Rani lived and died against the backdrop of the Great Rebellion of 1857, called by the English the Sepoy Mutiny. It was without doubt the most written-about event of three centuries and more of British presence in India. Hundreds of military memoirs and regimental histories chronicled the events of 1857 from the British perspective and witnessed the horror and shock felt by English men and women both at home and in India. The Indian perspective was of course different, and Indian historians for many years have described the Rebellion as the first phase of India's war of independence, a glorious war fought by passionate heroic patriots.

The Rebellion was a watershed in the history of British India, preceded as it was by control by the East India Company and followed by rule by the British Crown. It also marked a turning point in relations between the English and the Indians. Earlier decades saw friendships and marriages between the two and relatively cordial relations in some parts of India, for example the Punjab. Post-Rebellion relations, on the other hand, were marked by hatred, anger, and suspicion in the wake of the violence of 1857 and 1858. Blood shed on both sides escalated a desire for vengeance that affected relations for another century. Because the Rebellion produced such a great impact both on the growth of Indian nationalism and on the English colonial imagination, it has also generated much historical debate. Was it, as nineteenth and early twentieth-century Indian historians had it, a war of independence, or at least the first stage in such a struggle? Or was it, as the English believed, simply a revolt of Sepoys, an Anglicization of "sipahi," the soldiers who manned the British-Indian Army under officers whose higher ranks were virtually all English? Were its causes limited to the kinds of complaints felt by Sepoys—matters such as postings overseas that caused them to lose caste and discrimination in pay and promotion and access to officers' clubs? Or were there signs of wider malaise that affected other sectors of the populace, for example, economic distress and dispossession of landed classes and rulers of princely states?

The causes of these series of events were themselves diverse and complex and, as such, are still the subject of continuing discussion among both Indian and English historians. I note briefly here some of the major issues that will be treated more fully in later chapters. In the decade prior to 1857 several states were annexed as part of the policy of the "lapse" enunciated and implemented by Governor-General Dalhousie. Dalhousie decided to resume control of states whose rulers died without natural heirs, or who on their deathbeds adopted heirs, in accordance with Hindu custom. Among these states was Jhansi, ruled first by the husband of the Rani and, after his death, by Lakshmibai herself. The annexation of these states was resented by their Indian rulers, as the Rani's protests and memorials attest. Another series of causes relates to the sentiments of Indians and to rumors that circulated in villages and markets, especially in North India and the region called Bundelkhand that included Jhansi. Suppression of such social practices as sati, or widow-burning, and thugi, or religious murder, was resented among some classes. More widespread was the fear of forcible conversion to Christianity, a fear fed by the presence of missionaries in various parts of India. Rumors circulated that flour sold in the markets contained ground cows' bones.

Other rumors were less tangible and in some cases reached the ears of only a few English, who at times were at a loss to interpret them. Some of these rumors lay in the realm of myth or folk culture. Among Indians, for example, it was generally known that many Brahmins had predicted that the English would be driven from India one hundred years after the Battle of Plassey, fought in 1757. From this perspective, the hour of the English had come. Another phenomenon puzzling to the English who heard of it was the circulation of chapattis through the countryside of North India from village to village. What this portended was not clear to officers of the Raj. Some English recalled the circulation of chapattis prior to the outbreak at Vellore in 1906; others suggested it might be designed to prevent an outbreak of cholera. Yet no one knew what it portended.

One of the most notorious of the causes of the Rebellion was the introduction of the new Enfield rifles, whose percussion caps were greased with the fat of cows and pigs and thus defiling to Hindu and Muslim alike. This, if nothing else, served to unite the Sepoys in their antagonism to their officers and helped to precipitate the first spark of revolt when those officers called their men to parade to prove their loyalty. (For a fuller discussion of debates over the causes and historiography of the Rebellion see the historiographical essay at the end of the text.)

About the Rani's role in the events of the Rebellion there is also much scope for dispute among historians, English and Indian alike. Was the massacre of the sixty-six English men, women, and children at Jhansi in 1857 done at her order? Was she in fact aware of the plans of the Sepoys before they were carried out? Could she have done anything to prevent the massacre had she known of it in advance? Whatever the answers to these and other questions about her role in the Jhansi uprising, there can be no doubt about her exploits from late March through June of 1858, when she engaged in battle at the forts of Jhansi, Kalpi, and finally Gwalior, where she died in action.

Another issue of vital interest to the historian concerns the process of the metamorphosis of the Rani of Jhansi into a rebel. How and why did she go from a maharaja's widow with a working relationship with English officials in Jhansi to a rebel leader, one of the principal commanders of the forces that held out in Central India for nearly a year after the recapture of Delhi by the British? What were the major events or psychological changes in this woman that made the metamorphosis possible if not inevitable? And what was her relationship to the other major rebel leaders, Tatya Tope, Nana Sahib, and Rao Sahib? Whether or not the Rani was actively implicated in the events at Jhansi, the assumption that she was involved became the official position of English administrators, who planned to bring her to trial and punish her for her alleged complicity. Official India remained unconvinced of her innocence and helplessness against the rebels, innocence she professed in her letters following the outbreak at Jhansi.

Finally is the question of whether the Rani was a conscious nationalist or simply a ruler fighting for her small state. She left no diary, memoirs, or letters other than those written in protest to officials in Fort William (present-day Calcutta). Assessment of her motives is thus a problem. Whether or not Lakshmibai actually wrote the memorials to Calcutta herself is beside the point. There is evidence from British official accounts that she was a most skilled and spirited debater, more than able to meet English officials on their own legalistic ground. In any event, the memorials expressed her strong objections. And while she may not have argued for the independence of an Indian nation, she did in her memorials make a lucid case—even if it failed to persuade opinion in Fort William—for the return of Jhansi to her rule as regent for her late husband's adopted heir and for the legitimacy of Hindu custom in this regard. The question of whether the Rani was an early nationalist or fighting only for her own state in a sense poses a false dichotomy. And to argue that her contribution was principally in her fight in Jhansi and death at Gwalior is not to detract from the importance of that contribution to the growth of nationalism.

In postwar independent India and even among communities of Indians overseas, the meaning of the Rani is being reinterpreted in new ways. She is being read, for example, as a feminist, as a champion of the rights of labor and of the cause of the oppressed in places far beyond her home.

1

Jhansi and the Rani

Trained she was in the martial arts . . .
The spear and sword, arrows and bow

—*From a popular poem by Subhadra Kumari Chauhan*

Geographic Setting

The life and legend of the Rani have their genesis in the heartland of India, where today is situated the town of Jhansi, formerly a small princely state. Jhansi lies south of the Gangetic basin and Yamuna River and north of the outer scarps of the Vindhya mountain chain on a vast dusty, rocky, nearly treeless plain. Scrub and tamarind thorn growth is all that subsists today in the arid, sparsely watered soil, providing scant forage for cattle, buffalo, goats, and sheep. Where wells and irrigation are sufficient, wheat, rice, and gram crops can be grown. Accounts of a century ago describe dense, forested jungle in the hinterland surrounding Jhansi. The rainfall may have warranted the description at that time, but in no sense was it even then the kind of impenetrable jungle found in Southeast Asia.

Igneous sandstone rock outcroppings rising abruptly from the level, barren plain punctuate the landscape and provide ideal natural defensive sites for the forts built throughout the Bundelkhand heartland by warlike Maratha and Bundela rajas and Delhi sultans. From a distance these rocky outcrops are often themselves mistaken for forts, so abruptly do they rise to command the surrounding plains.

The state of Jhansi was from all indications approximately 3,000 square miles in area in the early 1850s. A map of 1863 shows that the district had shrunk to 1,471 square miles in area; part of the state had been handed over to Gwalior by the English in 1861 as a reward for Maharaja Jayaji Rao Scindia's loyalty during the Rebellion. By 1909 the district had again been enlarged to 3,634 square miles, part of it reannexed from Gwalior in 1886.[1]

In a part of India known as Bundelkhand, Jhansi was bounded to the north and northwest by Jaloun district and the native states of Datia, Samthar, and Gwalior. To the west Jhansi's neighbors were Gwalior and Khaniadhana, with the boundary line formed for a distance of over sixty miles by the Betwa River. To the south was the British district of Saugor. Jhansi was adjoined on the east by the state of Orchha, with the dividing line marked for over thirty-six miles first by the Jamni River, then by the Dhasan River. The Jhansi border with Orchha brought that state to within three miles of Jhansi town. Moreover, Jhansi's borders with all its neighboring states were interlaced in an intricate maze that defied symmetry. Some villages enclosed within Jhansi's borders actually belonged to the maharajas of Orchha, Datia, and Samthar, a fact that provided an irritant to perpetuate old rivalries among these neighboring states.

To the north, the level, barren plains are relieved by rocky hills and ravine-cut river beds, and the soil stretching north to the Yamuna is called "black cotton soil." In the south, as the plain extends to the scarps of the Vindhya range, it is scarred by deep nullahs and rocky outcroppings, with red gritty soil that supports only scrub growth. These rocky outcrops disappear to the west but deepen to the east into a maze of ravines and intersecting deep-bedded streams reaching toward the town of Kalpi on the road to Kanpur. Most of the central part of the district around Jhansi is a stony waste of reddish soil with scrub growth and acacia or tamarind thorn trees. Streams and rivers meander northeast toward the Yamuna, Betwa, Dhasan, Pahuj, and Jamni rivers, being fringed by a wide belt of rocky ravines useless for cultivation except for scattered patches of alluvial soil. The rocky escarpments are primarily gneiss formations, those in the south forming ridges running northeast-southwest.

Both the soil and rainfall of Bundelkhand are ungenerous. During the hot weather streams dry up and often disappear completely. The monsoon rains swell them into torrents that cut ever-deeper ravines before disgorging onto the countryside around. This is typical of the Betwa, Jhansi's largest river. This part of Central India is particularly dependent on rainfall and vulnerable, accordingly, to alternating cycles of agricultural prosperity and depression. Irrigation is not sufficiently widespread to provide a stable supply for all seasons. The whole area suffers from continual excessive drainage, erosion, and leaching of the soil, a process arrested in some places by the building of tanks and reservoirs of square stone, which also function for irrigation. If the harsh climate and poor soil were not enough, Bundelkhand is also marked by a prehistoric scourge—a weed called kans, whose roots extend five to seven feet below ground rendering the soil impervious to the plough.[2]

By early March or even February the millions of people living on the plains of Central India between the Ganges and the Vindhyas can feel that the cold of winter has passed and the hot season is well under way. The earth begins to dry up, and at this time a heavy rain is not necessarily a blessing to farmers hoping for a good harvest. By mid-April the parched earth cracks open as the temperature climbs well above 100 degrees. Mid-May finds the mercury closer to 120 in the shade. Flowers and plants shrivel, people walk more slowly, and by ten in the morning birds quiet down and lassitude overtakes all forms of life. Only crows and quail have the energy to challenge the heat of mid-afternoon to make their shrill presence known. The relief of dusk permits a renewal of hesitant activity. Only the scrawny tamarind trees seem to thrive during this hot season. The scorching dry windstorms of late April and early May incinerate insects, even mosquitos.

May and June of 1857 and 1858 found most of the English in the area suffering, as in other years, from various forms of dysentery, hepatitis, malaria, typhoid, cholera, and often from a combination of two or more diseases. A walk through any foreigners' cemetery of a century ago in India confirms the heavy toll these diseases took and the resulting low life expectancy. A gravemarker for a person over fifty is a rarity, and graves of children abound. It is not that the Indians lived longer, but perhaps they had immunity to some bacteria to which the English were vulnerable. The English soldier, accoutered in a high-collared, long-sleeved military uniform and carrying a heavy pack and rifle, had a less-than-even chance before the first shot was fired. Two hours in the searing midday sun was all the average Englishman could endure before collapsing from sunstroke and heat exhaustion. It was, as Gen. Hugh Rose remarked, a matter of simple arithmetic to calculate how long his force could fight under such conditions against native forces more accustomed to and prepared for the scorching glare of the sun.

Dust storms are another unpleasant feature of Jhansi's climate. Anyone who has experienced the burning winds of March and April in this part of the country understands why these winds are called locally "the devil's breath." These winds are often accompanied by paralyzing dust storms that cast a lurid light over everything. At night they can be terrifying, stopping humans and animals dead in their tracks.

Fort and Palace

As you approach Jhansi from whatever direction, the first thing that catches the eye is the fort. Built atop Bangra Hill and overlooking the old town to the east, the massive stone structure commands the countryside for many miles. The Bundela chief of Orchha, Bir Singh, built the fort in 1613 as part of a defensive circle of forts which included the larger fortresses of Orchha and Datia nearby. The Jhansi fort is constructed of huge blocks of reddish sandstone, the principal building material of the Bundela Rajputs. It is roughly square in plan, with an outer wall following the contour of the hill and enclosing not only the fort but also the old town north and east of the fort. The larger outwork is approximately three miles in circumference and contains ten gates. The fort walls are fortified with twenty-four bastions, the largest of which is the city bastion facing the main gate looking south. The walls are six to eight feet thick and battlemented around the top with gun emplacements cut at short intervals all the way around the main fort wall for defensive security. Part of the fort is protected by three tiers of battlemented walls. The second of the two gates to the fort faces north-

Fig. 1. Jhansi fort

east toward the old city. Access to the main gate today traverses a barren plain, which a century ago connected the fort with the British cantonment.

Inside the main gate of the fort stands a cannon thirty inches in diameter, which is said to have been manned by Jhansi's famous gunner Gulam Ghaus Khan, a Pathan, or valayati (Afghan mercenary). This gunner is reputed to have taught the famous dancer Moti Bai to fire the cannon. People in Jhansi say Moti Bai was a courtesan of the maharaja and that she also joined the Rani's women's army. The gravestones of Gulam and Moti Bai lie together, near the cannon, within the fort. Another famous cannon in the fort is said to have shattered the best gun of Nathe Khan, who invaded Jhansi from neighboring Orchha shortly before the Rebellion.

The old town still abuts the northeast wall of the fort. In the northeast corner of the fort an extension was built onto the original by Naro Shankar, the Maratha subahdar of Jhansi, and is named after him. He is credited with enlarging the town as well, and in all probability he added to an earlier village.

Like most forts built by Indian kings and princes, the Jhansi fort was virtually invulnerable to siege. Forts generally had an internal supply of water that enabled them to hold out against prolonged siege. Bribery to induce someone inside to open the gates was historically the most effective means of reducing a fort,[3] a critical point to remember when considering fortifications and tactics of warfare in India.

Inside the fort stand two Hindu temples: one near the northeast gate, the temple to the elephant-headed god Ganesha, and a Shiva temple at the bottom of a staircase. Today, as formerly, this temple is the focus of Jhansi's Shivaratri festival in February.

The inner fort contained quarters for troops, a palace residence, or mahal, used by the Rani, a well to supply water in case of siege, a prison, and an execution platform. It also featured a garden in the northeast corner of the courtyard, which the Rani and her army were said to have enjoyed.

The Rani's mahal was, as much as the fort, central to her story. Like the fort, it was said to have been built during the governorship of Shankar and is approximately seven hundred yards from the fort as the crow flies. These two facts—that the palace was built by Shankar's order and was quite close to the fort—lend credence to the belief still widespread in Jhansi that an underground tunnel connects palace and fort. Townspeople say that tunnels radiate from every fort in Central India in various directions. Some of these tunnels purportedly run to a distance of up to sixty miles, as in the Jhansi and Gwalior forts. While construction of these reputed tunnels does not appear plausible (existing technology did not and does not make it feasible to dig a tunnel of this length that would run not only underground but also under rivers), it is nevertheless possible that a tunnel may have run between the Jhansi fort and palace, since most forts in this part of India were in fact provided with short tunnels from inside to outside the fort walls to provide for secret escape. Some in Jhansi say that they have seen the tunnel entrance inside the fort. It is also possible that the tunnel entrance, if it existed, was simply the entrance to an underground chamber to be used during hot weather or in times of danger. Such rooms still can be found under some old houses in Jhansi.

The palace is a two-story stucco structure. A local legend holds that the palace was originally four stories high but that the British destroyed the upper two levels.[4] The durbar hall faces the palace entrance across the central courtyard. To the right on the ground floor are bathing rooms, and to the left is the long music hall with two prison cells beyond, one for men and one for women. A stairway to the left of the front gate leads to the large sleeping quarters of the Rani and her female attendants. From here the Rani could have looked down on her stable. This long room occupies the whole left wing of the upper floor above the music hall and includes a smaller dressing room beyond for the women of the court. Both the music hall and the sleeping quarters are boldly decorated—pillars, archways, and walls are covered with brilliant scarlet, gold, and green paintings of the late Bundela school. The motifs are predominantly leaf, bird, and geometric designs.

All the rooms of the palace were furnished richly with Persian carpets, chairs, ottomans, tables, couches, and silver bedsteads with covers of scarlet satin, silk, and gold thread. Purple glass chandeliers hung from the ceilings, and mirrors on the walls reflected the rich hues and added to the atmosphere of opulence. This palace was one of the most decorative in this part of India during the late eighteenth and early nineteenth centuries, though it was not as elaborate as those in Orchha, Datia, and Gwalior.

The temple to Mahalakshmi on the eastern edge of town was dedicated to the deity worshipped by the ruling Newalkar family. The young Rani took her adult name from Lakshmi, the goddess of wealth. The temple stands near a huge tank, or lake, with ghats that is said to have been used daily by the maharaja for bathing. This reservoir is surrounded by several smaller temples to deities worshipped by the Gosains, who controlled Jhansi briefly during the decade of the 1760s.

Historical Setting

Bundelkhand fell under the rule of monarchs of both the early Maurya and Gupta empires, as numerous temples and other remains attest. Following these empires, Bundelkhand was invaded in the eighth century by Rajputs and a century later by Chandellas, who also claimed Rajput descent. Stone tanks and temples bespeak the solid traditions created by three centuries of Chandella rule. Ultimately weakened by repeated Muslim attacks from the north, Chandella rulers succumbed in 1203 to the assault of the Delhi sultans, and peace and order were lost in Bundelkhand for over a century. The Khilji sultans of Delhi scattered the Rajput clans, but the Bundela Rajputs emerged in Bundelkhand in the thirteenth and fourteenth centuries, consolidating their power in the region and confronting the Delhi sultans of the Lodi line. During the sixteenth century, in the reign of the great Mughal emperor Akbar, several battles were fought between Mughal and Bundela forces. A particular target of Akbar's armies was the Bundela chief Bir Singh Deo, who formed a friendship with Akbar's rebellious son Prince Salim, who later became Emperor Jahangir.

Bir Singh was the greatest builder of the Bundelas. Among the forts erected by this chief and his father were the spectacular Orchha fort and palace, which they used as their capital. Bir Singh built the Jhansi fort also as part of the defensive ring of forts circling his kingdom. Tradition has it that one day as Bir Singh was entertaining the raja of Jaitpur on the roof of the Jahangir palace at Orchha fort, the chief pointed out his new fort six miles away and asked his guest if he could see it. The Jaitpur raja, shading his eyes and peering into the distance, is said to have replied "*Jhainsi*," "shadowy." Jhansi fort and town, the story goes, took their name from this incident.

The friendship between Prince Salim and Bir Singh deepened when Salim, in disfavor with his father, persuaded Bir Singh to assassinate Akbar's renowned Persian adviser, Abul Fazl, who was antagonistic to Salim. When Salim succeeded Akbar as Emperor Jahangir he rewarded

Bir Singh with a royal sanad and conferred on him the title maharaja of all Bundela possessions. The friendship between the two rulers ended in 1627, when both men died. Their sons continued the alliance formed by their fathers.

Bir Singh built the magnificent Jahangir palace in the Orchha fort for his Mughal friend. The Orchha palace was provided with a camel stable and a zenana for palace women. Both buildings were decorated with elegant wall paintings in vibrant hues. Bir Singh also built the imposing Datia fort a few miles north of Jhansi, which is comparable in scale and style to the Orchha fort and palace. Inner walls of the Datia palace, like those at Orchha, are decorated with paintings of floral motifs, elephants, birds, and geometric designs in brilliant scarlet, gold, and blue. The Orchha and Datia palaces were built on a grander scale than the fort and palace at Jhansi, though all were built of the same sandstone. The minarets and domes of the Datia and Orchha palaces are traced with decorative metal and stone grillwork. Bir Singh also built smaller outpost forts as part of the defensive ring, including those at Dinara and Karhra a few miles west of Jhansi.

The greatest Bundela ruler of the eighteenth century was Maharaja Chhatrasal of Tikamgarh. Chhatrasal served the Mughals during campaigns against Shivaji, founder of the Maratha Confederacy. When Chhatrasal met Shivaji, however, he was so impressed by the leader's spirit and military prowess that he learned the art of guerrilla warfare from him. And when Chhatrasal returned to Bundelkhand he determined to expel the Mughals and found a kingdom of his own. In 1671 he began the process.

The Marathas emerged in Bundelkhand when they answered an appeal by Chhatrasal in 1729. Chhatrasal at the time was being besieged by the subahdar of Allahabad, and Peshwa Baji Rao I rushed to the rescue. In gratitude Chhatrasal declared Baji Rao his adopted son and bequeathed him a third of his kingdom when he died in 1731. Baji Rao, though himself not a Maratha, served as their chief minister. Through him, then, the Marathas acquired a toehold in Bundelkhand, which they augmented by annexation and by fomenting succession disputes among Bundela Rajput chiefs. The Bundelkhand states of Orchha, Datia, and Chanderi were subdued and the Marathas, seeking a central military headquarters, took Jhansi from Orchha state in 1742. Jhansi became a Maratha stronghold under its first Maratha subahdar, Naro Shankar, who established Maratha ascendancy over Orchha and

Datia. The Marathas were then attacked by Afghan forces and by Nawab Shuja-ud-daula of Oudh. Jhansi was ultimately recovered by the Marathas, who benefitted from disputes among various Bundela states.

During the time Naro Shankar served as subahdar in Jhansi, he enlarged the fort and built up the town around it. He invited to Jhansi many Maratha families from the Deccan and made it an essentially Maratha town. His able rule ended when he was recalled by the peshwa in 1756, though he was reappointed briefly when Maratha control was reestablished there.[5] It was Naro Shankar who, in a dispute with Bir Singh, imprisoned Bir Singh in the Jhansi fort and burned Orchha to the ground. In 1761 Jhansi was attacked by a force of Shuja-ud-daula, nawab of Oudh (the Mughal emperor's viceroy at Allahabad), who considered himself the legitimate ruler of Bundelkhand. The peshwa was betrayed by an officer in Jhansi who negotiated with Shuja-ud-daula and imprisoned his Maratha colleagues in return for being taken into Mughal service. Shuja later besieged the Jhansi fort, expelled the Marathas, and reestablished imperial rule there.[6]

Jhansi was reconquered four years later by Holkar and became the object of the contending Rohillas, Jats, Rajputs, and Gujars. For seventy-five years Jhansi was ruled by governors with varying degrees of allegiance to the peshwas. When the power of the peshwas waned in the eighteenth century the governors in Jhansi ruled more independently. British power advanced into this vacuum at the turn of the century.[7]

Maratha power was marked at this juncture by conflicts between the peshwa and his officers—Holkar, Scindia, and other Maratha chiefs. In 1802 the peshwa was driven out of his capital, Poone, by Holkar and sought refuge with the British, with whom he negotiated the Treaty of Bassein. By the terms of this agreement the British promised to restore the peshwa's authority in Poone in return for stationing a British force there, with a cession of territory to maintain the troops. British troops accordingly ejected Holkar from Poone in early 1803, and the peshwa returned to the Maratha capital. War erupted between the Marathas and the British in 1817 when the Marathas in turn tried to expel the British from Poone. The attempt failed and the peshwa fled the capital and ceded all his territorial claims in Bundelkhand to the British.

The Rani married into the ruling Newalkar family in Jhansi. First scion of the Newalkar line there was Raghunath Rao, like the Rani a Karhada Brahmin. He ruled Jhansi as a peshwa appointee from 1769 to

1796, when he retired to Varanasi and was said to have drowned himself in the Ganges, a death that conferred automatic salvation. While he ruled Jhansi he was under continual pressure from Shuja-ud-daula but got little aid from the peshwa in Poone. He was succeeded in Jhansi by his brother Sheo Rao Bhow, who visited the British camp with a request for agreement in 1803. The treaty signed with the British in 1804 confirmed his possessions under the suzerainty of the peshwa and the protection of the British. When Sheo Rao Bhow died in 1814 he bequeathed his rule to his eight-year-old grandson, Ram Chand Rao. The will stated that Gopal Rao Bhow would act as regent until Ram Chand Rao reached majority.

The peshwa, in June 1817, ceded the British all his territory in Bundelkhand by the Treaty of Poone, including Jhansi. Ram Chand Rao accordingly concluded a new treaty with the East India Company in November 1817 which recognized him and his successors as hereditary rulers of the territory held by the late Sheo Rao Bhow. Ram Chand Rao aided the British by carrying grain to troops in Burma in 1824 and in return was sent a dress of honor and an official letter of thanks. In 1825 he agreed to pay an annual tribute of seventy-four thousand rupees to the Company and to maintain a body of troops, which later formed part of the Bundelkhand Legion. In 1832 Governor-General Lord Bentinck conferred on him the title Maharajdhiraj Fidvi Badshah Jamjah Inglistan (Devoted Servant of the Glorious King of England), and he was permitted to use the British flag. The Newalkar title thus rose from subahdar to maharaja. Despite his exalted title, however, Ram Chand Rao was a weak ruler, and under him revenue fell from eighteen to twelve lakhs before he died childless in 1835.[8]

The maharaja's death precipitated a struggle between four claimants to the Jhansi throne: Raghunath Rao and Gangadhar Rao, both sons of Sheo Rao Bhow and therefore Ram Chand Rao's uncles; Krishna Rao, alleged adopted son of Ram Chand; and Narain Rao, a relative of Ram Chand. The East India Company settled the dispute in favor of Raghunath Rao II. His brother Gangadhar Rao unsuccessfully protested this decision on the ground that his brother had leprosy and was thus disqualified by the Shastras and established usage. Under Raghunath the state revenues fell sharply to three lakhs, and he had to mortgage part of his territory to Gwalior and Orchha before he too died childless in 1838.[9]

Another succession dispute ensued. Once again four rivals claimed the throne: Janki Bai, Raghunath's widow; Krishna Rao, the same adopted son of Ram Chand; Ali Bahadur, Raghunath's illegitimate son; and Gangadhar Rao, last surviving son of Sheo Rao Bhow. Gangadhar Rao was recognized by a specially appointed commission but was kept from actual power until 1843 because of British apprehension that he would prove as inept as his brother. Gangadhar's own succession was opposed by Sukhubai, redoubtable mother of Ram Chand Rao. She seized the fort and surrendered it only after military coercion. Popular tradition in Jhansi relates that it was she who killed Raghunath Rao II.

Jhansi town became known throughout Bundelkhand for the manufacture of spears, bows, and arrows, all essentials of the martial lifestyle of the Bundela Rajputs. Jhansi was moreover at the convergence of five roads leading to Agra, Kanpur, Nowgong, the Nerbudda valley, and Indore. As a result Jhansi grew to be a town of some wealth and importance. These roads were heavily traveled by traders in cotton, grain, sugar, and salt. The transit duties on these goods produced a handsome revenue for Jhansi. Well-constructed houses, wells, tanks, and enclosed gardens added elegance to the town, and some of these landmarks still stand today. By 1855 the population had reached about forty thousand.[10]

The Historical Rani

Myth and fact intertwine closely in the story of the early life of the Rani of Jhansi. It is difficult, if not impossible, to extricate the one from the other. Nor in a sense can we speak of the "early life" of the Rani, for her life was all early, abbreviated by the events of the Rebellion. Even the date of her birth is debated.[11] She was born in Varanasi to a Karhada Brahmin, Moropant Tambe, and his wife. Birth in the holy city of Varanasi is viewed by Hindus as particularly auspicious, purified as it is by the Mother Ganga, the Ganges River. Moropant was son of an officer in the Maratha army and became adviser to Chimnaji Appa, brother of Baji Rao II, last of the Maratha peshwas. When the British deposed the peshwa in 1817, Chimnaji was offered a jagir holding worth two million rupees a year. Moropant advised Chimnaji against accepting. Chimnaji took Moropant's advice and left Poone to settle in Varanasi, accompanied by Moropant and his wife, Bhagirathi.[12]

While in Varanasi Bhagirathi gave birth to a daughter, who was named Manikarnika, one of the names of the sacred river Ganga. She was called Manu until the time of her marriage, when she took the name Lakshmi after the Hindu goddess of wealth and victory. Bhagirathi was probably illiterate, as were most women of the time, but was said to be intelligent and versed in the Hindu scriptures. While still a small child Manu lost her mother.

Moropant's employer died when Manu was three, and Moropant, thus deprived of his livelihood, moved to nearby Bithur, where the peshwa had settled after being deposed. Baji Rao gave Moropant a salary and place in his retinue.[13] There Manu attracted the affection of the ex-peshwa, who nicknamed her Chhabili.

It is said popularly that at Bithur Manu's childhood playmates were Nana Sahib (a Chitpavin Brahmin and the adopted son of the last peshwa), Rao Sahib, Bala Sahib, and Tatya Tope, the latter a special companion of Nana Sahib. In the company of these boys at the peshwa's court Manu learned to read and write, unusual skills for a girl at the time, even a Brahmin. Even more exceptional and important for her later career, she became adept at horsemanship and the use of the sword and other weapons, possibly even guns. She flew kites, ran races, fenced, and jumped. While these were the proper skills for boys growing up in high-born court families, they had no place in the traditional socialization of a Brahmin's daughter. Since Manu's mother had died when she was a small child, she was deprived of a traditional nurturing feminine influence. She was left almost entirely to the companionship of male playmates and shared their games and tastes as well as their education. Her father, whether from indulgence, indifference, or design, did little to deter her or to steer her into more conventional feminine directions and pastimes.

One popular story relates that Manu's older playmates, who disdained to take a girl on their rides whether on horseback or elephant, refused one day to take her with them. When she begged Nana Sahib to lift her onto his elephant so that she might join him, he refused. She replied indignantly, "I will show you! One day I will have ten elephants to your one. Remember my words!"[14] Another popular story, part of the legend of Manu's childhood, is told to demonstrate her bravery even as a child of seven or eight. An enraged elephant, it is related, ran rampaging through the streets of the city. Manu, finding herself in the path of the raging beast, leapt onto its trunk and from there onto its tusk, calming the elephant so that it halted its destructive course.[15] Since the elephant symbolizes kingship in India, these episodes with elephants were significant portents of her later role as well as early demonstrations of her bravery and spirit.

Manu's unconventional and lively childhood was brief, cut short by the traditional marriage at puberty. Her father was not a wealthy man, dependent as he was on the largesse of the ex-peshwa. He was ambitious for his daughter, his favorite child, and no doubt also for himself.

Maharaja Gangadhar Rao Newalkar of Jhansi was widowed and looking for a wife. Moreover, as he was childless, it was essential that he have an heir. Without an heir there would be no one to mourn or perform the traditional ancestral observances when he died. The brother he succeeded, Raghunath the Leper, had also died childless, as had his predecessor, Ram Chand Rao. A third successive death of a maharaja without a son would create difficulties for the state as well as for the family rites. Gangadhar was getting on in years by the standards of the day, being probably between forty and fifty, and he was all the more desperate for an heir. Manu came to the maharaja's attention through the peshwa, who urged Moropant to accept the excellent prospect for his young daughter.

Gangadhar Rao was known in Bundelkhand as a man of highly sophisticated tastes, a bibliophile and a patron of the theater and its actors and actresses. He himself even made stage appearances on occasion. Moropant may have hesitated, uncertain about whether a man of these refined tastes would be a proper husband for his daughter or even an effective ruler of a state surrounded by aggressive rival Bundela Rajput chiefs. The fact that Gangadhar Rao was considerably older was not a deterrent; it was, in fact, a customary age gap, particularly among the upper castes.[16]

Delighted at the unexpectedly good prospect, Moropant overcame any reservations he may have had and agreed to the match, first consulting the astrologers to see that the horoscopes matched. The astrologer said that Manu had the qualities of all three principal Hindu goddesses combined: Lakshmi, Durga, and Saraswati, deities of wealth, valor, and wisdom respectively. Her future was most auspicious by these traditional signs as well as by her birth in Varanasi. Moreover, the couple's horoscopes posed no deterrent.

Most Indian sources agree that the marriage was celebrated in May 1842 with cannons booming a salute, fireworks blazing, and all the splendor Gangadhar Rao's court could command. If it is true, as tradition has it, that Manu was only eight years old at the time, the marriage would not have been consummated until Lakshmi, the name she took at marriage, was fourteen, presumably in 1849.[17]

The ceremony was marked by a grand procession through the streets of Jhansi. Coins were distributed to the people of the city, who crowded the streets to catch a glimpse of the bride and to shower the couple with roses and lilies. The Rani glittered with Newalkar family diamonds and emeralds. When the wedding party reached the Ganesha temple they walked the prescribed seven times around the sacred fire. The priest, whose duty it was to tie the ends of their robes together, trembled as he did so and the ends came loose. Suddenly the assembled guests were startled by a voice ordering in ringing tones, "Tie the knot tightly!" People gasped when they realized that it was the young bride who had spoken out so strongly, and on her wedding day at that. The priests of the Ganesha temple where the ceremony was held repeat the story to this day. From that moment, they say, the Rani regarded Jhansi as her home and its people as her own.[18]

At the wedding durbar, tradition locally has it, Lakshmibai was told she would be granted three wishes. She considered carefully. Her first wish was that her friend and maidservant Mundar be allowed to remain with her always. Her second wish was that an elephant be sent to Nana Sahib as a gift from her and a reminder of her childhood promise to him. Her third wish was that her father also be granted a request. Moropant then turned to the priest with the wish that the priest look after Lakshmibai and make her a worthy rani. The priest promised the wishes would be granted. To the priest, then, was entrusted the education and training of the young bride.[19]

But Lakshmi did not find life in the court seraglio to her liking. The circumscribed life of a queen was too abrupt a change from the martial games and company of male playmates that she had enjoyed in Bithur. She chafed under continual surveillance and the atmosphere of suspicion that surrounded the court, especially the zenana. Life in purdah was a hardship.[20]

Relations between Lakshmibai and her husband must have been difficult in these circumstances. The Jhansi novelist Vrindan Lal Verma, who has fictionalized the Rani's life and thus added to the legend, has it that the maharaja was not only aging and suspicious but also short-tempered, capricious, and unbalanced in his political judgement. British sources more than confirm this view. Rewards and punishments were meted out without regard to justice. The punishment of retainers for failure to salute him reflects a certain pettiness on the maharaja's part. Even Indian sources assert that he depleted the treasury of Jhansi. British accounts relate that both Gangadhar Rao and his brother Raghunath Rao were incompetent rulers. George B. Malleson maintains that Gangadhar Rao, who succeeded his brother in 1835, was an "imbecile," which made it necessary for the government to administer the state through an agency. When financial stability was eventually restored in 1843, the government was handed back to the maharaja.[21] Gangadhar Rao has given neither historians nor poets cause for celebration, and but for his marriage to Lakshmi he would have passed unnoticed into oblivion.

Lakshmibai begged her husband to allow her to spend some time outside the zenana, riding and training with arms as she had done in Bithur. Gangadhar paid little attention to his bride's unusual request. This alleged difference in character and concerns of the maharaja and his wife is indicative of the popularity of the young Rani compared with her husband. Here too we see the genesis of the legend that she trained a regiment of women in Jhansi. She gathered her maidservants, including Mundar, and taught them horsemanship, jumping, and swordsmanship, say the people of Jhansi. The Sohrab Modi film portrays the Rani planning a military review of her regiment. British officers in Jhansi who were invited demurred on the grounds that they could not come on a Sunday. The Rani replied that wars often begin on Sunday,[22] and charged that their failure to appear would be a slight to Jhansi. In the film the review is held with British officers in attendance and saluting and the people of Jhansi cheering the Rani's regiment. The film's depiction of this event is meant to demonstrate the Rani's popularity with her people. Gangadhar purportedly was amazed at the review and remarked that he had not known his wife was serious about raising and drilling a women's regiment. It is more likely, however, that the Rani began drilling her unit after the death of her husband. Another key point to remember in assessing the Rani's strength and independence as a young bride is that her father, Moropant, accompanied her to her new home in Jhansi and was thus available to offer support when she needed it. This extraordinary arrangement meant that the Rani brought with her to Jhansi a kind of familial help that was not available to Hindu brides traditionally.

By this time Gangadhar Rao had begun to feel some affection for his unconventional bride, and in 1851, in order to please her and to attend to a religious duty, he took her back to Varanasi for a pilgrimage to her birthplace. Lakshmi revisited the temples where she had worshipped as a child. The maharaja called at the temple where the Newalkar family records were kept. The royal pilgrims fed thousands of beggars on the banks of the holy river and gave gifts to scholars and priests. When they returned to Jhansi they were welcomed by the people of their state with a special warmth. Rumors had already circulated in Jhansi that the Rani was expecting a child.[23]

The birth of a son and heir to the ruling couple was celebrated with great rejoicing in the palace and in the streets. The royal guard paraded in red uniforms with long Maratha lances. State elephants were loaded with sugar and sent throughout the state. The sugar was distributed to the people, a traditional sign of "sweet news." The poor were feasted and given clothing. The event seemed to augur a resurgence of the Newalkar line and of Jhansi's power. Gangadhar Rao, now a bit infirm, was especially delighted with his infant son. But the rejoicing did not last long. When the heir was only three months old he died, and the Rani was deprived of her major role as mother of the heir of Jhansi. The maharaja and his wife were disconsolate, and the people of Jhansi grieved with them. The maharaja seemed to age greatly following his bereavement. He fell into torpor and illness and died in November 1853, leaving the Rani a young widow, probably at eighteen. (The circumstances and events immediately prior to the maharaja's death occasioned so much controversy and had such wide ramifications that they will be examined in some detail in chapter 2.)

By the time the Rani reached the age of eighteen, when she began to drill her women's regiment, she was a striking presence. Unfortunately there are few extant descriptions of her in English or even in Indian languages. Several paintings exist in museums in India and England. There are also numerous folk paintings depicting her on horseback, sword raised over her head. The most frequently quoted description in English of the Rani is by John Lang, variously referred to as her legal counsel and as a novelist. Lang writes:

> She was a woman of about middle size—rather stout, but not too stout. Her face must have been very handsome when she was younger, and even now it has many charms—though, according to my idea of beauty, it was too round. The expression was also very good, and very intelligent. The

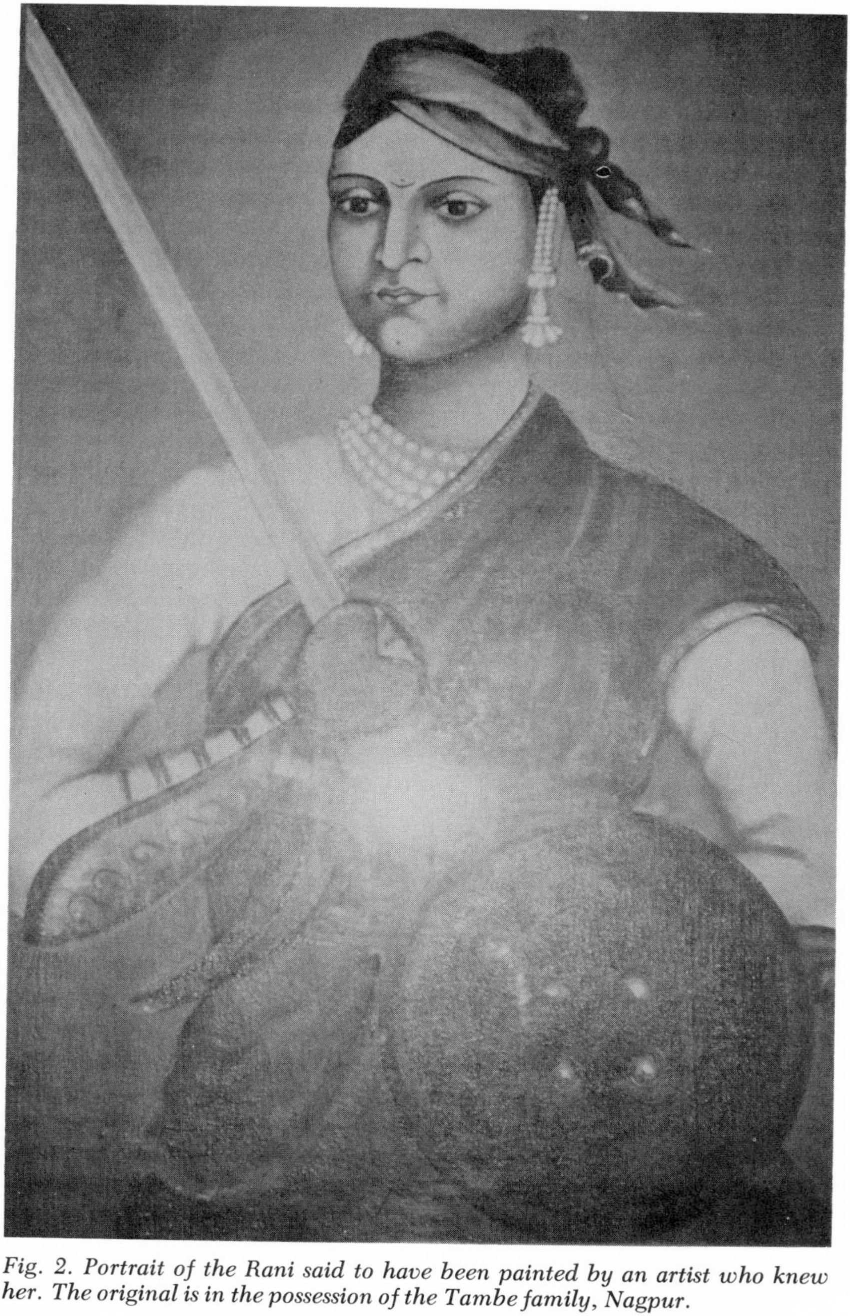

Fig. 2. Portrait of the Rani said to have been painted by an artist who knew her. The original is in the possession of the Tambe family, Nagpur.

> eyes were particularly fine, and the nose very delicately shaped. She was not very fair, though she was far from black. She wore no ornaments, strange to say, upon her person, except a pair of gold earrings. Her dress was a plain white muslin, so fine in texture, and drawn about her in such a way, and so tightly, that the outline of her figure was plainly discernible, and a remarkably fine figure she had. What spoilt her was her voice, which was something between a whine and a croak.[24]

We may be justified in questioning Lang's description in that he admits it was based on a brief glimpse caught as the curtain was pushed aside momentarily by her small adopted son. Moreover, descriptions from local Indian sources do not completely concur. Descendants of Moropant, the Tambe family in Nagpur, suggest that the painter who did the portrait discovered at Indore had seen her; she is portrayed in this portrait as tall, with long arms and large luminous eyes. Some confirmation of the descriptions of her eyes is evident in other portraits of her as well, in particular the one in the Victoria and Albert Museum, which appears to be very close to the one in the possession of the Tambe family. Another description comes from T. Rice Holmes, who wrote in 1897, "Tall of stature and comely of person, she bore all the outward signs of a powerful intellect and an unconquerable resolution."[25]

What made the Rani's presence so striking was not her physical appearance alone. She impressed also with her strength of will and unwavering determination. While most Brahmin girls of the time had virtually no formal education, she had spent her childhood with boys at the peshwa's court, keeping company with them as they were taught to read and write. She is said to have been literate even in Persian, official court language of the Mughals. Her childhood time spent with Nana Sahib, Rao Sahib, and Tatya Tope served her well during and immediately after the Jhansi uprising.

Even more extraordinary than her literacy was her prowess with weapons and her skill as an equestrienne. She gained a reputation even among some Englishmen of being one of the best judges of horses in India, high praise for Englishmen of the day. There are those in Nagpur who say that she carried her predilection for strenuous exercise to the extent of practicing pole climbing and wrestling with women of her military unit in Jhansi.

Added to these capabilities was the evidence from several sources of her extraordinary determination and forcefulness, even on her wedding day. The Tambe family holds that Moropant, advised of her exceptional horoscope at birth, specifically groomed her from childhood for the role of a queen with an army. It is evident too from popular sources that she had an ebullient, spontaneous nature that was reflected in a face radiating a healthy glow. The Rani was moreover, by all English accounts, logical, effective, and forceful in debate. Endowed thus with a potent intellect and character, she had the potential of the charismatic leader she became.

This, then, was the impressive young woman who inherited the throne of Jhansi in 1853 on the death of her husband. To the Rani and her ministers fell the challenge of dealing with British officials on matters of state in the months following November 1853. The steps taken by this young Rani were more than any Indian or Englishman could have anticipated that November.

2

The Rani Appeals the Lapse

The worst of Dalhousie's annexations
—Historian Sir John Kaye on the lapse of Jhansi

The Maharaja's Death

In early November 1853 English officials in Jhansi knew that Gangadhar Rao was gravely ill and not likely to survive much longer. Maj. D. A. Malcolm, political agent at Gwalior for Bundelkhand and Rewah, wrote Major Ellis, political assistant at Jhansi, advising him how to proceed should the maharaja suddenly die intestate. Malcolm suggested it was possible that the maharaja might wish to adopt an heir before he died. Malcolm instructed, "The adoption cannot be allowed or recognized without the special authority of the Government of India." Moreover it would be the duty of Major Ellis to assume charge of the state. It would be up to Ellis to preserve peace and order and take charge of the treasure pending further orders from Fort William. Malcolm requested Ellis to suggest an appropriate allowance for the support of the Rani and her retainers should this happen.[1]

Ellis wrote Malcolm that in view of the maharaja's health it would probably be necessary to carry out these instructions and asked for specific orders. Malcolm responded that Ellis should act as a temporary stopgap until instructions came from Fort William. Should Ellis meet opposition which might require the use of force, however, he should report the circumstances to Malcolm.[2]

Governor-General Dalhousie had already anticipated the need for a policy decision on Jhansi. His stance toward states whose rulers died without natural heirs was in fact an established and tested doctrine: lapse of the state to the British. Dalhousie's hard line on the issue of adoption and his policy toward it had already earned him a reputation as author of the "doctrine of the lapse." Should the maharaja—Dalhousie referred to him as raja—die without adopting an heir, the state would lapse to the paramount power. Should he seek to adopt, the case would be considered and decided by the government.[3]

On 21 November 1853 Gangadhar Rao breathed his last, and the Rani became a teenage widow. On his deathbed the maharaja adopted as his heir Damodar Rao, alias Anand Rao, a five-year-old relative. The maharaja had been careful to invite Major Ellis and a certain Captain Martin to his bedside on the previous day so that they might officially witness the adoption. The two Englishmen arrived at the maharaja's bedside in time to hear his will read aloud; they were furnished copies of the testament. It commended to the government the record of the Newalkar family's loyalty to the British government even before British authority was firmly established in Bundelkhand. In his will Gangadhar Rao entrusted the charge of the state during his heir's minority to Rani Lakshmibai.

Gangadhar Rao's will referred to Damodar Rao as, "my grandson through my grandfather Baneerah Juddee."[4] This is translated elsewhere as "a descendant of my grandfather," which makes better sense in English. The degree of consanguinity between Gangadhar Rao and Damodar has been described variously, but the principle for purposes of adoption was that they were of the same gotra, or exogamous unit of their Brahmin subcaste.

Ellis duly informed Malcolm of the maharaja's death, and Malcolm in turn reported the death and adoption to Fort William. Malcolm, at Ellis' recommendation, suggested that the sum of five thousand rupees per month (or six thousand pounds per annum) be settled on the Rani as a lifetime pension for herself and her retinue. Malcolm acknowledged to Dalhousie his belief that the Rani was "a woman highly respected and esteemed and . . . fully capable of . . . assuming the reins of government" in Jhansi. At the same time he recommended that a force of not less than "a Regiment of Native Infantry and one of Irregular Cavalry" be kept at Jhansi as a precautionary measure against the zamindars of the district.[5]

Dalhousie Proclaims the Lapse

Jhansi was a British creation and could be disposed of by British authority, Dalhousie announced in a lengthy minute on 27 February 1854. The Rani was stunned but not taken totally by surprise. Dalhousie's chief argument rested on an 1837 minute by Sir Charles Metcalfe, in which Metcalfe distinguished between ancient Hindu sovereign princes and chiefs who held land by grant from the sovereign or paramount power. Adoptions were recognized if they were "regular." They were "regular" if made by "ancient hereditary kingdoms of India," though how ancient was not specified by Metcalfe or Dalhousie. Adoptions were not recognized—were "irregular"—when the state or ruler existed under a grant from the paramount power (England), which was thereby entitled to limit succession to terms of the grant. Said sovereign or paramount power was "entitled to limit the succession and to resume on the failure of direct heirs of the body." This meant natural male heirs, which according to Metcalfe's minute, precluded adoption. "Sound policy combines with duty" in the case of Jhansi, the minute went on, to dictate that the paramount power "should act upon its right, refuse to recognize the adoption of Gangadhar Rao, and take possession as an escheat." Not only was the principle laid down by Metcalfe and accepted by the supreme court in 1837 regarding petty states in Bundelkhand, but it was also enunciated by the court in 1849. Dalhousie cited the precedents in Nagpur and Tehri as well.[6]

Dalhousie held further that the raja had left no heir, nor was there any heir whatever of any raja or subahdar of Jhansi with whom the British had ever had relations at any time, and moreover the raja was not expected by his own people to adopt.[7] The source of the latter assertion is not clear from archival evidence.

It is noteworthy that Sheo Rao Bhow's original grant from the British in 1803 contains the provision that in the event that the peshwa in the future should make over Jhansi to the British, "let a *Jaidad* be assigned to me for the support of my cavalry and infantry, and for the maintenance of myself and family in perpetuity." The treaty that followed contains no mention of heirs of any kind.[8]

The governor-general's rationale also noted that Jhansi had been misgoverned, revenues had declined, and order was not being maintained under Newalkar rule. Both brothers—Raghunath Rao and Gangadhar Rao—had been incompetent; the government took control of the administration of Jhansi before handing the state over to Gangadhar in 1842. Dalhousie's contention was supported also by Sir John Kaye. This leading historian of the Rebellion regarded Gangadhar as an imbecile and predicted, "Under his sway, disorder, far from being checked, would be increased ten-fold." Kaye further charged that the administration of Raghunath had been no better. British control, Dalhousie observed, had served in Jhansi to revive the revenues that had dwindled under native rulers. In 1843, after amputation of a limb of territory there to support the Bundelkhand Legion, the administration had been restored to Gangadhar Rao, who "ruled Jhansi for eleven years, neither very wisely nor very well." This situation was the result of the policy of "permitting adoptions and irregular successions in Jaloun and Jhansi" and could not be allowed to continue.[9]

Dalhousie argued moreover that Jhansi's incorporation within British territory would greatly benefit the people of the state as it had in the past. Dalhousie's argument reflected the two streams of Victorian Evangelicalism and Victorian Liberalism, for which his policy acted as a powerful catalyst in India. In this conviction of the benefits of British rule he combined emotional impulse with the rationale for annexation.[10] For Dalhousie, as for other governors-general, the construction of roads and railroads in India was one proof of the benefits of civilization. Sir John Kaye, however, commenting on Dalhousie's conviction about the blessings of British rule, noted later, "The results of experience have since shown to what extent the people of Jhansi appreciated the benefits of that incorporation." Kaye judged Jhansi "the worst of Dalhousie's annexations."[11] An Indian historian more recently has offered a positive if provocative assessment of the impact of Dalhousie's policy. In this view annexation contributed unwittingly to the political unification of India and thus became the foundation of the Indian nation.[12] This interpretation would no doubt have startled Dalhousie.

Dalhousie argued that altruism prompted his policy in Jhansi. He wrote following his proclamation that the British government would not derive any material advantage whatever from possession of Jhansi, either in terms of area or revenue. Situated as it was in the midst of other British districts, British possession of Jhansi would tend to "improve the general internal administration of [British] possessions in Bundelkhand." Moreover, Dalhousie said, he was even reluctant to take these measures. And in the case of another state, Nagpur, wrote Dalhousie, "I am sorry Nagpore has fallen just now, for we did not want it; but as it did fall, a ripe cherry, into our mouths, I think justice and expediency bid us swallow it, stone and all."[13]

Dalhousie felt later that his policy had been misinterpreted, and in his own defense stated that he had applied the lapse only to subordinate states created by the British government, or those in a relationship to it that gave it "the recognized right of a paramount power in all questions of adoption." Criticized after the outbreak of the Rebellion for his policy, Dalhousie stopped keeping copies of his private correspondence and forbade publication of his private papers until fifty years after his death. As finally published, his letters contain no mention of Jhansi.[14] The governor-general's council was of course nearly unanimous in his support. Councilman J. Low, however, partially dissented and suggested a more moderate course, of modifying British involvement in Jhansi so as to prevent future misrule. But Low, like the rest of the council, was convinced by Dalhousie's authority and position, if not by his rationale. The governor-general's ruling was forwarded both to the Court of Directors of the East India Company in London and to Major Malcolm at Gwalior. Malcolm sent it on to Ellis, who was to inform the Rani immediately of the government's decision.

In the 1850s women were rulers of several native states in Central India by virtue of their husbands' deaths. This fact in all probability did not accord with Dalhousie's concept of governing authority or with Victorian notions of the appropriate role of women. In neighboring Tehri in Orchha, for example, another maharaja had died, this one under somewhat mysterious circumstances. Ellis consequently sent an agent there to investigate the death. Ellis wished both to know whether the maharaja had been poisoned and to prevent any disturbances until the government decided the matter of succession. Ellis reported to Malcolm in December 1853 that, in the interest of preserving the public peace, the Larai rani and her party should be excluded from any interference in governmental affairs until the question of succession could be decided.[15] Malcolm concurred with Ellis but felt there was no alternative to having the widow of Maharaja Soojan Singh carry on with government at least temporarily.

Dalhousie's doctrine of the lapse added great tracts of territory to the area of the Raj, or what became the Raj proper after the Rebellion. The lapse was applied consistently to "dependent principalities" from 1848 onward. The Punjab, Sikkim, part of Cachar, Lower Burma, Satara, part of Sind, Oudh, the Central Provinces, Baghat, Sambalpur, Jaitpur, Udaipur, Jhansi, the Berars, and part of Kandesh all fell under British rule through Dalhousie's policy.[16] Not all British officials were happy with the consequences.

Disagreement within the Raj

Dalhousie's doctrine of lapse had opponents both in India and in England, though in India they were not always free to express their views openly. One such was Col. William Sleeman, renowned for his role in uncovering and suppressing thugi, ritual murder in Central India carried out in the name of devotion to the goddess Kali. In fact, the heart of Bundelkhand where Jhansi is situated was a major center of thugi operations and to this day the area harbors bands of marauding dacoits. Sleeman referred to Dalhousie as "the Deity." Dalhousie, charged Sleeman, wished to destroy the princes and territorial chiefs of India, and nothing remained but "to consider the means by which they can be driven mad in the shortest possible time." Dalhousie, he continued, believed all such native princes to be bad and unpopular among their people, though he and his apostles had never even seen such princes and were acting simply on what the newspapers said.[17] Sleeman was not alone in condemning Dalhousie for his actions. In India, however, those who disagreed had to keep their own counsel or lose their postings in Dalhousie's administration.

Another critic of Dalhousie's policy, Maj. Wilberforce Bird, in a lecture in London charged that British ignorance of Indian affairs had greatly damaged many princes and other inhabitants in India and had "impeded our progress in introducing the benefits of Western civilization to the extent that we might have done." Bird agreed with Sleeman that annexation and confiscation were incompatible with British relations "with this little independent state."[18] Although the resumption of Jhansi thus occasioned both official and unofficial opposition, Dalhousie had the final word, at least until 1857.

While the Rani was shocked at Dalhousie's action, she may have had some intimation of his intention. Soon after her husband's death she began conversations with the British official closest by, Major Ellis. In conversations with the Rani, Ellis had, according to Malcolm, "allowed a doubt as to the finality of the decision of Government regarding the lapse of the state of Jhansi to rest on the mind of the Ranee." This doubt, and Ellis' alleged role in fostering it, prompted much correspondence between Fort William and Bundelkhand as well as between Fort William and London. Strong opprobrium at Ellis' conduct was expressed up the line in the official hierarchy as far as Fort William.

Ellis' position warrants some explanation. It is apparent that as the local official most closely involved with the Rani and with Jhansi, he had some sympathy with her and the logic of her case. He had served in Sleeman's famous Thug̃i Department. He had, furthermore, gone on record on 7 November in opposition to the government's plan to place him under the political agent for Gwalior, Bundelkhand, and Rewah, namely, Malcolm. Finally, the reasons for his reluctance to work under Malcolm were several, apart from sympathy for the cause of the Rani. Malcolm and Ellis were known, for example, to have disagreed on the British role in settling boundary disputes among various states of Bundelkhand. The tone of the correspondence between Malcolm and Ellis reflects their strained relationship.

Malcolm wrote Ellis on 23 April castigating him for delay in carrying out instructions and for creating false hopes in the Rani's mind. Malcolm was particularly disturbed that the maharaja's troops had not been discharged immediately as the first step in transferring Jhansi to the British. The reason Ellis had not discharged them was, as he explained to Malcolm, that he could not do so without being authorized at the same time to replace them.[19] Malcolm also took Ellis to task for not taking immediate steps regarding the police force in Jhansi. Malcolm was moreover perplexed about the revenue arrears Ellis reported in the state. Malcolm added that Ellis should have informed the Rani immediately of the pension arrangements the government planned for her. His failure to take all these measures had fostered false hopes in her mind regarding the finality of the government's decision, hopes that served to "prevent her accommodating herself as she must eventually to the new order of things."[20]

The exchange continued, Malcolm asking Ellis in May for a statement of accounts from the date of the maharaja's death the previous November until Jhansi was resumed by the government. The tone of Malcolm's letter clearly reflects his annoyance with Ellis. Ellis responded that he had already called on the Rani on 19 April, informing her of arrangements for her support and asking her for a list of old servants she wished to have pensioned. The phraseology of this letter was what caused consternation up the line in the British bureaucracy. Wrote Ellis, "But she seems to entertain an idea that the orders of the Government in her case are not considered as final, and as long as this impression lasts will, in all probability, continue to defer furnishing the required statement."[21]

Ellis had a grievance of his own. He felt that Malcolm was not giving him his due, and he asked Malcolm to forward his request for a change in title (or promotion) to the governor-general through his agent for Central India at Indore, Sir Robert Hamilton. The reply from Fort William disappointed Ellis: his appointment was nothing more than its title implied.[22] Hamilton moreover remarked that he, himself, after reading Malcolm's report on Ellis, had considered relieving Ellis of his post because of his conversations with the Rani.[23] Ellis attracted so much negative attention from officials that in May 1854, when the lapse went into effect, he was posted to Rewah as "a more convenient headquarters" for his work as political assistant in Bundelkhand. But since there was no house available at Rewah he was ordered to Nagode. His salary was reduced and his appointment as assistant in the Thugi Department revoked.[24]

Correspondence between Malcolm and Ellis regarding boundary settlements also bespoke their different approaches to local problems. Malcolm favored a general survey and settlement of boundaries in Bundelkhand by the superintendent of the Revenue Survey rather than intervening in individual boundary disputes. Ellis, on the other hand, objected in the case of states having boundaries with British villages and advocated instead gradual determination of boundaries under the supervision of local political officers and their native assistants.[25] The reason for Ellis' strong reaction on this issue was that he, himself, had been closely involved in settling such disputes for ten years. He felt that much progress had been made and that interference with procedures he had used would jeopardize pending settlements. This difference of approach between Malcolm and Ellis illustrates a phenomenon general in the Raj. The lower the rank of the official and the closer he was to his district, the better informed about it he was and the more he tended to identify with it and its inhabitants. This generalization could be applied up the ranks of British officialdom to the governor-general, who was, as Sleeman suggested of Dalhousie, totally unconcerned with Indian sentiment.

Ellis had not remained as inactive as Malcolm charged. Ellis had taken immediate steps to preserve peace and order. At the fort where the treasure was stored and 250 prisoners were interned he put seals on the locks to the treasury and occupied the fort gates with a 115-man guard of soldiers from Scindia's Gwalior Contingent. They were ordered to cooperate with the Jhansi troops. For four days prior to Gangadhar's death Ellis held conversations with officials around the maharaja to warn them of the need to prevent an outbreak of prisoners should the maharaja die.[26] Ellis suggested at the time that it would be advisable to keep a full regiment at Jhansi.

Malcolm warned Fort William that the Rani was about to make a direct appeal concerning her grievances and that she had employed for the purpose a British barrister named John Lang.[27] Lang was being sent to Agra, where he was to be joined by one Kashmeree Mul, a vakil formerly attached to Malcolm's office. Malcolm complained to Hamilton that Ellis had given him no information about Lang or his activities, although Lang was known to have visited Jhansi. Malcolm must have been particularly piqued that a former employee of his own office had apparently become involved in the case.

Differences between Ellis and his superiors, especially Malcolm, continued in the months that followed the death of the maharaja of Jhansi. When the Rani cited precedents of allowing adoptions in Orchha and Datia, Ellis wrote a lengthy opinion to Malcolm in which he remarked that he could not see any difference that would justify recognizing adoption in one state and not another. He continued, "It appears to me that it would be opposed to the spirit of enlightened liberality . . . if the privilege was to be now refused to families created by ourselves as a reward for the services rendered to the British Government on the grounds that they were not of so ancient an origin as others."[28] The logic of Ellis' argument made no impression on his superiors in the months following, when the Rani pressed her appeal.

Malcolm, in reply to Ellis, asserted that neither Orchha nor Datia was comparable, since these states were independent and antedated the Maratha entry into Bundelkhand. Nor was Jaloun comparable, since it belonged to a Maratha family from the Deccan whose chief had made a treaty with the British in 1806 without reference to the peshwa. By this treaty, noted Malcolm, the British had recognized Jaloun as the chief's hereditarily and had taken some territory from him in exchange. And while a second treaty with the same chief in 1817 mentioned subordination to the peshwa, the chief was assured his heirs and successors were hereditary rulers of the territory.[29]

Lakshmi must have been prepared for this rejection. She had drafted yet another appeal dated 18 July requesting that papers indicating the grounds on which the state of Jhansi had been resumed be furnished her so that she might make a fresh statement of her claim. She was notified by the British just one month later that her requests were "wholly inadmissible" and that orders for the resumption of Jhansi would not be revoked by the government.[38]

Undeterred by Dalhousie's curt refusal, the Rani persevered. She pleaded this time that Jhansi had been well governed under her late husband. "The people of Jhansi were contented under the rule of the late Rajah, and of your memorialist, and were in as good a condition as those under the British rule."[39] Good roads, tanks, and bridges had been constructed, and "spacious bungalows were erected for the accommodation and comfort of travellers passing through the territory," an argument specifically designed to appeal to Dalhousie's concept of beneficent rule. Moreover, a large mansion had been provided rent free to officials of the governor-general, and Jhansi maintained an efficient police force. Under this good government the people had no complaints nor did they wish to be transferred to the East India Company. Sheo Rao Bhow, Raghunath, and Gangadhar all had an unassailable right to the territory and government of Jhansi, subject to certain tribute to the peshwa, who had been compensated through a cession of territory to the Company, she continued.

The Rani asserted that she would have been legal heiress and representative even had her husband made no will. Yet the adoption, she noted, had been recognized by the government for purposes of inheritance of private property, as even Malcolm admitted. "It is the effect of that adoption which your memorialist presumes that Government disowns," that is, for succession to the state. She questioned if, in disowning that effect, the government gave the East India Company a "right to Govern, and a right to possess and enjoy the territory and revenues of that state?" "Does it," she asked, "entitle them to seize the Government and territory of Jhansi? Does it entitle them to seize your memorialist's Treasury—to pension off your memorialist on a pittance of the Treasures of the State, payable only during the period of your memorialist's life, and to deprive your memorialist's ward, or the heirs of the late Rajah, of their entire inheritance, except the petty reversion of his personal estate?" If the government wanted to bring the state of Jhansi under its rule it should have followed the course of negotiation and agreement rather than the "exercise of the power, without the right, of the great and strong against the weak and small." She again invoked the government's sense of justice to the Newalkar family, which had served the East India Company for fifty years, and asked that it not despoil the family without just cause. She argued that there was no reason to conclude that the family's rule would be anything but beneficial to the government of India in the future, as it had been in the past. She again alluded to sanctioned adoptions in neighboring states, this time including Scindia in Gwalior.[40]

The Rani concluded her lengthy and spirited plea with three fresh and arresting arguments. The dispossession of the Rani and her ward constituted, she continued, "gross violation and negation of the Treaties of the Government of India . . . and if persisted in they must involve gross violation and negation of British faith and honor." Second, she pointed out that the government decision regarding Jhansi had "created great disquietude among the native Princes and Chiefs of upper India," and remarked that they awaited the government's reply to her memorial "with intense interest." And finally, she remarked on her own distress at the deprivation of her "authority, rank and affluence" and her reduction to a state of "subjection, dishonor and poverty."[41]

Lakshmi rested her case by pointing out that for four months following the maharaja's death on 21 November 1853 she had conducted the affairs of state in Jhansi. She emphasized that it was only after she had been carrying on the administration of Jhansi during this time that the government order came to resume the state and seize the property and treasury of Jhansi. Though she had already demonstrated her capacity to continue in charge of state affairs, she maintained, the government had ignored her competence to rule. The tone of the Rani's pleas had grown increasingly insistent and spirited during the half year following the maharaja's death, yet Dalhousie did not alter his resolve or revoke his decision.

3

The Lapse of Jhansi

Fall it did, like a ripe cherry.
—*Governor-General Dalhousie*

Administrative Arrangements

Jhansi lapsed to the Raj in May 1854 along with Jaloun. Both were brought under the supervision of Capt. W. C. Erskine, commissioner of Saugor and Nerbudda territories at Jabalpur. A new superintendent of Jhansi and Jaloun, Capt. Alexander Skene, and deputy superintendent, a captain named Gordon, were placed under the authority of Erskine. Erskine in turn answered to Lieutenant Governor Auckland Colvin of the Northwest Provinces at Agra in the chain of command in the new official dispensation.[1]

When Skene first arrived in Jhansi in late June 1854 to assume his new duties, rumors were circulating among the populace that the state would ultimately be restored to the adopted son of the maharaja. No doubt the Rani's many appeals to Fort William had helped to foster these rumors. The effect of these reports, Skene found, was "to unsettle the minds of the inhabitants," and he accordingly had Gordon issue a proclamation that the annexation of the state was total and irrevocable and calling on the inhabitants to "conduct themselves in every way as subjects of the British Government."[2]

Many details of administration had to be settled following the lapse of Jhansi. The Rani was required to vacate her splendid fort, it having been deemed a public building that had lapsed along with the state. She was allowed, however, to keep the palace in town as her private residence. A pension of five thousand rupees per month was authorized for the support of the Rani and her retinue, the sum originally recommended by Ellis and Malcolm. Other arrangements occasioned dispute among the officials involved. Revenue was a focal concern of the Raj everywhere in India, and Skene was ordered to submit correspondence regarding revenue and administration and to assume immediate charge of both.[3] The problem was a matter of accounting: when should the Rani's collection of revenue cease and the East India Company's begin? Ellis, who remained in Jhansi until the transfer of Jhansi to the Northwest Provinces, disagreed with Malcolm over the precise date when the Rani's collections should cease. The disagreement arose because of a disparity in the methods of reckoning the fiscal year; British and Indian fiscal years did not coincide. Erskine said he was inclined to differ with Malcolm's definition of the official year and to agree with Ellis.[4]

The first of May was finally fixed as the dividing point between revenue collected on the Rani's account and that collected on behalf of the Company. All disbursements made by Major Ellis between 1 May and the date of transfer to Captain Gordon had to be adjusted on "Major Ellis's responsibility." The new officials announced, moreover, that both Malcolm and Ellis had had only temporary control over Jhansi affairs and that appointments made by them were subject to review.[5]

British officials also failed to agree over arrangements for the Rani's support. Malcolm proposed that the private property of the late maharaja be given to his widow contingent on payment of her husband's debts. This suggestion infuriated Lakshmi. Even Dalhousie found Malcolm's suggestion unacceptable. "It is beyond the power of the Government," Dalhousie responded, "so to dispose of the property of the late Rajah, which by law will belong to the boy whom he adopted. The adoption if regularly made was good for the conveyance of private rights though not for the transfer of the principality."[6]

Lakshmi at first refused to accept the property willed to Damodar Rao on the ground that she was required by Ellis to give security for it. Fort William ruled, when Hamilton inquired, that Ellis had been in error in requiring her to execute a written agreement, and that it should be made over to her upon simple receipt, but that she should also be responsible for "the debts of the state, as far as the assets go."[7] This condition was likewise unacceptable to the Rani, who argued that she should not be held responsible for debts of state, since the property in question was private. The debts were state debts, not personal debts contracted by herself, and the pension was for her personal support and maintenance. Angered, she initially refused the pension with its attached conditions and considered leaving Jhansi to return to her birthplace, Varanasi, to live.[8]

Hamilton was asked by Lieutenant Governor Colvin to visit the Rani to urge her to accept the pension and to try to dissuade her from leaving Jhansi, "as her so doing would be most injurious to her Town." She received Sir Robert in her palace in full durbar, in the presence of Damodar, Moropant, and other of her advisers. Sir Robert found her "civil and polite, quite the lady, and easy in manner and in conversation." He did not comment on her appearance or detect any signs of hostility in her manner during this first interview. He wrote Sir John Kaye, "My impression was that she was a clever, strong-minded woman, well able to argue and too much for many."[9]

Hamilton was accompanied during the long interview by the two new officers at Jhansi, Skene and Gordon. When Hamilton inquired if the Rani was planning to move to Varanasi, she pointed to Gordon, saying, "The Sahib *wishes* me to go to Benares." She commented that Skene was a good man and her friend, but hinted that her feelings toward Gordon were not as friendly. Hamilton then asked if she intended to accept the pension. She replied that she could not, since it would mean acknowledging the lapse of Jhansi, something she could never do. In several fictional accounts she cries, "I will never give up my Jhansi!" Hamilton then urged her to take the income from the pension, and she promised to consider the suggestion.

Hamilton noted that on one issue—that of the police entering the palace precincts—the Rani was very irate. She threatened to leave Jhansi —apparently her chief bargaining ploy—if the police were allowed to enter her palace. Hamilton begged Lakshmi to remain until he could convey her views to Colvin and promised she would hear from him further. In his report to Colvin, Hamilton supported Lakshmi's view that the state debts were unrelated to her pension. He suggested that if this principle were recognized it was probable that she would prefer to remain in Jhansi but exempt from the jursidiction of the magistrate. Hamilton's recommendation regarding state debts did not prevail with Colvin.

Hamilton again visited Jhansi during April 1855 on a tour of inspection of "the seven houses of Bundelkhand" and received an invitation to call on the Rani. At this second meeting the Rani received Hamilton in the durbar room, but she observed purdah and remained seated behind a curtain. A year after his first meeting with the Rani, Hamilton noted no change in her. "She talked very cleverly and clearly." She made it plain that she was hurt by Colvin's decision to make her responsible for the maharaja's old debts. Hamilton expressed sympathy, feeling she had been harshly if legally treated in the matter.

The Rani made no mention during the interview of her appeal regarding recognition of her husband's adopted heir, which by now she must have seen as a hopeless cause. Instead, she thanked Hamilton for not placing her under the jurisdiction of British courts and police. Her purpose in requesting the meeting with Hamilton, according to him, was to request that she be placed under his authority as governor-general's agent for Central India rather than another arrangement, a "degradation" in her view. She must have realized that she might expect better treatment under Hamilton than under Colvin. He was favorably inclined regarding this request and wrote that he felt it would not be inconsistent with the decision to exempt her from the jurisdiction of the government's courts. He again noted that otherwise she might leave Jhansi for Varanasi, a possibility viewed by the people of Jhansi with "great sorrow and apprehension, as such a step would entail a serious loss on the town, in which she was the cause of a good deal of money being circulated."[10]

Lakshmi pleaded earnestly, leaning forward against the curtain so that Hamilton was able to see her despite the barrier that separated them. He also saw that she was completely alone this time, without attendants of either sex. He was impressed with the firmness of her appeal and assured her that the government had no desire to degrade the widow of someone who had held so high a position and been so faithful to the government. He recalled later that he urged her to continue to maintain her high reputation.[11] It is interesting that Hamilton felt his advice on this topic might carry weight with her.

Hamilton's favorable report on his visit to the Rani continued by recounting what Skene and Gordon in Jhansi had said of the Rani's conduct. They had assured Hamilton that the Rani had responded in a very satisfactory way to various requests they had made in carrying out the arrangements for the resumption of her state. She had vacated the fort without protest. This suggests that none of the officials directly concerned with Jhansi had any sense that she might be resentful at Dalhousie's decision. This is of particular interest in view of accounts by contemporary British historians that she was harboring resentment and nursing grudges (see chapter 4).

The Rani's wish that she be put under the authority of Hamilton was interpreted by Erskine at Jabalpur as "either oriental flattery, or possibly she thought she would have a better chance of having the State restored to her or her adopted child." Erskine agreed with Colvin that this arrangement would cause confusion, conflict of jurisdiction, inability of magistrates to pursue criminals if in the palace, and would further lower Superintendent Skene and Deputy Gordon in the eyes of the people of Jhansi. Erskine suggested that he, himself, be appointed agent to the governor-general in Bundelkhand and Rewah and that Skene be made his political assistant, combining the Revenue and Police departments.[12]

Hamilton and Erskine were vying for authority over Jhansi. Hamilton's solution to the disagreement was to combine the agency at Bundelkhand and Rewah with the agency for Central India at Indore, to put both agencies under himself, and create a political assistant post at Rewah, where Ellis had been posted. He argued that such an arrangement would be more economical, pointing out, too, that communications between Indore and both Jhansi and Gwalior were direct via a well-used dak road. Malcolm was out of the picture, having been transferred from Gwalior to Baroda by this time.[13] It is noteworthy that both the Rani and Hamilton showed willingness to mediate at this juncture. It is also tempting to conjecture what the result might have been had Hamilton's suggestion been accepted regarding supervision of Jhansi.

The grudging nature of measures taken for the Rani's support was apparent in areas other than her pension and inheritance of property. Erskine, for example, proposed that she be given grassland for her use for life but added, "I see no reason why she should have a firewood preserve also, as fuel can be purchased in any quantity in the town of Jhansie."[14] Skene had suggested she be given a firewood preserve. Jhansi grasslands had been the private property of the maharaja and were claimed as such by Lakshmi. Erskine had also directed that a promissory note from the Court of Directors to the maharaja be cancelled, though Ellis had protested this action. State buildings were pronounced state property and therefore considered to have lapsed to the government, except for the palace.

Several official measures taken after the lapse offended the religion of the Rani and the people of Jhansi. Refusal to allow Lakshmi to draw on the maharaja's trust for Damodar Rao for the boy's ceremonial investiture with the sacred thread was an affront to all Hindus. Another measure particularly galling to the Rani as to all Hindus was the lifting of the ban on cow slaughter. Before November 1854 the slaughter of cattle had been strictly banned in Jhansi. The prohibition was common to all Hindu native states at the time and remains a factor in Indian politics today. After the lapse this restriction was removed over the Rani's protest, whereupon she and her subjects protested again. Although these pleas were referred through several echelons of Company officials, they were ultimately rejected, and cow slaughter was allowed by Fort William. It has been suggested that one possible motive on the part of the government may have been to curry favor with the Muslims.[15] If so, the attempt was singularly unsuccessful; Muslims played a prominent part in events of the uprising at Jhansi.

Yet another offense to religion related to the support of the temple of Mahalakshmi east of the town wall, a temple closely associated with the Newalkar family and frequented regularly by the Rani for worship. Some years previously an ancestor of Gangadhar Rao had made over the revenue of two villages for the support of this temple, and the arrangement had been continued by Gangadhar Rao. Gordon, the new deputy commissioner, recommended that the arrangement be continued. He was overruled, however, and it was ordered that these two villages be resumed along with the rest of the state. Lakshmibai's protests were futile. The resumption of these villages was about to take effect when the insurgence erupted at Jhansi. These measures were a significant factor in fostering wider popular resentment. Their abhorrence to Hindus must have fanned the fear widespread among Hindu and Muslim alike that the people were about to be forcibly converted to Christianity.

As late as 6 January 1856 the Rani was vainly persevering in her pleas to the governor-general. All her appeals had been ignored. Her husband's debts had been deducted from her pension; the ban on cow slaughter had been lifted; revenue from the two villages supporting the temple was being resumed; and she was not allowed to draw on the trust for her son's sacred thread ceremony.

The previous November, Hamilton had forwarded to her a confirmation of the resumption order from the Court of Directors in London. In her response Lakshmibai referred to the order as "only a confirmation of my bad fortune." She cited her own letter of May 1855 to the governor-general in which she requested to be placed under Hamilton's authority and explained that her only motivation had been the preservation of honor and name. "The delay in the same being complied with . . . assures me of the influence of my adverse luck." Nothing else could explain the rejection of such a request by one who could "without any difficulty grant a chief help or create a King." She referred again to her personal honor and the record of obedience of her family to British authority. "You are well aware that as a fallen party, whose state had been lost, I have stretched out my supplicant hands for the protection and favor of this Government," she remarked. She recalled Hamilton's visit to Jhansi and his advice to her to accept the stipend. She recollected, too, that her only desire was to avoid disgrace, "being looked down upon" by neighboring chiefs. She expressed her hope that the loss of her estate would not bring with it the loss of the honors due to her rank. "I have been exempted from the jurisdiction of the Courts. I pray to be relieved of the degradation which separation from the Agency must involve." The financial arrangements were, for her, "a disgrace which renders it quite impossible . . . to live from day to day."[16] Fort William remained silent.

Several features of these exchanges are especially noteworthy. One is the tone of the Rani's appeal. She consistently portrays herself as helpless, at the mercy of Hamilton and Fort William, at the same time referring repeatedly to her honor and status as widow of a chief. Another point is her curious mention twice in the 1856 communication of her adverse fate, a conviction that was becoming increasingly prominent in her consciousness and calculations. Still a further concern of the Rani that also gains significance in light of subsequent events was her desire to avoid being looked down on by neighboring states and chiefs, who were, she said, watching events in Jhansi. And finally is the fact that the governor-general continued to ignore her many pleas. All these issues, including the repeated failure of government to respond to specific points in her appeals, must have had a cumulative impact on the Rani's sentiments regarding the East India Company. That she was still addressing the British in early 1856, despite the rejection of all previous entreaties, is also a matter of some importance in assessing her role in the Jhansi uprising of the following year.

What emerges in the Rani's response to the lapse is a dogged, unrelenting determination to retrieve her state or, at the very least, to have her case heard in Fort William and possibly London as well. Instead the list of measures taken by Fort William in disregard of her protests merely lengthened. It is no wonder that Englishmen of the day, when contemplating this list, expressed the view that the Rani must be harboring resentments. Yet British officials at Jhansi anticipated no problem there in early 1857. As was generally the case in most of India among the hundreds of officials and army officers who manned the apparatus of the East India Company, complacency prevailed as May of 1857 approached.

4

Uprising at Jhansi

Many had a feeling mutiny was a matter of destiny, the Benares Brahmins having predicted it.

—*"Narrative of the Mutiny of the Force at Nowgong in Bundelcund"*

The Spark Ignites

As May of 1857 approached, a few British officers became apprehensive, warning of malaise among the Sepoys, of their anger at the possibility of losing caste by being posted overseas and their resentment at having their allowances reduced. They were reported to be especially indignant at the introduction of the greased cartridges of the Enfield rifles. Odious and defiling though the cartridges were to both Hindus and Muslims, the British viewed the new rifles as a welcome improvement over the old muzzle-loading rifles. The Enfields had greater range (a ratio of four to one), speed, and accuracy. Because of these advantages they were introduced to units of the Bengal Army in the final months of 1856 and beginning of 1857.

Added to these very real causes of unrest among the Sepoys were rumors circulating not only among the troops but also among the civilian populace. In the Indian countryside rumor often looms larger than objective reality and can assume a power of its own for influencing events. Such was the case with the circulation of chapattis among the villages of North India, a situation that fostered an air of anticipation among villagers and a feeling of uneasiness among some English. The traveling chapattis suggested to those English who learned of them that all was not well, certainly that all was not under their control. Such was the case, too, with rumors among both Hindus and Muslims that forcible conversion to Christianity was imminent and that flour mixed with ground cow bones was being sold in the markets. Yet those officers who warned their superiors of impending trouble were transferred elsewhere for their efforts.[1]

Official opinion was no more responsive to princely resentment at the annexations of Oudh, Jhansi, Satara, Nagpur, and other states, as the Rani's case attests. Oudh was significant both as the recruiting ground for the Bengal Army and as the Bithur seat of the government of Nana Sahib, the last peshwa's adopted heir and Lakshmi's childhood playmate.[2] In Delhi, too, Bahadur Shah, last of the Mughal emperors, sat unhappily on his throne, nursing grievances. Not even the great numerical superiority of Sepoys to English officers and troops (a ratio of at least eight to one on a countrywide average) aroused much apprehension among most officers of the army in early 1857. British confidence and complacency formed an effective insulation against the real sentiments of Indians. Revenue treasure was left in the districts as a kind of proof of business as usual, of confidence in the Sepoys. Anything else would have been an admission of lack of confidence or failure of nerve on the part of British officers, even of their ineffectiveness as officers. Not even Sepoy outbreaks in February at Berhampur and Barrackpur over the introduction of the Enfield rifles shook the confidence of the British. But the spark that had been ignited in February would soon catch fire all across North and Central India in units of the Bengal Army.

Sunday, 10 May, dawned under a fierce sun in the town and district of Meerut, some forty miles northeast of Delhi. Two weeks earlier the native cavalry, which included high-caste Brahmins, had refused the greased cartridges; a court martial meted out sentences of imprisonment at hard labor. Some time later, on 9 May, at a general parade, the old commander, Maj. Gen. W. H. Hewitt, ordered the offenders dismissed and their sentences executed. Hewitt was deaf to the pleas of the offenders, Sepoys who had until then served in the army with unwavering allegiance.

The Meerut cantonment was one of the largest military stations in India, covering an area five miles in circumference and including infantry, artillery, and cavalry regiments. The morning after Hewitt's order, the servants vanished from the bungalows of the English officers, and men in the bazaars armed themselves. The sun set, marking the hour of the evening vesper service. Ignoring the warning signs, God-fearing Englishmen took their families to church. Meanwhile, as the troops were called to the parade, they shot their officer, a Colonel Finnis, and broke ranks in general revolt. Men from the bazaars ran along the British lines burning the bungalows, and Sepoys broke into the jail to release the prisoners. English men, women, and children emerging from the unfinished church service were all murdered. While the revolt was in progress in one part of the city, in another part, at the treasury, the Sepoy guard stood loyally at its post, revealing by its inaction the absence of a prior concerted plan.

The commanders at Meerut were caught off guard and failed to act in time to check the egress of insurgents from the city. The Sepoys left for Delhi, spreading revolt with them to the old Mughal capital. Three native regiments reached Delhi, where Emperor Bahadur Shah and his retainers waited, poised to join the rebels. In Delhi the arsenal inside the city wall was guarded by native troops only, as was the main magazine, which had been moved three miles from the city as a precaution. By sunset on the eleventh all the English in Delhi had been killed, captured, or had escaped or hidden, and the city was in the hands of its Sepoy liberators. The same afternoon the telegraph lines from Delhi were cut, and the city was isolated from British garrisons elsewhere. When the news spread, British India was numb with shock, English men and women were struck with terror at word of the Meerut massacre and the fall of Delhi. It was several months before the British could retake Delhi, and in the interim, rebellion spread in the Bengal Army across North Central India, leaving disruption and death, fear and hatred in its wake.

Uprising at Jhansi

Jhansi was a station to watch, situated strategically as it was in the heart of Bundelkhand at the junction of four important roads. One road ran northeast toward Kalpi, Kanpur, and Lucknow, and another northwest to Agra and Delhi, all major centers of the Rebellion. A third headed south across the Central Indian plateau to the Nerbudda River and South India, and the fourth ran east to Allahabad. The great strength of the Jhansi fort further added to its military significance. At this critical time the garrison there consisted entirely of Indian troops: the left wing of the Twelfth Native Infantry and the right wing of the Fourteenth Irregular Cavalry of the Bengal Army. The opposite wings of each of these units were stationed at Nowgong.

Sir Robert Hamilton, reporting on relations among the houses of Bundelkhand following his April 1855 tour, characterized the armies of the chiefs as an "assembly of idle, dissipated men in parties independent of each other, under no proper control, and ready for any broil."[3] Bundela Rajput chiefs harbored grievances against the British for actions taken in their states as well as designs on each other. Raja Mardan Singh of Banpur hoped to regain the whole kingdom of Chanderi, the former possession of his ancestors. Many Thakurs (landlords) broke into rebellion in the region even before the troops rose at Lalitpur, the district headquarters. Mardan Singh was said to have visited the Rani of Jhansi following the death of her husband and thereafter to have kept in touch with her at frequent intervals. Some said the Rani had elicited promises of support from neighboring landowners of Oodgaon, Nonir, and Jigna. Jawahar Singh of Nanikpur and Mangal Singh of Jakhlon were also disaffected because their states had been partially or totally resumed. Jawahar Singh began plundering before the outbreak at Jhansi. The British had intelligence too that the Thakur landowners of Karhra a few miles from Jhansi intended to attack.[4]

At Almora another officer of the Salt Excise, an Englishman known locally for his knowledge of the language and customs, referred to the general atmosphere of unrest and disorder in Central India just prior to the Rebellion. "There were several gangs of robbers in Bundelkhand just waiting for an opportunity to plunder," he wrote.[5] This explosive situation in Bundelkhand belied the calm the English in North India displayed.

In Jhansi, Superintendent Alexander Skene was not particularly alarmed when news of the revolt at Meerut reached him. Though he had no English troops at Jhansi, he felt secure with his small contingent of native infantry and cavalry. "The troops here," he reported on 18 May, "I am glad to say, continue staunch and express their unbounded abhorrence of the atrocities committed at Meerut and Delhi. I am going on the principle of showing perfect confidence, and I am quite sure I am right." A few days later he reported signs of unrest in the town, especially among Thakurs, merchants, and bankers, but he was still confident: "All will settle down here . . . on the receipt of intelligence of success."[6]

Skene's nonchalance was reflected, too, in his offhand dismissal of the "small Rajahs and Chiefs." "They saw enough of rebellion, fourteen years ago, to give them a salutary dread of it. The Oorcha and Chutterpore and Ajeegurh men are children; the Dubbah man is off to Bithoor in a moribund state; and the Sumpther man is mad and a prisoner in his own fort; the Chirkaree man and the Punnah men almost the only chiefs worth mentioning, and they have kept out of everything of the kind hitherto—so I trust we are all safe." He added, "But for the feeling that this mutiny is universal I should say the men here are perfectly staunch."[7] Apparently none of the rumors yet disturbed Skene's sleep.

On 2 June, nonetheless, Skene finally took note of a rumor of an intended attack on Karhra by Thakurs and ordered Commander Dunlop to send a party to protect the town. Forewarned, the Thakurs took no action. Skene's continuing confidence on 3 June is difficult to explain. Two days earlier in broad daylight two bungalows in the Jhansi cantonment had been burned. This was the signal in many districts that the Sepoys were ready, poised for revolt. Skene still sensed no great danger. Captain Dunlop was similarly trustful of his troops. Reports from his spies about their difficulty in infiltrating the Sepoy lines also failed to arouse his suspicions. Neither Skene nor Dunlop took any precautions following the firing of the bungalows.

Captain Dunlop did, however, forward letters by Skene and Gordon to Major Kirke, commander at nearby Nowgong, a few days before the eruption at Jhansi. The letters told of rumors from separate sources that "Luchman Rao the servant of the Rani was doing his best to induce men of the 12th Native Infantry to mutiny." It was not known by these men, however, "if the Ranee authorized these procedures."[8] Dunlop still sensed no problem with the Jhansi troops.

Deputy Superintendent Gordon also had intimations that trouble was brewing in the ranks of the Sepoys. He was informed several days before the outbreak that "an adherent of the Ranee named Bolanath used to hold long private conferences with the native officers of the Jhansi troops, who frequently visited the Ranee's palace, and that some treachery was intended."[9] The head writer for the deputy commissioner's office, a man named Scott, similarly claimed there was "good reason to know that a mutiny was intended, and that the Ranee and the troops were one."[10] On 30 or 31 May, another Company employee by the name of Andrews went to Gordon and urged that precautionary measures be taken immediately regarding the fort and magazine. Andrews was convinced that the troops planned mutiny, and that the Thakurs were in collusion with the Sepoys. Gordon replied that he had already suggested some such measure to Skene, but Skene was convinced that any precautionary move would only precipitate mutiny at once.[11] Faced with the obvious need to balance military preparedness and caution with a show of confidence in Sepoy loyalty, the Jhansi officers clearly opted for a show of faith.

Apart from these warnings, none of the Rani's protests—those over resumption of the state, lifting of the ban on cow slaughter, use of funds for her son's sacred thread ceremony, or resumption of the villages that supported the temple—convinced Skene of the need for any precautions. Nor is there evidence that he was very concerned about the Sepoy grievances and malaise over the cartridges, the rumors of forcible conversion, or the night runners with their mysterious chapattis. After news of Meerut reached Jhansi, the Rani asked Skene for permission to raise a bodyguard of armed men for her own protection; Skene apparently agreed without hesitation.

The cantonment lay beyond the walled town of Jhansi, and within the cantonment the treasure and magazine were stored in an area called the Star Fort. It was this small fort rather than the Jhansi fort proper that was the focus of the first act of open mutiny. It happened on the afternoon of 5 June (4 June in some accounts). A company of the Twelfth Native Infantry, cheered on by gunners, marched into the Star Fort and occupied it. Captain Dunlop and his officers rushed to the parade ground, where the other four companies of the regiment denied any knowledge of the actions of the offending company and professed that they would stand by their officers. Still credulous, Captain Dunlop called for a parade the following morning. This was the usual response of a British commanding officer when faced with the first signs of revolt. The parade was intended to effect a show of confidence on the part of the British officers and to demonstrate loyalty and solidarity among the Sepoys. Dunlop, in fact, had implicit faith in the assurances of loyalty on the part of the Sepoys assembled at the parade ground that morning. After dismissing the troops, he made preparations to deal with the company that had occupied the Star Fort. He wrote letters and reports of the events and mailed them himself to other stations, including Nowgong. The same day he wrote Major Kirke at Nowgong saying simply, "The Artillery and Infantry have broken into Mutiny and have entered the Star Fort where are the guns and treasure. No one has been hurt yet. Look out for stragglers."[12]

On the afternoon of the fifth, Captain Skene sat in his office hearing petitions when Sepoys began firing in his direction. One shot fell at the door, the next flew over the house. Skene rose, rushed out the door, and seeing the Sepoys firing, shouted for his wife and four children. At the same time he ordered his carriage made ready at the stable. Faced with delay, he hurriedly took his wife and children by the hand and led them on foot toward the main fort, leaving instructions to his servant to take the carriage to Captain Gordon. Gordon sat in his bungalow writing a report when Skene's coachman and carriage arrived. He immediately took the carriage and made for the fort, overtaking the Skene family on the way. They joined him in the carriage and the party arrived safely at the fort. Skene then ordered his coachman to take the horses and carriage to the Rani's artillery sheds. His confidence in her was unshaken.[13] It was by then four or four-thirty, and the other English in the cantonment were all converging gradually on the fort, clutching a few possessions. Only four of the English inside the fort were military men.

Skene's servant related later that when the English entered the fort they tried to maintain their usual daily routine. A few servants were still able to slip unobtrusively into the fort with food and their English employers had them bring in dinner the first night and breakfast the following morning. The servants were directed to bring coal, wood, chickens, eggs, and sweetmeats to the fort on the night of 6 June. By later the same evening most of the servants had been apprehended. Skene's servant, however, testified that he was freed the next morning and made his way toward the fort again with some loaves of bread and bottles of milk. Gordon and Skene, looking over the fort wall, saw the servant and lowered a rope to haul up the provisions. As the servant returned from the fort he was apprehended by insurgents for the second time and was unable thereafter to provide Skene and his party with food.[14]

During the night of the sixth the armed watchmen and Thakurs who had entered the fort with the English deserted, either through fear or a change of heart. Some inside the fort suggested escape during the night as the only possible hope for the besieged English. Several possible routes were studied, but this prospect was abandoned as too dangerous. Dawn was already visible and the only two gates of the fort were being closely watched, both from without and within. From the main fort the English could see between 100 and 125 mutineers posted at the door of the magazine and around the treasury of the Star Fort.[15]

During the morning of the sixth, Gordon wrote pleas for help to nearby Datia, Tehri, and Gursarai, all of whose chiefs professed loyalty to the British. He also wrote the tehsildar (revenue collector) of Jhansi and several Thakurs for aid.[16] Soon after the English made their way into their refuge, Gordon ordered the police to garrison the fort, which they did. Shortly thereafter, early in the morning, several cavalrymen came to the fort with a message from Captain Dunlop to the effect that only thirty-five Sepoys had mutinied and that the English might therefore return in safety to their bungalows. Skene, however, was not ready to trust this message. Later in the morning, about nine o'clock, a second message arrived from Dunlop, this one in writing. This time Skene and Gordon, together with Dr. McEgan, the cantonment physician, returned to the cantonment to meet Dunlop. Dunlop told them that the mutiny was only partial, that only thirty-five men of the cavalry had mutinied and were holding the Star Fort. Dunlop tried to induce Gordon to let him have some powder and ammunition, reiterating that the mutiny could be quelled with those who remained loyal. Gordon, unconvinced, feared that the munitions would only fall into the hands of the insurgents to be used against the English inside the fort. Even after Skene and Gordon returned with McEgan to the fort at ten o'clock, Dunlop still sought their aid through written messages. The morning conversation between Dunlop, Skene, and Gordon was not recorded, but their servants understood the nature of their disagreement.[17] The servants were ordered back to the bungalows to look after the houses and belongings of the English.

On the morning of the sixth when Gordon's servant again brought tea for Gordon and the others, it appeared that the whole force had mutinied; guards had been posted outside the fort and were clearly visible to the English inside. The guards were given instructions not to allow anyone to pass with food or water for the English or even to speak to them, according to Gordon's servant. There is some disagreement in both Indian and English accounts regarding the exact timing of events of the four days following 5 June.

Sometime after meeting with Skene and Gordon, probably the morning of the sixth, Dunlop took the precaution of preparing some shells and went to post his letters. Returning from the post office, he passed near the Twelfth parade and was attacked and killed by men of the Twelfth Native Infantry, an ensign named Taylor with him. Lieutenant Campbell, officer of the Fourteenth Irregular Cavalry, was shot and wounded but made it into the fort clinging to the back of his horse. (In some versions it is Taylor, not Campbell, who rides into the fort wounded and clutching his horse's mane.) Another lieutenant, Turnbull, was on foot nearby and climbed into a tree to escape but was discovered and shot down.[18]

Some accounts relate that a mullah named Ahsan Ali called all true Muslims to prayer as the signal for the troops to mutiny. The mutineers stormed the jail and there the daroga, or warden, Bakhshish Ali, released the prisoners. This marked the beginning of the general plunder and burning of the bungalows in the cantonment. On the afternoon of the sixth the mutineers, joined by the freed prisoners and police, all joined the siege of the fort. The English officers inside returned the fire of the insurgents. The rebels brought a gun up to the Orchha gate and began firing on the fort wall. They attempted an escalade but could not get over the wall because of the English guns pointed at them through the parapets of the walls.

Gordon's servant testified that Gordon wrote a letter, which he threw down over the fort wall, calling on "the Ranee's servants" to cease firing and take his letter to the Rani. The servants brought back a reply from the Rani, which the English pulled over the fort wall on a string. The Rani's reply, according to Gordon's servant, stated that she was helpless, that the Sepoys had surrounded her palace and accused her of protecting the English. She reported, moreover, that the Sepoys wanted immediate surrender of the fort and some assistance from her. She claimed she had replied to the mutineers that she had no power to evict the English from the fort, but in order to save her life she had sent some of her men and two guns to the mutineers. The servant later alleged that she advised the English that if they wished to save their lives, they must leave the fort and Jhansi as well, though she did not specify how. The besieged English replied by the same messenger that if they had a carriage they would leave in whatever direction the Rani proposed. She did not respond.[19]

Skene became increasingly convinced that the English could not hold out in the fort indefinitely. In his view the only hope lay in escape from the fort through the good offices of the Rani. Why Skene reached this decision after only two days in the fort is not clear. The fort had its own water supply, but undoubtedly the English were short of food and also suffering from shock and various discomforts. For whatever reason, Skene decided to send envoys to talk with the Rani and solicit her aid. Four men were chosen: Scott, Andrews, and two Purcells. Of the fate of these men Kaye relates, "They were sent by the Rani to our own revolted Sepoys, who deliberately murdered them."[20] According to Gordon's servant, Andrews disguised himself as a native in a turban and tried to seek a meeting with the Rani. Escaping from the fort, he made his way to the Rani's cowshed, where he was recognized by her servants. He offered them ten rupees if they would spare him. They took the rupees, murdered him, and thew his body onto a hayrick. The English in the fort were anguished to learn of the fate of their messengers.[21]

The rebels moved a gun up toward the inner Ganesha gate and began firing at the fort wall. Within the fort, rifles had been distributed, women assigned the tasks of cooking and preparing ammunition, and even children enlisted to help pile stones behind the gates. Each person in the fort had an assigned post. The rebels were surprised at the vigor of the defense. On the morning of the eighth the mutineers tried to scale the walls of the fort but were shot down from the walls and the escalade aborted. Renewing their attack, the insurgents toward afternoon captured the lower part of the fort wall. Two Indians still inside the fort, anticipating that the escalade might succeed, had tried to open one of the gates to let the mutineers in. They were immediately shot by Captains Gordon and Burgess, but in the skirmish another captain, Powys, was killed. Captain Gordon's fire toward the gun at the Ganesha gate had kept the rebel gun silent for some time. He decided to look through one of the gun emplacements on the wall to see what effect his firing had had and ascertain exactly what the rebel strength was. Just as he peered through the parapet emplacement a bullet struck him in the head and he fell dead. Gordon was the ranking officer in the fort and the key to the morale of the English defenders. The death of "the life and soul of the garrison" was a serious blow to the besieged.[22] Attempts to get help from outside, from Gwalior, through Anglo-Indian messengers failed when they were intercepted and killed. Messages sent to Orchha and Datia similarly elicited no aid.

Massacre

On the afternoon of the eighth, three days after the beginning of the siege, Captain Skene hung out a flag of truce, hoping to negotiate terms. Despite the fort's water supply, the English were short of food. Gordon's death, furthermore, had ended any hope of continued military resistance from inside the fort, and there was still no sign of any relief from nearby stations. The intensity of the siege on the afternoon of the seventh and morning of the eighth was surely a factor in Skene's decision. Responsible for the lives of some sixty English men, women, and children crowded into the fort in these circumstances, Skene saw no alternative.

Leaders of the insurgents, among them the jail daroga, came to the fort gate to hear what Skene had to say. They "swore oaths, both Hindu and Muslim," that the English could leave safely if they would vacate the fort, lay down their arms, and surrender. The question of who authorized the promise of safe conduct has prompted much debate among historians. Many English accounts have it that the promise was given on authority of the Rani. It seems unlikely, however, in view of her earlier warning to the English of her helplessness against the Sepoys, that she would have given such an assurance, or, even if she had, that Skene would have been credulous enough to accept it. Yet most accounts agree that Skene did accept someone's promise of safe conduct. No doubt he felt he had no other recourse. Skene, then, led all the besieged —men, women, and children—down out of the fort and into the area beyond the main gate. What happened next was one of the horrors of the Rebellion.

The rebels tied the English together and led them in a procession through the town to an area called Jokhun Bagh beyond the city wall. Men were separated from women and children. The cavalry and infantry troops then declared they were acting under orders of the rissaldar, the cavalry commander. The jail daroga and his assistants began the massacre, Bakhshish Ali himself cutting down Captain Skene first. The rebels wielded swords and spears until every English man, woman, and child lay dead or dying on the ground. Gordon's servant watched the grisly scene and later related that "Captain Browne's sister begged very hard for her life. She said she would remain wherever they told her and held the hand of the Sepoy, but they would not spare her and she was killed too." Mrs. McEgan, the doctor's wife, threw her arms around her husband in a desparate attempt to save him, but she was beaten and pushed aside. Dr. McEgan was then killed, and his wife threw herself on his body, where she was killed also.[23]

The bodies of the English were left for three days on the road where they fell and then were thrown into gravel pits and covered over. In the evening after the massacre the rebels issued a proclamation: "The people are God's; the country is the King's; and the two religions govern."[24]

Only one adult escaped, an Anglo-Indian named Mrs. Mutlow, taking her two small children with her. She later told how she eluded the notice of the insurgents and hid with her children in a temple at Jokhun Bagh. She remained there in terror of her life for a month before she managed to get help and escape. Her husband was among those killed at Jokhun Bagh. Two other Anglo-Indians who had remained in the cantonment also managed to escape: a man referred to as Conductor Reilly and a clerk named Crawford. Reilly made his way toward Burwa Saugor, and Crawford somehow got out of the fort on the night of the seventh and went toward Samthar and Kanpur. Gordon's servant testified that he, himself, was detained in Jhansi for ten days before being allowed to return home to Saugor.[25]

For a brief interlude it was uncertain if the rebels would allow the Rani to retain the throne. They brought to Jhansi a Newalkar relative and former claimant to the throne, Sadasheo Rao Narain, from Unao twelve miles away. The Rani was thus coerced into promising the rebels more money and aid than Narain had offered in order to retain her throne. The insurgents then issued a second proclamation: "The people are God's, the country is the padshah's, and the Raj is Ranee Luchmee Baee's."[26] With that the rebels took the road for Delhi on the eleventh. Narain also left Jhansi with three hundred men and on 13 June seized the small fort at Karhra. There he appointed his own officials, levied taxes, and proclaimed that he had seated himself on the throne of Jhansi. The Rani sent troops against him shortly thereafter, and he fled to Nurwar, in the territory of Maharaja Scindia of Gwalior. When Jhansi was retaken by the British, Narain was taken prisoner and transported for life.

The day after the departure of the rebels from Jhansi the Rani wrote the first of two letters to Erskine giving her account of events and deploring the murders. In it she reported that the government troops at Jhansi, "through their faithlessness, cruelty and violence killed all the European civil and military officers, the clerks and all their families." She expressed regret that, having "only 100 or 50 people guarding her house," she had been helpless to assist the victims. She had herself been victimized by the rebels, who "behaved with much violence against herself and servants and extorted a great deal of money from her."[27] She had been compelled to pay large sums to the rebels in property and cash "to save her life and honor," as she had been threatened in messages "through the Tehseeldar of Jhansi the Revenue and Judicial Mukhtadar Courts and Superintendents Courts to the effect that if she at all hesitated to comply with their requests they would blow up her palace with guns."[28] She had urged the police to remain at their posts after the outbreak and hastened to send this report to Erskine as soon as the rebels left Jhansi for Delhi.

Two days later she sent a second letter to Erskine, this time informing him that disorder and plunder were prevalent and that it was "quite beyond her power to make any arrangement for the safety of the District." She had no funds and had sold her personal property "to save the town from being plundered." She was doing her best to maintain order in Jhansi but did not believe she could hold on much longer "without a competent Government force and fund." She therefore requested orders from Erskine. With this letter she sent a more detailed account of events at Jhansi. She related that when the English entered the fort (she dates this the fifth), she had "sent a few of her own guards to the Fort for their aid." On the night of the eleventh the rebels left and she hoped would "go straight to hell for their deeds." The mutineers had compelled one hundred fifty of her men to join in their assault on the fort on the eighth.

Erskine received both letters and sent a reply on 23 June, which he followed up with another dated 2 July in case she had not received the first. In his reply he gave no indication that he doubted the veracity of the Rani's report. He said he hoped to send officers and troops soon to restore order in Jhansi, but pending the arrival of a new superintendent in Jhansi, he authorized her to manage the district for the British government, collecting the revenue, raising such police as necessary, and making other proper arrangements. He assured her that the new superintendent would repay her for her losses and expenses and "deal liberally" with her. Erskine sent with the letter two proclamations: one with his seal authorizing the Rani to rule the district until further orders, and another issued on presumption of the retaking of Delhi.[29]

Erskine naturally forwarded copies of his correspondence with the Rani to Fort William. In his cover letters describing the steps he had authorized the Rani to take, he commented, "It will be seen by the Ranee's own account she in no way lent assistance to the Mutineers and rebels," that on the contrary she herself was plundered. Unlike Erskine, however, Fort William was unconvinced by the Rani's account. The governor-general's reply came through his secretary to the effect that he did not blame Erskine for accepting the Rani's account or for authorizing her to manage the government under the circumstances. "Yet this circumstance will not protect her if her account turns out to be false," the governor-general warned. Moreover, from Major Ellis' account, it appeared to Fort William that "the Ranee did lend assistance to the mutineers and rebels and that she gave guns and men."[30]

Erskine, to be strictly accurate, should have made it clear that in both her letters and account the Rani did state that she had complied with rebel demands, though under duress, and that her men had been compelled to participate in the assault on the fort. Erskine may have anticipated some official criticism, and in his attempt to support both his and the Rani's actions may have overstated the case for the Rani's noninvolvement.

Fort William in October proclaimed a reward of one thousand rupees each for two men who were designated as ringleaders in the murders at Jhansi. The accused were Rissaldar Kalee Khan of the Fourteenth Irregular Cavalry and Ahmad Hassein, tehsildar (local revenue official) at Jhansi.[31] It is noteworthy that neither the Rani nor the jail daroga were designated culpable at this time. Somewhat later, questions were raised by English officials regarding the Rani's role in the uprising and massacre at Jhansi.

5

The Rani's Role

I hope [the rebels] will go straight to hell for their deeds.

—*The Rani's letter to W. C. Erskine, 14 June 1857*

The Revolt Spreads

The contagion of revolt spread rapidly across Bundelkhand. When word of the Jhansi uprising first got out, relief parties started out from several neighboring stations, but each party was stopped either by insurgents within its own ranks or by news of the murder of the English at Jhansi. With nearly the whole of Bundelkhand in revolt, Gwalior was regarded by most English as a safe haven, and many fugitives from the insurgents accordingly made their way toward Gwalior. Some arrived while others, less fortunte, were captured and imprisoned or killed along the way. In Lalitpur another Captain Gordon was coerced into signing over the administration of the district to the raja of Banpur out of fear that refusal would endanger the lives of his party of fugitives; he also distributed treasure among the cavalry as a means of guaranteeing the safety of the English. This Lalitpur party was protected by the tutor of the young raja of Orchha, Prem Narain. Narain later was rewarded by the government and subsequently by the raja of Shahgarh, who himself vacillated between friendship and hostility toward the English. The party of fugitives finally reached the safety of Saugor on 14 September.[1]

When news of the uprising at Jhansi reached the nearby state of Jaloun, some officers attempted to send relief. This was the plan of a certain Captain Browne, but before he could leave Jaloun with a force, news came on the ninth of the massacre at Jhansi, and he abandoned the idea. Instead he accepted the aid of the Gursarai chief which the chief's sons had offered. As Browne left the town of Orai he found the whole of northern Jaloun in confusion—customs officials in revolt, police calling for their pay, and "petty chiefs ready to rise at any moment." Chief Kesho Rao of Gursarai took over the government of Jaloun in the name of the British government. He kept control briefly, protecting English fugitives from the mutineers, including two deputy collectors from Orai, before being deposed and imprisoned by the revels led by Tatya Tope.[2]

Thakurs rose and plundered in other districts surrounding Jhansi when news of the Jhansi revolt became known. Disorder spread through Lalitpur, Chanderi, and Talbehat. In the view of Capt. J. W. Pinkney, some Rajput rajas, including the Banpur raja, were playing a double game, professing loyalty to the government and criticizing other Thakurs while at the same time actually siding with the mutineers.[3]

At Almora station near Jhansi, Deputy Commissioner J. V. Sturt learned of the Jhansi outbreak immediately after it erupted on the fifth. He was ordered to go to the relief of Jhansi fort with half his small force of one hundred fifty men. Many of the men made excuses of family crises to avoid going with him. Several deserted, slipping away under cover of dark as Sturt approached Jhansi. Ten miles out of Jhansi Sturt got news of the massacre and was uncertain as to what course he should take. It was possible that his men might murder him and desert when they heard what had happened at Jhansi. Sturt quickly decided to go back to collect the rest of his men, but by then all his troops had deserted. Sturt's extant report notes, "The very men we trusted with such blinded sight were made the instrument of our destruction." He returned to Talbehat and, learning that the troops at Lalitpur had also mutinied, he ordered the gate of the Talbehat fort guarded. By dawn of the seventh, however, Sturt found himself alone except for a few domestic servants. He then disguised himself as a native, mounted his horse, and managed to persuade one servant to accompany him. He took the road to Banda in hopes of reaching Fatehgarh to join his family. He avoided the roads through Jhansi and Gwalior and also skirted Mau Ranipur, which he discovered was in the hands of the rebels.

Sturt on the thirteenth met another European in flight and learned that both Kanpur and Fatehpur were in the hands of the insurgents and that Banda was expected to fall next. He subsequently encountered a party of Europeans fleeing from Nowgong and told them that their destination, Banda, was expected to fall momentarily. Sturt had his horse and all his money taken, and was separated from the party. He was then shown the road to Hamirpur instead of the road to Banda. After further harrowing adventures he reached Charkhari and was given asylum there for a month by the maharaja. He eventually made his way to Kanpur, where he volunteered in defense of the fort against the siege by Tatya Tope. Sturt's extraordinary escape was made feasible by his unusual command of local languages and ability to deal with villagers along his route. Sturt later related that he felt able to go into villages for food and water because he "looked native, knew every class of country lingo, and used the name Ram Gopal."[4]

In Nowgong, where the opposite wings of the Jhansi units were stationed, Major Kirke received Dunlop's letter telling of the capture of Star Fort. Kirke prided himself on the loyalty of the right wing of the Twelfth Native Infantry; as a show of confidence, the officers of that unit slept among their men. Nevertheless, when Kirke found some of his men inciting others to mutiny, he discharged them on the spot and sent them away from Nowgong under guard. When he got word of the uprising at Jhansi he despatched a force of thirty cavalrymen to relieve the English there. They halted en route, however, when they heard that all the English at Jhansi had been murdered. Despite Kirke's confidence in his troops, on 10 June at sunset they too mutinied, three Sikhs taking the lead. Since it was apparent that the whole force was in revolt, the English fled toward Charkhari and Mahoba. Kirke and several other officers died during their flight.[5]

At Mhow, another station near Jhansi, a deputy collector named Thornton made an unsuccessful attempt to raise troops to go to the aid of Jhansi. Thornton wrote Erskine that he had warned Gordon at Jhansi not to rely on the Sepoys there as it was "well known" that both at Jhansi and Nowgong the troops "were holding nocturnal meetings which boded ill for the English." Moreover, Thornton felt that "had the least precautionary measures been taken at Jhansi and even the local corps for which the Lieutenant-Governor given his sanction been raised, the catastrophe at Jhansi might have been averted." Unfortunately Skene and Gordon were so convinced that the men at Jhansi were staunch that they would take no precautions.[6] Erskine in his report to Fort William noted that Skene and Gordon had sent off expresses in every direction for assistance and were trying in particular to get aid from the Jhansi Thakurs who, Erskine feared, "would be much more likely to plunder the Sepoys than to aid the European officers."[7]

It was apparent by now to most of the English in India that the whole of North India was in revolt and no troops whose loyalty was assured were available to go to the relief of Jhansi or any other station in Bundelkhand. It would be several months before the situation could be reversed.

The Rani's Role

What precisely was the Rani's role in the uprising and massacre at Jhansi? Critical though this question is to an understanding of the motives and aspirations of the Rani, the evidence unfortunately is conflicting. From her own pen we have two letters from the time of the events in question, June of 1857. Similarly scant evidence remains from among her closest Indian contemporaries in Jhansi. Eyewitness testimony from the events of June comes from three individuals: the two servants of Skene and Gordon and the Anglo-Indian woman who escaped the fort with her children. These three accounts are at times conflicting (the servants, for example, contradict each other). There are also British accounts from three officials who dealt with the Rani and subsequently assessed her actions: Erskine and an official under him at Jabalpur, Captain Pinkney, and Robert Hamilton at Indore. Other extant narratives from officials in districts near Jhansi also survive, for example, from Jaloun, Mhow, and Almora, but the information they provide on Jhansi is fragmentary and peripheral, often based on hearsay. Then there are numerous accounts by other British officials more removed in both time and place from Jhansi and the Rani. The accounts of writers such as Kaye, Charles Ball, and G. W. Forrest, leading early historians of the Rebellion, are among them.

The dearth of written sources from the Indian perspective is tantamount to silence. It is not until after the battles of 1858 that even oral Indian sources occur, and they begin ten or more years after the events. Beyond these categories there are numerous British memoirs of service in India, some of them nearly contemporary but reflecting the rumor and bias that permeated English official ranks. Finally, as is true of the Rebellion generally, there are secondary sources, assessments by present-day historians, both English and Indian.

Addressing the question of the lack of contemporary Indian accounts of 1857, the historian P. C. Joshi alludes to the traditional Indian disinclination to keep historical chronicles. He also suggests as an equally cogent reason for the gap in documentation the fact that any Indian attempt to keep records in 1857 was made at the risk of an Indian's life. Joshi therefore concludes that our understanding of the Indian side of the story is incomplete.[8] Moreover, what sources we do have are likely to be partisan, inflamed by emotion and the horrors perpetrated by both sides.

Consider the Rani's predisposition before the uprising at Jhansi in May of 1857. What hard evidence is there regarding her views and attitudes, her goals and sentiments toward the English? It is clear from her own writing, or at least from the memorials submitted in her name during 1854 and 1855, that she was unhappy about a number of official measures taken by the British. But in 1856 and early 1857, apart from her distress over British policy, the Rani must have been mindful of the fact that Jhansi was a small state surrounded by many rapacious Bundela Rajput chiefs, some of whom had designs on Jhansi and other neighbors. The threat from the rival chiefs became all too apparent to the Rani and her advisers following expulsion of the English from Jhansi in 1857. Under the circumstances, then, she must have felt in May that her security lay with the preponderant and paramount British power, a feeling that may have remained with her even in June.[9]

Survival among the Bundela Rajput states in nineteenth-century North Central India surely required considerable diplomatic acumen as well as military power. Chiefs who had succeeded before the British advent there did so through long decades of experience amid contending Maratha, Mughal, and Rajput rajas. In June of 1857 the Rani must have recognized her predicament: if she gave wholehearted support to the English she would be killed by the insurgents, while if she gave unequivocal aid to the rebels she would be killed by the English.[10] It was hardly a situation to encourage complacency. There seems to be no quarrel with the view that her major concern was protecting, if not regaining, her lost state in the extremely precarious situation in which she found herself in June of 1857.

What are we to make of British allegations that she was "nursing grievances," waiting for an opportunity to avenge the wrongs done her? Pinkney's narrative provided an immediate source of this perception, and was subsequently widely quoted by contemporary English authors. Pinkney enumerated the Rani's grievances as evidence of the ill will she harbored toward the Company. "She wanted revenge," wrote Pinkney, "and she like many other Mahratta women of rank, possessed a masculine spirit, well fitting her to carry out her designs."[11] Pinkney's error in characterizing her as a "Mahratta woman" reflects his inadequate knowledge of facts about the Rani, facts which have remained obscured by the errors of those who have relied on Pinkney subsequently.

Another English author referred to the Rani as "a woman of indomitable personality," whose perception of "real or fancied wrongs inspired . . . a smouldering hatred of the British race."[12] This author admits, nevertheless, that there is room for doubt about the Rani's guilt in the massacre, since the Sepoys were not under her control at the time. Pinkney, on the other hand, referred in his narrative to the warnings of Head Writer Scott at Jhansi, who "mixed with the natives and had much better information of what was going on." Scott, according to Pinkney, "persisted in avowing that a mutiny was intended, and that the Ranee and the troops are one."[13] Again, Pinkney's assessment of the Rani's motives and actions is based not on direct evidence but on secondhand knowledge and conjecture of what the English guessed was going on in her mind. His report, it should be noted, was written in November 1858, several months after the Rani was killed.

English officials like Pinkney recognized the legitimacy of the Rani's grievances because many English acknowledged that she had been dealt with unfairly and unwisely. Apart from racial bias and hatred fanned on both sides by events of the Rebellion, some English no doubt harbored feelings of guilt at the treatment of the Rani, including the fact that she was killed in action by British troops. These British sentiments are apparent in official accounts of her death, as we shall see. It seems reasonable to conjecture, too, that the attribution of rebellious sentiments to Lakshmi before June 1857 may have been a retrospective reading based on actual events occurring later in 1857 or even 1858.

What finally can be concluded about the Rani's actions in June of 1857 when the Rebellion broke out in Jhansi? T. A. Martin, a man who claimed he was at Jhansi at the time, later wrote both Sturt and Damodar Rao denying that Lakshmi was implicated in the massacre or even anxious to rebel. According to Martin she hesitated and debated for some time before taking up arms. His letter to Damodar Rao has been quoted by numerous Indian historians.

> Your poor mother was very unjustly and cruelly dealt with, and no one knows her true case as I do. The poor thing took no part whatever in the

> massacre of the European residents of Jhansi in June 1857. On the contrary she supplied them with food for two days after they had gone into the fort, got one hundred matchlock men from Kurrura and sent them to assist us. But after being kept a day in the fort they were sent away in the evening. She then advised Major [*sic*] Skene and Captain Gordon to fly at once to Duttia and place themselves under the Raja's protection.[14]

Erskine, in Jabalpur, gave credence to the Rani's account of events in early June, as we have seen. Hamilton, the official at Indore who had twice met with the Rani, similarly wrote in support of her innocence. "Not a paper incriminating the Ranee did I find nor did there appear any evidence that she desired or was privy to the murder of any Europeans . . . The English were induced to leave the Fort by the persuasion of the Darogah of the Jail . . . and a Ressaldar of the Irregulars. The Ranee was not present or any man on her part."[15] Erskine, at a later writing, apparently revised his initial reaction to the Rani's account, for he alleges later that the English on leaving the fort "were most basely and treacherously murdered by order of the Rani."[16] Still another official, Deputy Collector Thornton at Mhow, depicts an even more active role for the Rani. "It is the 'General Impression,' that the mutineers were about to leave Jhansi and were persuaded by the Rani to attack the fort, for which she furnished armed men."[17]

There remains the puzzling question of who offered the besieged English safe conduct out of the fort. Later English writers are certain that the Rani was responsible for the massacre, "predicated on her hatred of the English race." This conclusion is shared also by Forrest and Malleson.[18] One contemporary official at Jaloun reported that the tehsildar suggested to the Rani that the massacre of all Europeans was the means to regain her state, and that she therefore induced the troops to carry out the deed. Another Englishman at Agra cited as evidence of the Rani's evil influence the difference between the behavior of the insurgents at Jhansi and those at Nowgong, who did not harm their officers.[19]

The eyewitness testimony by the fort survivor, Mrs. Mutlow, claims the Rani was the one who offered the English safe conduct. It is interesting that Pinkney's narrative does not support this claim, although he does state that the envoys Scott and the two Purcells were sent on her orders to the lines of the insurgents where they were killed. The safe conduct promise, however, Pinkney attributes to a written communication from the rissaldar of the Fourteenth Irregular Cavalry. Pinkney also alleges that it was on order from the rissaldar that the English were killed,[20] and that the jail daroga began the grisly work.

One local official, Thornton again, alleges that not only did the Rani sanction the killing of the English, but she paid the insurgents thirty-five thousand rupees plus two elephants and five horses to carry it out. If it were true that the Rani authorized the killings, one early historian saw no need for further communication with her or for any other action except to hang her.[21]

In several English accounts, both contemporary and later, actions of the Rani's servants, such as the murder of the envoys, are taken as synonymous with her orders. However, in the confusion and crisis of events of 7 and 8 June it is entirely possible that those in her service were using her name without her sanction or even knowledge to achieve their own ends.[22] Moreover, had Lakshmi been in complete control at Jhansi, it would not have been necessary or possible for the insurgents to bring in another claimant to the Jhansi throne to challenge her authority.[23]

Numerous letters allegedly written by the Rani have come to light in connection with the 1957 centenary of the Rebellion to provide "evidence" that the Rani worked to organize revolt even before the outbreak at Meerut. One such letter, written in bad Hindi, refers to the greased cartridges before the date of their introduction into India. The letter is, in the opinion of historian Surendranath Sen, an obvious fabrication by those anxious to depict the Rani as organizer of the revolt and therefore heroine of the first war of independence.[24] The nationalist view of the Rani as organizer and leader of the Rebellion ironically coincides with the opinion of contemporary Englishmen who judged her guilty. This guilt, however spurious it may be, made her at once a martyred heroine in India and a treacherous "Jezebel" in England.

This concern to portray the Rani as heroine of the first phase of the independence struggle motivates historians such as V. D. Savarkar to depict her as organizer of the uprising at Jhansi.[25] If, on the other hand, the Rani is cleared of all complicity in the uprising and massacre, does she still remain a heroine and martyr to the cause of independence? Manmohan Kaur, addressing this intriguing question, asserts that the Rani was neither coerced into helping the rebels nor was she faithful to the English. Otherwise, she argues, the Rani would have taken refuge with the English as did Scindia.[26] There is, nonetheless, considerable evidence that she was coerced by the insurgents. It might further be argued that the degree of her reluctance to fight the British is not really an issue in the final assessment of her heroism, since in the end she did take up arms and die valiantly on the battlefield at Gwalior.

Yet another aspect of the question of her complicity relates to the role of her father, Moropant, and her relationship to his "plans." One British document has it that "the Rani's father Moro Pant was one of the chief instigators of the rebellion in that part of the country." In this view, he could not possibly have kept Lakshmi in the dark about the impending revolt. He must have sought her advice and assistance.[27]

The Tambe family of Nagpur, descendants of Moropant, throws more light on the relationship between Moropant and his daughter. G. R. Tambe was the son of the Rani's half brother, Chintaman Rao, Moropant's son by the second wife he married in Jhansi. G. R. Tambe in his unpublished manuscript asserts that Moropant specifically moulded Lakshmi's character to groom her for her future role. The extraordinary training Moropant's young daughter received was the result of an astrological prediction given when Manu was in her infancy. Manu, according to the astrologer, was destined for an outstanding career; she would become a ruler and have an army of her own. According to G. R. Tambe's son, E. G. Tambe, Moropant's influence on Lakshmi was critical from the time of her childhood through the period when she was rani and lasted until after the siege of Jhansi when he was killed.[28] Though it is quite likely that Moropant was unhappy with British rule and may even had urged his daughter to fight, his access to the plans and actions of the Sepoys remains a debatable point. The account of Skene's servant of the events in Jhansi alleges that it was the Rani's father who ordered the servant taken to the rissaldar to be "murdered or to be blown from a gun" because he had supplied Gordon and Skene with food.[29] The servant nevertheless managed to survive to give his testimony, while Moropant was captured and hanged after the British retook Jhansi.

Sir John Kaye, leading historian of the Rebellion, concludes: "Whether the Rani instigated this atrocity, or to what extent she was implicated in it, can never be clearly known. I have been informed, on good authority, that none of the Rani's servants were present on the occasion of the massacre. It seems to have been mainly the work of our own old followers."[30] Senior Indian historian R. C. Majumdar takes Kaye's conclusion even further. He charges that the failure of Kaye and Pinkney to take note of Erskine's reply and action regarding the Rani's resumption of administration in Jhansi is part of a "conspiracy of silence," a governmental failure to clear the Rani of charges in connection with the uprising. Majumdar also finds it strange that Pinkney made no mention of the Rani's assurances of loyalty in her letters to Erskine. Erskine's judgement as the highest British official in the region is convincing evidence, in Majumdar's mind, that the Rani was not implicated.[31]

Yet Erskine's judgement at the time was not accepted by his English superiors, who were convinced that the responsibility and culpability for the events at Jhansi were the Rani's. Following Erskine's reply to her correspondence of 12 and 14 June, all her subsequent communications to British officials went unanswered. The British failed also to take a stand during the September-October invasion of Jhansi by forces from Orchha. As late as January and February of 1858, Lakshmi was still addressing letters to Erskine, Hamilton, and others. No response came.

Charles Canning, Dalhousie's successor as governor-general, in February wrote Hamilton from Fort William with instruction on the treatment to be accorded the Rani in the event she should fall into British hands.

> She must be tried, not by a Court-Martial, but by a Commissioner appointed for the purpose . . . If for any reason it would not be possible to deal with her at once and if there should be any difficulty in keeping her in custody in or near Jhansi, she may be sent here. But it is desirable that the preliminary inquiry into her conduct which will decide whether there be grounds for a trial should be completed before she arrives here. She must not come here with any doubt as to whether she deserves to be tried or not.[32]

Thus it was that the Rani came to be viewed by the English as a rebel. She must have guessed from their failure to reply to her letters after 14 June that her communications were falling on deaf ears. Even as Gen. Sir Hugh Rose's Field Force was advancing on Jhansi in March of 1858, Lakshmi was still desperately sending off letters to Jabalpur, Jaloun, and Agra. They met silence.

6

The Rani and the British Make Ready

> Although the news of the total defeat of the rebels at Cawnpore and that of the advance of British forces has been received by the Rani, she seems to entertain no fears.
>
> —*Secret Consultation, 8 March 1858*

The Rani's Rule in Jhansi

Following the departure of the insurgents from Jhansi, the Rani assumed control there as Erskine had authorized her to do pending arrival of a new British superintendent. Her administration of Jhansi was vigorous and firm. She opened a mint, distributed food and clothing to the indigent, and saw that the public peace was preserved. Laskhmi also went regularly beyond the city wall to worship at the temple of the goddess bearing her name. She moved easily among the townspeople, sometimes in a white widow's sari. Jhansi residents say she was beloved by residents there, more so than her husband or his two predecessors, who had not distinguished themselves in any way.

Yet she did not behave as an orthodox Brahmin widow. She did not shave her head, break all her bangles, or dress exclusively in the traditional widow's white. She instead took to wearing a style of dress more suited to her active life. For this she was criticized by some of the more orthodox Brahmins in Jhansi. In portraits the Rani is portrayed in one of two styles of clothing, each of which would have enabled her to ride and pursue her vigorous lifestyle. One was a modification of the Maharashtrian sari, which differs from the sari elsewhere in India. It consists of ten yards of material draped through the legs like a man's dhoti to create a kind of loose trouser. The other garment she is shown wearing is trousers and a long tunic, loose-belted and reaching to the ankle. With either costume she is shown wearing a wide-belted silk blouse with a diamond-studded sword in her cummerbund or sari end.

On her head she often wore a cap and silk turban decorated with a string of pearls, as in her better known portraits. In her dress and bearing, then, she proclaimed that the time had come to prepare seriously for the problems facing Jhansi, not least of which were military. Far from conforming to the image of the helpless young widow some of her

Fig. 3. Popular-style painting of the Rani. The original, a gift from the late Jaya Appasamy, is in the author's possession.

hostile neighbors anticipated, she revealed instead a woman to conjure with.

The Rani decided after she resumed control to celebrate the annual festivities honoring the principal Newalkar deity, the goddess Lakshmi. The Haladi-Kunku festival was held in the durbar hall of the palace, where an image of the goddess was bedecked with ornaments, roses, lilies, and marigolds. The floors were covered with rich carpets, on which offerings of fruit, sweets, and silver were placed. All the women of Jhansi were invited and streamed into the palace to honor the goddess. The Rani moved among her guests wearing a white sari and pearl necklace.[1] The annual round of religious festivals was traditionally a central part of government in India, and by these observances the Rani demonstrated the effectiveness of her rule. The festival also symbolized the importance the Rani attached to her bond with the women of Jhansi.

The Rani turned her attention particularly to the serious problems of security and defense. She enlisted troops, cast cannon, and manufactured other weapons. Since horsemanship, swordsmanship, and the imperatives of military strategy were hardly conventional pursuits for a Brahmin widow, neighboring chiefs must have wondered how the young Rani came to know of them.

An arresting analogy is provided by Joan of Arc. Joan's father was an innkeeper located on an important crossroad where generals, ministers, and other politically important persons were wont to stop. Joan must have listened intently to the conversations and discussions that took place in her father's inn. The question of how the Rani acquired her technical knowledge of weaponry is partly explained by her childhood in the company of the boys at the last peshwa's court. There she learned to ride and became an accomplished equestrienne, reputedly an excellent judge of horses. She joined her palace playmates in kite-flying contests and other boys' games. She learned to use the swords in the peshwa's extensive armory and developed an eye for swords as well as for horses. And when she was not allowed to participate actively in the boys' play, she sat on the sidelines and watched intently. The story of her resentment at not being allowed to ride an elephant with Nana Sahib is often repeated and appeared in the film version of the Rani's life. Although she was occasionally excluded because of her sex, she often managed to participate with her male companions, whose company she preferred to that of palace women.

The Rani may have had the edge over Joan of Arc in knowledge of weaponry and growth of astute generalship. Moreover, unlike Joan, she appears to have suffered no qualms when it came to using her weapons. Troops of the Bundelkhand Legion were stationed at Jhansi at least by 1842, and she could have watched them drill. Legend has it that when she went to Jhansi at marriage she created a women's military unit and personally drilled her maidservants and other women recruits. Once in battle, the exigencies of the moment must have served to sharpen her tactical skills. Surely sound judgement added greatly to her sense of strategy. Military acumen, spirit, and sense of timing in battle—those attributes of a good general—must have derived from her keen intelligence as well as from childhood training.

After the departure of the rebels from Jhansi in June 1857 the military defense and security of the state were her responsibility. She devoted special attention to the organization and training of her army, including the women's unit. The events of the outbreak at Jhansi left Lakshmi acutely aware of the vulnerability of her position. Her first adversary, Sadasheo Rao Narain, had sought rebel support against her. Leaving Jhansi, he had proclaimed himself in Karhra the raja of Jhansi. One of the Rani's generals, Jawahar Singh, pursued Narain there and drove him out of Karhra. He fled then to Nurwar, a fortress under the control of the Scindias in Gwalior. He was pursued again by Jawahar Singh, who captured him in Nurwar, brought him back to Jhansi, and imprisoned him.[2] This skirmish with the forces of Narain convinced Lakshmi, as did the Jhansi uprising itself, that it was imperative to strengthen her defenses.

British sources on the battles fought by the Rani in 1858 contain no information about her generals. It will be useful, therefore, to consider this feature of her military organization. The Rani's force was commanded by seven generals who fought both at Jhansi and in subsequent battles in April, May, and June. Their deeds are related in the Kalyan Singh Kudara ballad, the earliest to appear after the events described. Foremost among these generals was the famous gunner Gulam Gaus Khan, a valayati (Afghan mercenary) from Rahatgarh who had under him three hundred of the Pathans, renowned throughout India as the fiercest of fighters. This unit of Muslim Pathans was a striking feature of the Rani's army and a significant source of her military power. Mercenaries though they were, they were also reputed to be among her most loyal soldiers in battle.

But the Rani's military strength did not rest on Muslim power alone. An important Hindu general was Kunwar Jawahar Singh, a Parmar Rajput and jagirdar of the villages of Katili and Udgaon near Dinara. Two other generals, known only as Chunni and Jhadu, were of the subcaste of Ahirs, and were from the village of Ambari, now called Chandawara, also two miles from Dinara. A fifth general was Raghunath Singh of Nauner, about six miles from Dinara. Sixth was a Koli (weaver caste) named Gampat, whose descendants still live at Dinara. Finally, General Kashinath Chandarkar was also an important officer in the Rani's army. These Hindu generals all came from villages near Dinara and trained at the Dinara fort, within the domain of the Rani. Dinara was thus a significant area for the development of the Rani's military organization. Dinara fort still stands today, partially in ruins. These, then, were the Muslim and Hindu generals on whom the Rani relied for advice in developing strategy for the defense of Jhansi.

Invasion from Orchha

From the neighboring state of Orchha came the next challenge to the Rani's rule. In Orchha the Bundela ruler Hamir Singh was a minor, and his mother, the Larai rani, was his regent. Her chief minister, or diwan, was an official named Nathe Khan, who figures importantly in the ballad by Kalyan Singh as in Orchha's relations with Jhansi. Relations between the two states were complicated by the fact that Jhansi had once been part of the Orchha domains and was in fact carved out of Orchha territory.

Recall the manner in which Jhansi came into being. In the early eighteenth century a powerful Bundela chief, Chhatrasal, had served the Mughal emperors Bahadur Shah and Farruksiyar in Mughal campaigns against the Sikhs in the Punjab. In 1728, however, when the Mughals turned against Chhatrasal and expelled him from the Jhansi region, he called on Peshwa Baji Rao I for help against the Mughals. The peshwa responded, since the Marathas were eager to secure a foothold in Bundelkhand. When Chhatrasal died he bequeathed part of his territory to his sons and part to Baji Rao, including Jhansi. Jhansi accordingly became part of the Maratha empire under a Maratha governor and was lost to the Bundelas.

This loss of Jhansi to the Orchha Bundelas still rankled in the mind of the Larai rani. She and her diwan had viewed Gangadhar Rao as a usurper, and in his death and the subsequent uprising and collapse of British power in Jhansi they saw their chance. It seemed to them that British authority was on the verge of being permanently overthrown. Moreover, these two in Orchha must have judged that the British would not be averse to an attack on their enemy in Jhansi. The Larai rani sent a messenger to the raja of Datia, another neighbor, hoping for an alliance and joint campaign against Jhansi. Had the raja of Datia agreed, the subsequent history of Rani Lakshmibai and of Jhansi might have taken a markedly different turn.

The response of the raja of Datia was described in romanticized terms by his court poet, Kalyan Singh, who has the raja reply: "Oh messenger, against whom should I array my forces? She has lost her husband; she is in difficulty. For what reason should I kill her? She is a woman. She has no valor. If I attack her I will put a black mark against my caste. Do not forget that I am a jewel in the crest of the great Bundela line . . . Go back and tell your queen I cannot stoop to this extent."[3] The Datia raja was a Bundela Rajput and, like some others in Bundelkhand, had taken refuge against the Marathas in the protection of the British. Apart from the romantic motives ascribed to him by his poet, the raja may have been reluctant to alienate the British or to become involved in local struggles. The Orchha effort to ally with Datia against Jhansi consequently proved abortive.

The Datia raja's refusal, however, did not deter Nathe Khan or the Larai rani in their designs on Jhansi. Nathe Khan raised a large force, in some versions as large as twenty thousand, for the attack on Jhansi. In Jhansi the Rani placed a thread on the wrist of General Jawahar Singh, symbolizing her appointment of him as commander in chief of her forces.[4] She and her general readied the defenses of Jhansi.

The poet Kalyan Singh recounted a three-day invasion of Jhansi in September by the forces of Nathe Khan. The loyalties of the small chiefs of the region between Orchha and Jhansi were divided: Madhukar Shah of Manpura favored Jhansi, while Ramdhir Singh of Palera sided with Orchha. The two men clashed in a desperate sword fight. Ramdhir Singh was killed, but his followers surrounded Madhukar Shah and wounded him with a bullet. General Chunni and others rushed to his aid but could not save him. On the second day of fighting the forces of the Rani left the fort and attacked the Orchha invaders under command of a chief from Rathan Bagh. Some of the Rani's army were wounded and killed there.

Her army fell back to the fort at the end of the second day's fighting. On the morning of the third day, Orchha forces surrounded the fort with cannon. The Rani held a war council and martialled seven thousand troops for the decisive stand. This army succeeded in driving the Orchha forces off, despite their cannon, to Kumharra, a village two and a half miles from Jhansi. This success reassured Lakshmi about her guns and men. Nathe Khan then sent his men home to the Orchha capital at Tehri. He, himself, went off to Indore, where, in the ballad, he spoke against the Rani and persuaded British officials there (presumably Hamilton) that the Rani had actively aided the rebels at Jhansi and had been responsible for the atrocities. (As has been noted, most English officials were already convinced that the Rani was culpable.) While Nathe Khan professed loyalty to the British, at the same time his agents collected the revenue from a section of Jhansi territory still held by Orchha.

Contrary to the Kalyan Singh ballad, the Orchha invasion of Jhansi lasted not three days but closer to two months. On 10 August 1857 Orchha invaded Mau Ranipur and took Mau, Pandwaha, and Garautha before assaulting Jhansi. In the process the Orchha army drove off cattle and burned and plundered many villages in the areas it passed through. Nathe Khan took Burwa Saugar en route to Jhansi. The Orchha siege of Jhansi, which began in early September, was not raised until late October when the raja of Banpur came to Lakshmi's rescue and enabled her to reestablish her authority. Orchha troops were finally expelled from the whole area between the Betwa and Dassan rivers. The experience added to the Rani's sense of vulnerability. Moreover, since the British had sent no help in answer to her appeals, she strengthened her army to a total of between fourteen and fifteen thousand troops.[5]

Jhansi residents tell of another challenge to the Rani's authority. It came from Burwa Saugar, in a small fort sixteen miles east of Jhansi, where a dacoit chief called Saugar Singh eluded capture and refused to recognize the Rani as ruler of Jhansi. They say in Jhansi that she went to Burwa Saugar in person, challenged Saugar Singh to a duel, and defeated him decisively with her sword. Saugar Singh was so impressed that he swore lifelong fealty to the Rani, joined her cause, and helped spread her military reputation through Bundelkhand.

Lakshmi had few other allies in October of 1857, a time when allies were critical to survival among the small states of Bundelkhand. The British had failed to send forces to aid the Rani in keeping order, as

Erskine had promised when he authorized her to take temporary control. Now Jhansi was surrounded by several hostile neighbors all too willing to take advantage of the Rani's apparent vulnerability. Where was she to turn for help? The raja of Banpur was one chief who had already demonstrated his friendship to Jhansi during the Orchha invasion. Nana Sahib of Bithur and Kanpur, along with his general Rao Sahib, was another obvious possibility, but he was farther away. Tatya Tope, like Nana Sahib a childhood friend, was now a rebel leader and a potential ally, but he was engaged elsewhere. Other neighbors were controlled by chiefs friendly to the British, such as Scindia in Gwalior. There was no stable authority in Bundelkhand, and the Rani, increasingly uneasy, continued to seek contact with various officials of the government, in particular Hamilton at Indore.

Between late October 1857 and March 1858 the Rani gradually became disillusioned and disappointed with British failure to respond. She felt a growing apprehension that the British might capture and try her, even hang her. She pursued a dual policy: building up her forces and seeking allies among the chiefs around her, and at the same time attempting to resume communications with the English. The failure of many of these attempts is central to an understanding of the metamorphosis of the Rani into a rebel who, however reluctantly, finally resorted to taking up arms for the defense of Jhansi against the British.

The Central India Field Force

Maj. Gen. Sir Henry Havelock's army retook Kanpur on 16 July, followed by Bithur and in September Lucknow. John Nicholson's force from the Punjab finally recaptured Delhi on 22 September. The new commander in chief of the Indian Army, Colin Campbell, then turned his attention to Central India, where rebel forces still held control.

Central India and Jhansi in particular posed a threat to British power in early 1858, a threat both political and military. It was the last stronghold of the rebels still at large at the end of 1857. This was the part of India that had always been the last to feel the arm of the law, the part of India that had harbored the Kali-centered cult of *thugi* and is still infested with dacoits today.[6] Jhansi was especially significant in being located at the junction of several important roads. The immense Jhansi fort gave it added strategic importance. Moreover, in British India the demand for vengeance was a potent force in 1858. The Rani of Jhansi was the "Jezebel of India" in British eyes, the perpetrator of horrible atrocities and an affront to British sensibilities on a par only with Nana Sahib of the macabre Kanpur massacre. But apart from their desire for retribution, the British wanted to reestablish their authority and order in Bundelkhand where Jhansi was pivotal. Dalhousie's doctrine was established policy. All these factors combined to make Jhansi a prime target of the Central India Field Force, the army commissioned to reestablish British control in the wake of rebellion there. Commander in Chief Campbell wrote of Jhansi in January 1858 that until its capture his rear would always be at risk. He would, he said, be "constantly obliged to look back over his shoulder, as when he relieved Lucknow."[7]

Selected for the task of commanding the Central India Field Force to retake Bundelkhand was Gen. Sir Hugh Rose. Rose had acquired his earliest military training in Berlin, where his father was a diplomat at the Prussian court. He was promoted to the rank of brigadier and then major general for his exploits in the Crimean War. There were those who felt he should have been awarded the Victoria Cross for Crimea. Rose arrived in Bombay in September of 1857 with a distinguished war record but only the sketchiest knowledge of the country.

Rose was faced with immediate problems: inadequate numbers of troops, supplies, and transport, no maps of the roads or Jhansi fort, and scant knowledge of the terrain in Central India. Still, he possessed many qualities of a good general. He had the ability to elicit the best from his troops, to appraise his foes accurately, and to assess a situation and act instantaneously. He had, in addition, great energy and tenacity. He was a bachelor wedded to his duty and ended his career a field marshal. His personal military style and hallmark was his predilection for personal reconnaissance of a battle site before the first shot was fired. This habit proved critical in Central India in view of the scarcity of adequate maps.[8] Rose was selected to command the Central India Field Force in 1857 over the opposition of critics who suggested there were others who knew the situation in Bundelkhand better than he.[9] The British deemed the Rani of Jhansi a serious enough threat to pit a seasoned general against her.

With Delhi and Oudh recaptured, the major outstanding problem for the British was continued rebel resistance and presence in Central India. Pacification of rebels and guerrillas was the task assigned General Rose and his army. Since Rose lacked knowledge of this part of the country, Sir Robert Hamilton, the experienced agent at Indore, was asked to draft the campaign strategy and to accompany the general as political officer. Hamilton envisioned a two-pronged operation: one column marching from Bombay would be based at Mhow, while the second column pushing up from Madras would be based at Jabalpur. The goal of the two columns would be to converge on the area between Kalpi and Banda.[10] General Rose would command the column based at Mhow with the target of retaking Jhansi. The column based at Jabalpur would be commanded by Brigadier General Whitlock. Rose's force consisted of two brigades totalling 4,300 men in infantry, cavalry, and artillery units. The majority of the troops were Indian; the officers and a smaller number of troops were British.[11]

Rose's Bombay column reached Mhow and Indore in time for Christmas dinner, 1857. Whitlock's Madras column, however, had not yet reached Jabalpur. Hearing that the garrison at Saugor was under siege, General Rose decided to start out, despite the fact that Whitlock had not arrived at Jabalpur for the combined operation. It was 6 January. Hamilton's years at Indore had given him a knowledge of the people and terrain that was to prove vital to Rose's campaign, particularly before Rose's force arrived at Jhansi.

The Rani's Dilemma

During this two-month period the Rani's close military advisers gave her contradictory counsel, some arguing for peace with the English, others advocating war. In January, Bakhshish Ali of the jail asked the Rani if she would fight. One source has it that she replied she would not, and she would moreover turn over all the districts under her to the British when they reached Jhansi.[12] Bakhshish Ali then left Jhansi on the sixth in the service of the raja of Banpur.

In early February the Rani reportedly sent for the vakil Ajoodia Pershad in Gwalior to solicit his advice. He allegedly refused to go to Jhansi to help her. He gave as his reason, "Her advisers give her bad advice which she follows."[13]

Then Lakshman Rao, the Rani's diwan, posed to her the question of what was to be done, what with the British defeat of both the rajas of Banpur and Shahgurh and British forces advancing on Jhansi. News had just arrived that the raja of Shahgurh, a friend of Lakshmi, had been defeated at the Madanpur pass. Not only that, but some four hundred mutinous Sepoys who had fought for the Shahgurh raja poured into Jhansi with stories of the desertion of thousands of Bundelas in action against the British. A courier arrived by camel from Tatya Tope with the intelligence that Charkhari had been taken. Rebel leaders were converging on Jhansi with troops. Sher Singh, eldest son of the Banpur raja, came with sixteen hundred cavalry and infantry, plus six guns. Another ally with Sher Singh brought the ominous news that the British had reached Chanderi and that its fall was imminent.[14] The situation at Jhansi was critical, the Rani knew.

Moropant and General Kashinath left twelve hundred infantry and cavalry at Burwa Saugar and returned to Jhansi with more bad tidings for the Rani. Talbehat had been burned by Orchha and the Madras troops. The son of the raja of Nurwar had also fallen back to Pichore before the advance of the Gwalior force, and Chanderi in fact had just been taken by the British.

Lakshmi nevertheless took heart from the timely arrival at Jhansi on 15 March of the raja of Banpur. He brought with him twenty-five hundred infantry and cavalry, plus two guns, and the son of the raja of Nurwar with one thousand cavalry and infantry. There were rumors that both wished to join forces with Tatya Tope. Encouraged by these forces, the Rani issued a proclamation the next day: all military officers must be prepared to strike should the English appear. Anyone opposed should resign his appointment and leave Jhansi. All present affirmed their determination to fight.[15] The Rani moved from her palace into the fort and ordered the Jhansi flag flown from the fort wall. She sent out a small force to reconnoiter the British position.

On the seventeenth the Rani met for three hours in emergency council with her top officers. The raja of Banpur reportedly suggested she make terms with the English, since in the circumstances her forces could not succeed against them. General Kashinath and the paymaster Lalloo Bakhshi were of the same persuasion. "The English are masters of the country. No one ever made anything of fighting them." Submission would be advisable, they counseled.[16] Moropant and the diwan's son, Gangadhar, however, strongly opposed this view and urged that the state could not be surrendered without a fight. Kashinath and the paymaster then countered with the argument that there was a precedent. The state had in the past been made over to the English by the late raja himself.[17] Another English source, however, alleges that at the emergency meeting on the seventeenth, Kashinath, Gangadhar, and Jawahar Singh strongly advised the Rani to fight.[18] British sources thus not only have the Rani receiving contradictory advice from her officials, but getting contradictory advice from the same individual on the same day. What seems certain is that there was no consensus among the Rani's closest advisers on 17 March.

Hamilton's agent at Jhansi reported on the sixteenth that the Rani was being urged to make terms with the English and seemed inclined to accept this advice. She had allegedly sent another letter to Hamilton by courier and at the same time ordered the rajas of Banpur and Nurwar to leave Jhansi. Whether and why she did so is not clear, unless she hoped to expunge opposing views from her councils. They did leave, going toward Tatya Tope's army, in this version. The Rani was told her letter had been taken to the agent at Talbehat, which had fallen to the British. According to another source she also tried to contact General Rose on learning that his forces had reached Talbehat, but her officials who opposed this course intercepted her couriers before they could reach Rose.[19]

The Rani's attempt to communicate with the English prompted a reaction from some officials around her. They allegedly informed her that they had taken service with her because they assumed she would fight the British. If she wanted to make peace with them she should dismiss the officers with two months' pay. Meanwhile, another courier informed the Rani that he had delivered her letter to the agent, presumably Hamilton, but had not been given a reply.[20]

One Indian source alleges that the Rani issued a call on 14 February to all Hindus to defend their faith against the English destroyers, "perverters of all men's religion." This purported circular enumerated English efforts to contaminate the Hindu religion: "forcible remarriage of Hindoo widows, the abolition of the ancient rite of Suttee, the exaltation of those who may embrace the Christian faith." Moreover, the English had "powdered bones and mixed them with flour, and forced the army to used greased cartridges."[21] This presumed letter sounds more like a summary of rumors and general Hindu complaints against the English than a rallying call from the Rani. Moreover, it contains no mention of the affronts against religion specific to Jhansi. Further, it was reputedly printed in mid-Februry, while the Rani's debate with her advisers raged for another month.

As late as 18 March, then, the Rani was still of two minds—disposed both to make peace and to fight. She appeared to have relaxed her martial determination of two days earlier to send out reconnaissance against the English. And she was still receiving contradictory advice by those closest to her. Two factors helped to tip the balance. First, she had no reply to any of her February or March attempts to communicate with the English. She must have sensed that the English silence boded ill for her; perhaps she even had some intimation of British intentions to try her. As a matter of fact, in January 1858, Hamilton and the governor of Bombay were communicating on the matter of her trial. The suggestion was made that she be sent to Allahabad to await trial, as "a trial at Jhansi would take time."[22] And Erskine, whose tone had changed radically since the previous June, also wrote Hamilton on 4 January that both Lakshmi and the raja of Banpur "should be hanged when caught."[23]

Finally and irrevocably, the Central India Field Force was advancing on Jhansi. Gangadhar, reporting a letter from Tatya Tope, warned of the approach of four British companies from the direction of Kalpi (apparently an error) with more to follow. General Kashinath urged the recall of the official sent to Hamilton. Tatya Tope was also said to be advancing to the aid of the Rani with a force of nearly thirty thousand men.[24] There was now no option. The Rani prepared for battle.

7

The Battle for Jhansi

I will give my life but not my Jhansi!
—*From a song by Saxena,*
a Jhansi businessman

The British Assault

General Rose had no ready strategy for the siege and capture of Jhansi. He relied on Hamilton's knowledge of that part of the country and his general plan for a two-pronged attack. Hamilton urged Rose to clear the country around Shahgurh and Charkhari of rebels before advancing on Jhansi itself. Rose accepted the advice. He marched the Central India Field Force slowly toward Jhansi, reaching Rajwas on 1 March. There he had to decide between two possible approaches to Jhansi: one through the Narhut pass, the other through the Madanpur pass. The Madanpur pass, though guarded by the raja of Shahgurh, was thought to be the easier of the two. Rose determined to make a feint in the direction of the Narhut pass, which he learned the raja of Banpur had blocked with boulders, and then make for the Madanpur pass. The Madanpur pass was a narrow defile, overgrown with thick brushwood, good cover for entrenchments of the defenders. After a day's hard fighting Rose succeeded in driving the rebel forces from the pass, inflicting heavy losses, and so demoralizing the rebels that they put up no further resistance until Jhansi. Rose then advanced rapidly through Banpur and Talbehat, Rathgarh, Saugor, and Garhakota, capturing the towns in rapid succession.

The first brigade of Rose's force under Brigadier Stuart then besieged Chanderi as Rose advanced on Jhansi with the second brigade. What was intended as a combined operation suffered from lack of adequate communication between the two generals. Rose wrote Stuart on 14

March and excoriated him for not informing him of his operations. "I have several important operations on hand, but in consequence of the entire ignorance in which you keep me as to your proceedings I can do nothing." He complained, moreover, "When troops act together in combined operations, the first and indispensable condition for their success is the knowledge of their respective operations."[1]

On the night of 20 March, Rose and his force were encamped just fourteen miles south of Jhansi. He sent an advance party to reconnoiter. As he prepared to follow his reconnaissance party the next day, he made preparations for the final march on Jhansi. Just then an express courier rode up with two despatches from the governor-general, one for General Rose and the other for Hamilton. It transpired that the pro-British raja of Charkhari was being besieged in his fort by Tatya Tope and the Gwalior Contingent. The governor-general ordered General Rose to go immediately to the relief of the friendly raja, whose fort was eighty miles from Rose's present camp.

Rose was in a quandary. To follow the governor-general's order would mean abandoning the more important and closer fort at Jhansi, his main target. Rose was furthermore convinced that the best way to save Charkhari was to take Jhansi first. He made a difficult decision, particularly difficult for a disciplined soldier. He disobeyed his superior's order and proceeded with the campaign against Jhansi. Some British accounts of this decision offer an ingenious explanation. Rose was a general, a professional soldier incapable of disobeying an order from a superior. Hamilton, on the other hand, who also received the governor-general's letter, was not a soldier. He saw Rose's dilemma and offered him a way out. Hamilton would himself accept full responsibility for proceeding with the Jhansi campaign rather than being diverted to the less important Charkhari fort eighty miles away.[2] This version of Rose's solution, however, overlooks the obvious fact that General Rose, not Hamilton, was general in command and had received a military order. However much some authors may wish to evade the implications of insubordination, the ultimate responsibility must rest with Rose. As it turned out, Rose's military judgment was correct, and those who were concerned with the chain of command did not press the point.

Thus General Rose and the second brigade of the Field Force arrived a few miles from Jhansi, still minus a tactical plan or even description of the Jhansi fort and city. Clearly the situation required detailed reconnaissance before Rose could begin a siege. What Rose glimpsed of the fort impressed him greatly. Like most forts in Bundelkhand, the Jhansi fort was visible for miles, from as far away as the eye could see, built as it was on elevated rock. Rose remarked in his report on the excellent, massive granite masonry, the thickness of the walls (sixteen to twenty feet), their height (up to thirty feet), and the elaborate solid outworks with loopholes for musketry. The general concluded the fort would be extremely difficult, if not impossible, to breach. He noted also that the fortified city wall protected the fort as well, except on the west, where the abruptness of the rock itself served as protection. A high mound, or mamelon, on the south guarded that face and was itself fortified by a circular bastion partly surrounded by a moat.[3]

Rose's army was delayed by transport and supply problems, to say nothing of being plagued by the weather. There was no longer any hope for a cool day, which, as Rose remarked, was so salubrious to the health of European soldiers.[4] Rose's force was running directly into the heat of the subcontinent in March, before the monsoon breaks. One ameliorating factor was that the Central India Field Force had been issued new tropical uniforms of loose cotton trousers and blouses. This uniform was far more suitable to the intense heat and less visible to the enemy than the traditional red and blue uniforms with their high collars and tight, heavy jackets.[5] Yet the English found the terrain extremely inhospitable for infantry, even more for cavalry.

Rose's perspective as he marched toward Jhansi was far from negative, despite the many obstacles. Writing to General Whitlock on 18 March he remarked, "If they stand at Jhansi they must have improved since the last ten days, as it has been one general interrupted run." And, he continued, "They say the Palace is the best house in India and that it will make a charming barrack."[6]

Relying on his reconnaissance, Rose determined before the siege commenced that there was no means of breaching the fort and city wall, except perhaps from the south. But the south was flanked by the fortified city wall and mound which Rose had noted and described. A rocky ridge east of the fort was an excellent site for a breaching battery except that it was too far from the fort wall for firing range, some 640 yards away. Rose concluded that capture of the fortified mamelon to the south was therefore the first priority of the operation because it not only abutted the fort wall but also commanded the city and palace. The city would have to be taken before the fort. Concentrating fire on the mound would drive the defenders from the mound and south of the city and facilitate breaching the wall.

Rose on 23 March formed seven flying camps of cavalry around Jhansi as an investing force, each with outposts and guards. Each camp was to watch for any attempt to leave the fort.[7] Rose found it surprising that Jhansi had no defensive posts outside the city but concentrated the entire defense effort on the fort itself and the city walls. The investment, which began with the right attack on the mound, erected a battery and cleared the mound of rebels. Rose ordered long rows of hayricks in the south of the city burned. The Rani and her officers fired from the white turret and tree-tower batteries in the fort, and other defenders fired from the Saugor and Lutchmen gate batteries in the town. Rose was impressed with the abilities of the artillery chief, commenting that from some batteries the defense "returned shot for shot" and rapidly repaired guns and resumed fire almost immediately. One of the guns, which the English nicknamed "Whistling Dick," "never gave us time for precaution (bobbing one's head behind sand bags), for the puff of smoke was scarcely seen before the shot whipped over your head, or came with a heavy thud on the battery."[8] English attackers could see women working in the batteries and carrying ammunition. The resistance was unremitting. Rose's explanation was: "This was not surprising as the inhabitants, from the Ranee downwards, were more or less concerned in the murder and plunder of the English. There was hardly a house in Jhansee which did not contain some article of English plunder, and politically speaking, the Rebel confederacy knew well that if Jhansee, the richest Hindoo city, and most important fortress in Central India fell, then the cause of the insurgents in this part of India fell also."[9]

General Whitlock arrived from Madras on the twenty-fifth with the siege train and guns of the second army. The men worked all night constructing batteries on the rocky ridge and putting up cover for their guns for the left attack. By morning the guns were positioned, and they opened fire on the walls and continued to pound them for three days. The heaviest equipment and the key to dismantling the fort's defenses were two eighteen-pounders. One was deployed near the wall bastion of the mound. Rose reported that the fire of these two cannon was so efficient that toward sunset the parapets of the white turret, the black tower and the tree tower, which faced the left attack, were "knocked into shapeless heaps by the fire of the two eighteen-pounders."[10] Two ten-inch mortars also caused havoc inside the fort by blowing up a powder magazine.

Day and night the firing continued, but the thick granite masonry held and the defenders fired back. English artillerymen at the siege guns worked with wet towels wrapped around their heads against the heat of the blazing sun and the risk of sunstroke. On the fourth day Rose decided a breach was feasible. The Rani, meanwhile, personally supervised the defense, ordering the damaged wall retrenched with a double row of pallisades filled with earth. Rose ordered fire concentrated on this retrenchment, and as a result part of the stockade was destroyed.

The two batteries that put up the stiffest resistence were the wheel tower on the south and the garden battery on a rock to the rear of the west wall of the city. Rose directed that a new reenforced battery be constructed on a ridge to the east to silence the wheel tower and ordered a fresh assault on the garden battery. By the thirtieth most of Jhansi's guns were disabled and the defenses of the fort itself dismantled. Rose noted, nevertheless, that the obstinate defense continued, especially on the white turret, where they made "an excellent parapet of large sand bags, which they kept always wet, and still ran up fresh in lieu of disabled guns."[11]

The Rani's best artillerymen were killed during this siege, including chief gunner Gulam Gaus Khan and Khuda Bakhsh. Their tombs lie within the fort today. In the course of the siege the British exhausted so much ammunition that it became apparent that there was not enough left to effect a main breach in the south double wall of the fort.[12]

The Rani was constantly on the minds of the English attackers during the entire siege operation. They directed their field glasses toward the fort wall, where they hoped for a glimpse of her. One army surgeon recalls, "The dauntless bravery of the Ranee was a great conversation in the camp. Far-seeing individuals thought they saw her under an awning on the large square tower of the fortress, where she was said to sit and watch the progress of the siege."[13] It was from this same turret, the white tower, that the Jhansi flag furled. Englishmen with field glasses thought they could see that the Rani was young and beautiful. Adding to the Rani's mystique was the rumor among some young Englishmen that she was unmarried. "In the cool of the evening," in the words of one soldier, "the Rani of Jhansi with her handmaids, wrapped in bright, radiant vesture, went to the batteries and roused the zeal of her soldiers by her presence and fiery words."[14] One British account has it that a bombadier in charge of one of the breaching guns had in his gunsite one evening "the Queen and her ladies" as they visited a tower to see how the fight was going. He asked General Rose for permission to fire on them, "but he was told that kind of warfare was not approved."[15] Both

Indian and English versions of the siege feature such romanticized embellishments.

Given the shortage of British ammunition and the impregnability of the walls, the commander of the English artillery and engineers convinced General Rose that the only feasible way to take the city and fort was by escalade. Continuing the fire, Rose then made preparations on the thirtieth to storm the fortress walls. He hoped to mount the operation next morning near the mound. Meanwhile, however, something happened to delay Rose's plan for capturing the city by escalade.

Tatya Tope to the Rescue

On 29 March General Rose received intelligence from his telegraph on the hills east of Jhansi that Tatya Tope and the rajas of Banpur and Shahgurh were advancing from Mau Ranipur to the relief of Jhansi with at least fifteen thousand men, more likely, twenty thousand. The British referred to this force as "the Army of the Peshwa." Tatya Tope had captured Charkhari after a siege of eleven days, thereby adding to his store of guns. This was the operation that prompted the governor-general's order to Rose to divert from the Jhansi campaign. Tatya Tope's reputation as a remarkable and elusive guerrilla leader had also been enhanced by his victory over the British garrison at Kanpur. This victory was reversed only by the later arrival of British reenforcements. The main feature of Tatya Tope's plan to relieve Jhansi was to make a surprise attack. This plan, however, failed when Rose got advance intelligence of the march of the rebel army toward Jhansi.

Tatya Tope and his relief force crossed the Betwa River during the night of 21 March. A bonfire was lit at sunset to signal the Rani of his arrival outside Jhansi. Tatya Tope's intelligence sources mistakenly informed him that nearly the whole of Rose's force was engaged in the siege and investment of the fort, and the few who guarded the camp could easily be taken.

At dawn the next morning the Rani's pickets sighted in the distance thousands of men moving closer to Jhansi, beyond the British batteries. A roar went up from within the fort, and salvoes were fired to welcome Tatya Tope and his army. The Rani saw the prospect of crushing the British in a pincer between the two armies; her childhood friend had saved the day.

Tatya Tope had a master plan: attack the British with his main force and send another part of his army across a lower ford in the Betwa to turn the left of the British flank. The rebel relief force marched on, carrying colored banners, beating drums, and brandishing bayonets gleaming in the sun. But Rose, apprised in advance of Tatya Tope's strategy, ordered his first brigade to check the rebel maneuver. This movement left Rose minus a second line.

Rose quickly saw that the only way to prevent Tatya Tope from outflanking him was to seize the initiative, rolling up both enemy flanks in a lightning operation. He rapidly ordered both his flanks to advance against the rebel storm of fire. Three times Rose ordered the Hyderabad Cavalry to charge the rebel battery, and three times the charge was repelled by showers of grape and volleys from the valayati matchlocks. One British officer described the battle: "The Velaities jumped up in hundreds on high rocks and boulders to load and fire, but before they could re-load their matchlocks, Captain Need, leading his troop . . . penetrated into the midst of them and for a time was so hotly engaged that his uniform was cut to pieces."[16]

Tatya Tope's force, though it contained part of the crack Gwalior Contingent and was numerically superior, was fighting at some disadvantage. It was using the old slow-firing matchlocks; more important—though unknown to the Rani—90 percent of the men were untrained raw recruits.

While Tatya Tope's army was attempting to outflank the left of the British force, they pushed too far to their right, leaving their left exposed. Rose himself dashed in at the head of the dragoons with artillery and cavalry, routed the left flank, and advanced in line against the rebel front. Tatya Tope's green troops, disconcerted, began to retreat in disorder as the British turned both their flanks. The retreating army set fire to the jungle. The first line retreated under cover of smoke and flame toward the second line and the Betwa River beyond "in wild disorder." Tatya Tope's crack troops fought desperately, "matchlock and tulwar in hand, at times lying down and cutting at their pursuers who dashed through the blazing jungle toward the Betwa." In their flight, however, Tatya Tope's inexperienced troops abandoned most of their guns, including an eighteen-pounder drawn by elephants. Nearly all the guns Tatya Tope had brought from his Kalpi arsenal fell into British hands during the rout.

The Rani and her officers watched in dismay from the fort walls as their rescuers retreated. On the right bank of the Betwa, Tatya Tope's troops dug in for a fresh stand but could not regain the initiative. Meanwhile, General Rose kept up the siege of the fort. Rose reported the rebels lost between fifteen hundred and two thousand men in the Battle of the Betwa. All was silent within the fort; all hope of relief was gone.[17]

The Rani learned beforehand that her old friend Tatya Tope was advancing to relieve Jhansi. She calculated that with his numerical superiority he would be able to rout the English offensive and raise the siege. The rout of Tatya Tope's troops stunned her and made her realize that she could rely only on her own dwindling resources. One perplexing question remains. Why did the Rani fail to send out some of her forces from the fort on 1 April when Tatya Tope's army arrived and thereby effect a pincer against the English? Had she done so the English besiegers might have been overwhelmed, trapped by the numerical superiority of the two armies. The explanation for the Rani's failure to do this, some Indian authors suggest, is that she feared her men would desert if they left the fort.[18] Another, equally cogent explanation is that Rose's besiegers did not let up their bombardment of the fort even with the advance of Tatya Tope. As it was, the Rani found it hard to believe that the massive army of twenty thousand had failed to raise the siege against a British force one-fourth its size, a force which still kept up its assault on the fort despite the fact that it had been fighting for several days in alien terrain. What she had no way of knowing was that most of the relief army were raw recruits.

The Escalade

With the defeat of Tatya Tope, General Rose turned his attention again to the problem of an escalade. On 2 April the commander of the engineers informed Rose that preparations for the escalade were completed and a twenty-four-pound Howitzer was in place for enfilading the wall. At three o'clock the next morning storming parties advanced by moonlight on both the right and left attack into "a savage fire of round shot, musket balls and rockets." Bugles blared from up on the walls, muskets cracked, rockets hissed, and cannon boomed. The cacophony of sound and the fire momentarily checked the British advance, and the attackers hid behind the shelter of rocks. Then the engineers reached the walls, and the infantry, under cover of smoke, began to creep forward. Two officers who reached the ramparts were bayoneted and shot from the walls, another was struck by a rock in the face and fell. Three ladders broke, and the men on them were plunged into the ditch. The escalade on the right then failed because of the breaking ladders and because one ladder was too short for the thirty-foot wall. But the escalade on the left succeeded, punctuated by an Irish yell rising above the crack of musketry as men jumped over the wall. A column rushed through the breach that had been blown through a gate with a bag of powder, and English soldiers streamed into the city. Men clambering over the wall gained the mamelon and pushed into the streets. They fought from house to house in hand-to-hand combat. Skirmishing continued in the streets and houses as the English cut their way toward the palace against obstinate resistance.

The defenders set fire to trails of gunpowder laid against the entry of Rose's army into the palace. This ruse killed several of Rose's men. Rose concentrated both right and left attacks now on the palace, forming an oblique line from the northeast Burrahgong gate to the palace and a second line from the mound to the palace. The palace was defended with determined fury, and "the streets of the palace gate ran with blood." Clearing the city of rebels to the rear of the oblique line was only effected by bloody hand-to-hand fighting with heavy losses on both sides.

Defense of the palace stables by forty valayaties, the Rani's bodyguard, was described by Rose: "The sowars, full of opium, defended their stables, firing with matchlocks and pistols from the windows and loopholes, and cutting with their tulwars . . . they retreated . . . still firing or fighting with their swords in both hands till they were shot or bayoneted struggling even when dying on the ground to strike again."[19] In the looting that followed the taking of the palace the English captured the Rani's flag and a silk Union Jack, the same flag given by Governor-General Bentinck to Gangadhar Rao's ancestor. Destruction continued, "the British soldiers eagerly exceeding their orders to spare nobody over sixteen years—except women, of course."[20]

Townsmen and rebels who could not escape threw their wives and children into wells and jumped in after them. Jhansi became "a slaughter pen reeking under the hot Indian sun."[21] Some rebels escaped to a hill west of the city where they held out briefly. Among them was Moropant, the Rani's father, who was wounded, captured, and, on 20 April, hung with Lalloo Bakhshi in the garden at Jokhun Bagh, the same garden where the English had been massacred.

During the night of 3 April Rose issued orders for an assault on the fort the next morning. The assault began on schedule, but as it began Rose got the startling news that the Rani had escaped during the night. She had left the besieged fort with some three hundred valayaties and twenty-five sowars, and headed out the Bandher gate northeastward, in the direction of Koonch and Kalpi.

The Rani's Flight

The Rani and her officers realized that the British bombardment had seriously weakened the defense of the city and fort. The city was already invested by the English, and losses in the street fighting were heavy, estimated at up to three thousand on the Rani's side. A further problem—not apparent to the English until they entered the fort—was that the fort's water supply, a large tank covered by a tarpaulin, had gone dry.[22] Without water the defense of any fort was limited to a few days. With a full reservoir a fort's defense could hold out for a month, maybe two. The cause of the drying up of the fort's reservoir is not apparent, but it must have been a significant factor in the Rani's reckoning on 3 April. No doubt the impending monsoon rains that were expected to refill the tank had not yet begun. Finally, and most crucial in the Rani's decision, was that the British had a firm foothold in the city and had captured the palace. The fort was the final target, and the Rani knew an escalade of the fort wall would come at any moment.

The Rani, by what exit is not certain, left the fort under cover of darkness on horseback with, as popular tradition has it, "her adopted son on her back." According to legend and ballad, she galloped the 102 miles to Kalpi in one night. Other sources suggest she reached Bhander, 21 miles from Jhansi, though actually off the main road to Kalpi, and there she bivouacked for the night. The cavalry units sent by Rose in pursuit came upon her tent and unfinished breakfast, left behind as she resumed her flight. A British officer, Lieutenant Dowker, pursued the Rani and four companions across the town until he caught sight of her on her gray horse. He drew close enough to be wounded and struck from his horse. In the popular version, the blow was struck by the Rani's own sword.[23]

Rose's army occupied the fort without resistance the morning of 5 April. The fort was virtually empty, the Rani and all her troops having evacuated. Thus ended the siege of Jhansi, "one of the most remarkable wars of the Mutiny." It demonstrated both British success and the spirit and vigor of the Rani's defense. Some British estimates of rebel casualties rose as high as five thousand. A medical officer with Rose's force wrote afterward, "In Jhansi we burnt upwards of a thousand bodies . . . I believe we must have slain nearly 3000 of the enemy. Such was the retribution meted out to this Jezebel Rani and her people for the heinous crimes done by them in Jhansi."[24]

Rose was dismayed at the Rani's escape from the heavily guarded fort. A British account relates that her horse was brought to the fort moat under cover of darkness "with the connivance of a native contingent serving with Sir Hugh Rose, and that after being let down over the wall she was placed in the saddle, with her stepson in her lap, and thus escaped."[25] It is noteworthy that just as Indian accounts in Jhansi refer to treachery in opening the fort gates to the English, so also English accounts advert to the treachery of a conspirator in Rose's force in the Rani's escape. Her dramatic nighttime flight from Jhansi fort became part of the Rani legend, the implication being that a fort under siege could no more hold her than it could other legendary Indian heroes. Stories of the Rani's flight also contain elements of myth and legend. Some versions relate that she leapt off the wall of the fort. Bundelkhand's history is studded with heroes making spectacular leaps from the heights of fort walls, leaps that would kill ordinary mortals. The spot where the Rani is said to have leapt over is marked on the fort wall at Jhansi today.

The British press in India shared Rose's puzzlement at the Rani's disappearance from the fort. The Bombay *Telegraph and Courier* carried a report on 9 April. "We confess ourselves perfectly unable to comprehend this. Either the previous telegram must have greatly misrepresented matters or some connivance with our own native troops must have enabled the Rani to pass unnoticed through our Sentries and Pickets. Such a circumstance demands the strictest enquiry, and we hope it will not be slurred over."[26]

One version of the Rani's escape is that of Lt. Anthony Lyster, Rose's aide-de-camp at Jhansi. In it Rose asks Lyster one night for suggestions on how to capture the Rani. The aide-de-camp's first suggestion, "Try money," Rose rejects. Lyster then suggests leaving a loophole in the cordon surrounding the fort, a gap through which the Rani could escape. The Fourteenth Dragoons could then be poised for pursuit in the morning and, "catch her up before she can have got far." According to Lyster, his plan was followed by General Rose, thus enabling the Rani to make her escape through the intentional gap in guards around the fort. Lyster admits the rest of the plan did not work out, since after the Fourteenth Dragoons had pursued her about twenty miles they "had to give up, as the men and horses were quite done."[27] "It is surprising that women who had never been on horseback before could have ridden the distance in such a short time," Lyster then comments. This remark reveals his ignorance of the Rani, which Rose cannot have shared, and casts doubt on the veracity of his account. The Rani was reputed among other Englishmen in India to be "one of the best judges of a horse in India."[28]

By whatever means, escape the Rani did, making her way toward Kalpi. General Rose did not himself immediately follow after her. Rose's men had not taken off their uniforms or unsaddled their horses for seventeen days and nights. Apart from battle casualties, many had fallen with sunstroke and heat exhaustion, some of them fatally. Rose knew his men had earned a rest. They had successfully stormed their target, the strongest fortress in Central India. Moreover, he was expecting another unit of rebels in the Jhansi area. The rebels at Kotah had been defeated by General Roberts, and it was logical to anticipate that they might head toward Jhansi in their flight from Kotah. Major Orr's Hyderabad Contingent was sent to clear the country between the Betwa and Dassan rivers of rebels. It was not until 26 April that Rose and his army had recovered sufficiently to march from Jhansi toward Koonch, leaving Colonel Liddell with a small force to hold Jhansi. Rose could spare no troops to occupy the Chanderi district, which was overrun once again with rebels as the general headed northeast with his partially recovered army.[29] The Rani's whereabouts were to concern Rose and his army for another two months.

8

The Rani's Last Battles

The Rani charged to attack
Now to the right, now to the left . . .
They many, she alone.

—*From a popular poem by*
Subhadra Kumari Chauhan

The Battle at Koonch

As General Rose's force took the road to Kalpi after the Rani's flight, a distraught Hamilton wrote the governor-general suggesting a reward be offered for the capture of the raja of Banpur and "the Baee of Jhansi." The governor-general replied that he did not consider it expedient for the government to issue this offer of reward. He agreed, nevertheless, with Hamilton's suggestion of offering "rewards of up to 10,000 rupees for the Nawab and 20,000 rupees for the Baee."[1]

Both the Rani and Rose were headed, ultimately, for Kalpi, one hundred miles northeast of Jhansi on the road to Kanpur. It was the only important town remaining in rebel hands, critical too because it housed the principal rebel arsenal, a cache of guns and ammunition hidden within and under the fort. Kalpi was also an important crossing of the Yamuna River and could threaten the British advance base and communications center at Kanpur. Kalpi in rebel hands could prevent the union of the British armies from east and west, cutting them in two. Kalpi was, moreover, headquarters of Rao Sahib, the old cohort of the Rani and Nana Sahib. Though rebel forces had scattered in defeat, they were able to regroup at Kalpi, resilient and ready for yet another battle. Rao Sahib was joined there by Lakshmi and the raja of Banpur, and briefly, by Tatya Tope as well.

It was late April before Rose resumed his march northeastwards toward Koonch and Kalpi. The general, as was his habit, sent reconnaissance parties ahead. He hoped to clear Kotra, an important ford on the Betwa, of rebels before pushing on toward Kalpi. His reconnaissance groups found no rebels at Mau or Kotra, but at Koonch, forty-two miles southwest of Kalpi, they were present in force. Intelligence arrived on 27 April that the Rani was at Koonch, together with Tatya Tope, the subahdar of Koonch, the rajas of Banpur and Shahgurh, Rao Sahib, and an army of over ten thousand men.[2]

When she fled Jhansi the Rani had ridden northeast, arriving at the Kalpi rebel headquarters the same day as Tatya Tope. At Kalpi, the last defense post of the rebels, a war council was held. Rao Sahib presided. By British accounts, the Rani implored Rao Sahib to "give her an army that she may go and fight." The following morning at a parade of the troops, Rao Sahib responded by publicly praising Lakshmi for her defense of Jhansi. The troops on parade consisted of some regiments of the Gwalior Contingent, some of the regular Indian Army, units of various rebel rajas, and remnants of the Jhansi garrison. Rao Sahib reviewed the rebel troops, then ordered Tatya Tope to lead them against the English.

Lakshmi was acutely disappointed at being overlooked by Rao Sahib. She must have blamed male disposition and bias for the slight and for clouding the military judgment of the rebel leaders. Many in Jhansi and Kalpi still say that had the Rani been selected to lead the army the outcome of the battles at Koonch and Kalpi might well have been different.

Although the Rani had not been given a command, she offered a tactical proposal. She suggested that the army should not ensconce itself in the Kalpi fort to await Rose's attack, but should go out on the offensive before the British could reach Kalpi and fight on ground favorable to the rebels. She suggested Koonch, to the southwest of Kalpi and back toward Jhansi. Though the fort was dilapidated, Koonch offered the rebels several defensive advantages. The town was difficult to approach, surrounded as it was by temples, woods, and gardens, and protected by high mud walls. These features made Koonch difficult to attack and an ideal site for defensive retrenchments. The Rani urged Tatya Tope not to expend all his troops in the defense of Koonch but to keep some reserve for a fall-back position on Kalpi, and above all to watch his flanks. Tatya Tope failed to heed his friend's advice.

Rose, as he approached Koonch, decided that rather than mount a frontal assault, he would opt for a flank attack from the northwest of Koonch and at the same time threaten the rebel line of retreat toward

Kalpi. He attacked in three columns on 6 May, a month and a day after the Rani's flight from Jhansi. Rose described the battle: "As nothing puts the Rebels out so much as turneing their flank, or defenses; and as the excessive heat of the day rendered it advisable that I should not undertake a long operation against Koonch, much less a siege, I made a flank march with my whole Force to the Northwest . . . This position threatened seriously the enemy's line of retreat from Koonch to Calpee, and it exposed the northwest of the Town, which was not protected by entrenchments to attack."[3]

It was a brief battle, lasting but an hour, with siege guns all the while directed against the town. The flank attack caused the rebels to draw back, but they continued a vigorous defense and maintained their lines. For a time Major Orr's Hyderabad Contingent was pushed back by a brief counterattack of musket fire and Maratha swords. The English were becoming exhausted by their effort, debilitated by temperatures that were 100 degrees at sunrise, intolerable by noon. One thermometer burst at 130 degrees in an officer's tent. English soldiers observed that Maratha tulwars were sharper than British swords. A native sword completely severed the arm of an English lieutenant, another cut off part of a dragoon's foot, shoe and all.[4] Rose also discovered that the Enfield rifles no longer gave his men any advantage, for the heat made loading them extremely difficult and firing uncertain. Despite these difficulties Rose had Tatya Tope on the retreat. In the process the rebels abandoned all their nine guns and left behind nearly six hundred casualties.[5]

Tatya Tope and his army withdrew from Koonch along the Orai-Kalpi road, this time in an orderly retreat toward their arsenal town. At Kalpi the English later found Tatya Tope's order book, in which he praised the spirit of bravery of his men at Koonch. "If they would only fight so a few times more the infidel English would be exterminated."[6] Yet it is certain that the brief battle sowed dissension in the rebel camp. Infantry and cavalry accused each other of desertion and cowardice, and men in all units accused Tatya Tope of retreating more rapidly at Koonch than he had at the Betwa. Even the Jhansi cavalry was faulted for having left the field too soon. British accounts assert with a Victorian touch that the Jhansi force excused themselves "on the plea that they had felt bound to escort their Rani to a place of safety."[7]

The battle had exhausted the English even more than the insurgents, and Rose marched back to Koonch rather than press the pursuit. It was late April, on the verge of the most intense heat of the year. The worst enemies of the English were not insurgents but sun, exhaustion, and lack of water. Sunstroke was common, and the general himself had suffered four times from it. It was virtually impossible to imagine the English launching an offensive under conditions that barely permitted most men to keep moving at all.

Rose was grateful to his men in the face of such formidable odds and might have allowed them more time to recuperate but for an urgent message from the civil officer at Koonch. The message warned Rose that unless he marched at once to the right bank of the Yamuna, Tatya Tope and Lakshmi at Kalpi and the nawab of Banda at Nowgong would cut him off from joining Brigadier Maxwell's Second Brigade. Rose reluctantly ordered his exhausted men to make a forced march to Golauli, seven miles from Kalpi on the Yamuna.[8]

The Fall of Kalpi

The rebel army retreated from Koonch and fell back to Kalpi, their last hope. The fort at Kalpi was small but well situated for defense, poised as it was 120 feet above a bend in the Yamuna River. The original fort was built by the Chandellas in the tenth century, and later it housed part of the Maratha treasury. Walls of the fort were nine feet wide and the fort covered an area 440 yards square. What made it formidable was that it housed what was left of the rebel arsenal. The fort was surrounded by walled temples built of masonry. Beyond the city and temples was a labyrinth of deep ravines, deep enough to inhibit the advance of any army using whatever means of transportation. The ravines were an ideal line of defense, but of course might also conceal an English advance. So long as this rebel stronghold remained in the hands of the insurgents, it would prevent the union of the British armies in the east and west.

Rao Sahib, the Rani, and the nawab of Banda were now the leaders in the fort. Tatya Tope, after the defeat at Koonch, had headed for Charkhari near Jaloun, where his parents lived. From there he disguised himself and made for Gwalior. His goal was to attempt to win over Scindia's well-disciplined army of ten thousand.

The army at Kalpi now included part of the Gwalior Contingent, in Rose's words, "the finest men, best drilled and organized troops of all armies in India."[9] The nawab of Banda's army, some Bengal infantry, valayaties, and cavalry from Kotah completed the force. Rose related of the army, "All the Sepoy Regiments kept up, carefully, their English equipment and organization; the words of command for drill, grand rounds, etc. were given, as we could hear at night, in English."[10]

The rebels prepared five lines of defense to protect the fort to the front, while to the rear it was protected by the Yamuna River and precipitous rocks below the fort. The first line was entrenchments on the Koonch-Kalpi road; ravines on each side of the road provided serious obstacles. The second line was eighty-four temples built of solid masonry, two or three miles from Kalpi. The third line was another outwork of ravines. Fourth was the town of Kalpi, and fifth another chain of ravines between the town and fort. The final fall-back position was the well-armed fort itself.[11] Guns and ammunition, the major ordnance of the rebels, were stored within and under the fort.

General Rose devised his tactical plans for the attack on the Kalpi arsenal. He had to take into account "a new antagonist, a Bengal Sun, at its maximum heat. This formidable ally of the Rebel cause was more dangerous than the Rebels themselves; its summer blaze made havoc amongst Troops, especially Europeans . . . already exhausted by months of overfatigue and want of sleep, by continued night watchings and night marches."[12] Some of these same problems, of course, plagued their opponents. The temperature, already intolerable at Koonch, crept relentlessly upward as operations continued. One insurgent tactic was to attack in daytime, knowing the British with their light hair and complexions would be incapacitated by sunstroke and heat exhaustion. The sick list lengthened; worst afflicted was the Seventy-first Highland Light Infantry, newly arrived in India. All who suffered sunstroke collapsed and, unless they died, had to be carried on the march in dhoolies, or palanquins. Rose himself collapsed and was put into a dhooly but insisted on getting up. He thereafter had a man follow him to pour water over his head to prevent a recurrence. Rose remarked that "the prostration of the whole force had become a matter of arithmetical calculation, so many hours' sun laid low so many men."[13] A two-hour march prostrated half an English unit. The scarcity of water and forage added to the precarious situation.

Faced with these problems, Rose determined that a rapid assault on Kalpi was imperative. Morover, in view of the logistic situation and lines of defense in front of the town and fort, he knew he could not concentrate a force against the mutineers' stronghold. He decided to break off to the right of the main road to Kalpi and at the Yamuna near Golauli to rendezvous with Maxwell's force, sent by Campbell to unite with Rose. From that point Rose would advance up the right bank of the Yamuna toward Kalpi, covered by fire from Maxwell's batteries from the other river bank. To mislead the insurgents Rose ordered the Second Brigade to follow the main road from Koonch to Orai and Kalpi in a feint and take up a position at the village of Banda. This plan was foiled when the brigade lost its way and followed Rose instead. Rose marched the First Brigade to Golauli and ordered Major Orr to cover the rear of his march and keep up communication with the debilitated Second Brigade. The rebels destroyed bridges and commandeered all boats. Rose accordingly ordered pontoon rafts floated and was able then to unite his Central India Field Force from Bombay with Maxwell's force from the east. This rendezvous was an important feature of Rose's mission.[14]

Rose mounted a flank rather than frontal attack against the Kalpi defenses. Yet any advance against Kalpi meant advancing through the maze of ravines, a two-mile belt that could conceal friend or foe and provided an ideal cover for ambush. Against the need for a rapid assault Rose had to balance the debilitated state of his men. "My game was a waiting one, and I abstained carefully from playing that of my adversary, which was to disorganise and prostrate my force by continued exposure to the sun."[15] In planning the final assault Rose took into consideration also the nature of his adversaries. He noted, "The high descent of the Ranee, her unbounded liberality to her Troops and retainers, and her fortitude which no reverses could shake, rendered her an influential and dangerous adversary."[16]

This time Rose did not feel his opponents would repeat the story of the siege of Jhansi by shutting themselves up in the fort and becoming the "victims of an investment." Maxwell was constructing his battery on the opposite bank of the Yamuna to stage the shelling of the fort and to try to blow up its powder magazine and destroy its defenses. As Rose had anticipated, the mutineers did not remain in the fort awaiting his attack but made their stand outside the walls. Rose crossed the river to select the battery sites. For a while the ravines were ominously quiet. Rose became suspicious of the stillness, convinced that the ravines were swarming with rebels. On 20 May the rebels in fact advanced through the ravines under cover of smoke.

CARL A. RUDISILL LIBRARY
LENOIR RHYNE COLLEGE

Rose had fixed the twenty-third for the attack and refused to be drawn into action on the twentieth. When, on the twenty-second, Rose launched his attack on the left, the mutineers hit his right flank, which he was careful not to abandon. Reinforced by Maxwell's Camel Corps and some Sikh infantry, Rose moved with them to the right. He heard the fire there get fainter while the enemy's grew louder, and he realized that his right flank was in danger. Just then an orderly came from Brigadier Stuart and begged Rose to reinforce the right. At the foot of a hill on which the mortar battery with three guns had been emplaced, the British soldiers dismounted from their camels and rushed for the summit, led by Rose. There they met volleys of musketry coming over the crest of the hill. At the top, they were stunned by the sight of rebel troops advancing in mass over level ground against the mortar battery. The rebels yelled in triumph as they came on with volleys of musketry that killed all the horses of the British staff officers. The British could not reply; their Enfield rifles had become leaded and would not fire, and the men were debilitated by the sun. Their guns fell silent.[17]

Rose immediately took in the perilous position of his troops. He ordered the infantry and Eighty-sixth Cavalry to charge with bayonets. The Camel Corps gave a ringing cheer and dashed down the steep incline into the dense lines of mutineers, who far outnumbered them. For a brief moment the rebels stood, then wavered and turned, fleeing through rocky ravines followed by their English pursuers. The retreat spread to the whole insurgent line of battle. The fort offered no safety, as it was under a stream of shellfire from Maxwell's guns. Insurgents separated in their flight, in ones and twos across the difficult terrain to meet later at a predetermined rendezvous. This method of retreat made pursuit fruitless.

The Camel Corps had saved the situation for the British force but only at heavy cost; officers and men slumped to the ground in the heat. By evening all in Rose's camp were speculating on the capture of the fort and town the next day. By the next morning, however, the rebels had departed and the fort stood empty, the resistance evaporated. The Rani, Rao Sahib, and the nawab of Banda had all fled in the early hours of morning. The Rani's departure was reportedly hastened by one of Maxwell's shells, which burst into her room killing two attendants.[18] The insurgents headed across the rocky ravine-cut terrain toward Gopalpur, some forty-six miles from Gwalior, where they were joined by Tatya Tope.

Inside the Kalpi fort was the whole rebel arsenal, abandoned to the British. The English found a subterranean magazine of ammunition in the fort, excellent foundries, and facilities for the manufacture of guns. The quantity of weapons and ammunition amazed Rose. Also in the fort, Rose found a box of the Rani's correspondence which he hoped would throw "great light on the revolt and its principal authors." Everything pointed to the rebel view of the Kalpi arsenal as their final stand.[19]

What remains of the Kalpi fort today is a white tomblike structure. The walls facing the river have eroded away. Local residents say that the British hanged thirteen people from a tamarind tree in a Kalpi courtyard when they failed to reveal where the rebels had gone. And in Kalpi the inhabitants still deplore the fact that the Rani was not in command at the battle of Kalpi.[20]

Rose and the Central India Field Force and Maxwell's force were exhausted by their prodigious efforts. Nearly every man was suffering from sunstroke and exhaustion. The general thanked his troops for the conduct of the campaigns against Koonch and Kalpi and commended them for "the discipline of Christian soldiers," which had seen them through, "triumphant from the shores of Western India to the waters of the Jumna."[21]

With the fall of Kalpi, the campaign mission of the Central India Field Force was completed. Commander in Chief Colin Campbell had planned that Rose's army would be dispersed to Gwalior and Jhansi following the Kalpi operation. General Rose was ordered by his doctors to return at once to Bombay for treatment. Before he could leave, however, news arrived that shocked the officers and forced Rose to alter his plans.

9

Genesis of the Rani Legend

Then fell the Tigress Great
They many, she alone.

—*From a popular poem by Subhadra Kumari Chauhan*

Gwalior, the Last Battle

On 26 May Tatya Tope left the Gwalior bazaars, where he had been gathering intelligence, and rejoined the Rani and Rao Sahib at Burragaon eight miles from Gwalior. They held council over their desperate plight in a mood of gloom. Three British columns were converging on them and on the fourth side was one of the staunchest supporters of the English in India, Maharaja Scindia of Gwalior. Rao Sahib posed the question of where they should go next. The Rani, in one version, proposed advancing to Karhra, the home base of her generals. Tatya Tope suggested that "even Bundelcund would be better." Rao Sahib, in one version, felt this was bad advice. "There we should find the Boondelas hostile and no supplies," he is quoted as saying. "Our only course is to make for the Deccan, where all will join us. But we must go first to Gwalior, where the army is gained, and take it with us by the Sipree road. When that army shall come over, the Maharaja and the Baiza Baee will join us, and all the Princes of Hindoostan will rise."[1]

Military analysts later judged the insurgent plan to make yet another stand at Gwalior "a stroke of genius." Some English historians credit the Rani with the idea, as they consider her the best strategist among the insurgent leaders.[2] Others suggest it was the inspiration of Tatya Tope, who had already spent time in the Gwalior bazaars to test the mood of the Gwalior troops.

In Rose's camp sunstroke had cut a wide swath. Rose and the other generals were ill and desperately in need of medical attention and a respite. Now, just as Rose was preparing to depart for Bombay and his army to disperse to Gwalior and Jhansi, he got the sensational intelligence that the rebel force had crossed the Chambal River, regrouped, and were headed for Gwalior. Rose quickly took stock of the unexpected development and wrote Hamilton: "I was afraid the rebels would make a dash for Gwalior; they have numerous friends there with whom they are in understanding, and it is everything for them to make Gwalior replenish their coffers with a heavy ransom."[3]

Rose in late May met with Maj. Charters Macpherson, resident at Gwalior and adviser to the young maharaja. Macpherson advised Rose it would be expedient to send a strong force to Gwalior, for otherwise the loyal Maharaja Scindia would have "cause to complain of a breach of faith if a strong force were not sent after the fate of Calpee." Such a relief force would enable Scindia to carry out his plan to disarm Gwalior. Macpherson added that the size of the relief force could be reduced once the disarmament was accomplished.[4] Apart from Macpherson's proposal, Rose himself was convinced that the critical importance of Gwalior made fast action imperative. Rose set aside considerations of health and ignored his doctor's advice to return to Bombay. He did not even wait for orders from his superiors to proceed to Gwalior.

Gwalior, like Jhansi, had immense strategic importance, situated athwart the Grand Trunk Road and telegraphic link between Bombay and Agra. Scindia's army was renowned throughout the subcontinent as the best trained in India. It had been drilled by French and English advisers over a period of several decades. Rose knew Tatya Tope had gone to Gwalior to persuade Scindia's troops to join the rebel cause. It would be a combination that could only spell more trouble for the exhausted English officers and their men. Rose wrote Hamilton: "You should inform Scindiah without a moment's delay, that Col. Robertson with a British Force of all arms . . . has my orders to push on, and attack the rebels in the rear, whilst he attacks them in front. This will encourage him and his faithful troops, and discourage his unfaithful troops and subjects."[5]

Rose then sent a series of inquiries to Hamilton seeking information about the terrain around Gwalior. The monsoon rains were imminent, the worst time of the year for any military operations, and each day that passed made Rose's outlook dimmer. There was moreover the possibility of a rebel advance toward the Deccan to rally the south around the standard of a revived Maratha Confederacy, another major concern of the British. Rose was unfamiliar with the countryside and fearful of the effects of the rains on the Sindh and Pahuj rivers, surrounding roads, and supply lines. He wrote Hamilton on 6 June that he would take up a position in the cantonments east of Gwalior and make Agra his base, since he feared the rains would swell the Sindh to the point where communications with Jhansi and Kalpi would be cut off. Moreover, "From the nature of the country I fear Major Orr's and Brigadier Smith's forces will not be able to join me at the Cantonments. Could you tell me of any other road for them?" he asked.

Rose peppered Hamilton with more questions. "You say you can furnish supplies from Cawnpore, Calpee and Jhansi, but I suppose you mean only *before* the monsoon, because after they have begun the Scinde and Pahooj will rise so that our communications with those three towns will be completely cut off. Can you supply after the rains? In what way? If you cannot, will you be able to supply us after we have crossed the Scinde and are besieging Gwalior?"[6] Rose decided to send a party to protect the ford or bridge over the Chambal River on the Grand Trunk Road near Dholpur. Part of the force at Kalpi could not leave there until 8 June, when they would be relieved by another unit.

Rose was moreover apprehensive about Hamilton's suggestion to bring Orr's and Smith's forces to the foot of a difficult pass twenty miles from Gwalior. "I hear that from there to Gwalior it is a network of ravines, and besides, they are quite separated from me," he added. Rose pointed out that the Jhansi-Gwalior road crossed the Scindh River twice and questioned whether Smith, if he took that route, could get heavy artillery over the two fords. Orr was supposed to reach Gwalior the same day as his force, Smith a day later. But, Rose noted, "I hope that Brigadier Smith and Orr may unite, as Orr's force is weak and all native." Rose asked Hamilton to get all the information he could about the best place to attack Gwalior fort and town.[7]

Rose immediately sent out orders to Smith and Orr. He cautioned Smith on 8 June: "Look out for *treachery*, for that is the only thing they can beat us by. Pray have patrols out in every direction night and day." He ordered Orr on 11 June to march from Jhansi and effect a junction twenty miles from Gwalior with Smith's force, both of them to reach Gwalior by the nineteenth. "The rebels may not wait to be attacked by my force at Gwalior but make a dash at you or Brigadier Smith's column," he warned.[8]

Gwalior was known as the bastion of British support in Central

India, Maharaja Scindia's loyalty regarded as unshakable. Though the English counted Scindia their "truest ally," they were less certain about his troops. The devotion of the Scindia family to the British was partly due to the fact that the Scindias were Marathas surrounded by subjects who were Bundelas, Rajputs, and Jats. In their support of the British, the Scindias had traditionally found security against the possible rebellion of alien subjects. But Tatya Tope anticipated that the Gwalior troops might be vulnerable to an appeal to join the rebels and regenerate the Maratha Confederacy. The Rani, Rao Sahib, and the nawab of Banda, as they left Kalpi, approved of Tatya Tope's destination. They knew that Gwalior possessed a fort even larger than the fortress at Jhansi; its treasury and arsenal, furthermore, were legendary.

The critical factor in Gwalior, then, was the allegiance of Scindia and his army. Maharaja Jayaji Rao Scindia was a young man under the influence of his diwan, Dinkar Rao Rajwade, who in turn was influenced by the resident, Macpherson.[9] Moreover, the tie between Scindia and the English dated back several generations and could not easily be ruptured. A visit to the Scindia palaces and museum in Gwalior confirms the picture of close, long-standing bonds of friendship, of elaborate hunts, lavish parties, and maharajas attired in English hunting dress posing for photographs with their English friends and tigers' corpses.

The loyalty of Scindia's troops was less certain, however. This was why Tatya Tope had visited Gwalior on several occasions, one of the earliest being September 1857 on a mission from Nana Sahib to seek the allegiance of the Gwalior Contingent. The young Maharaja Jayaji Rao in June of 1857 had been unable to prevent the spread of the Rebellion to Gwalior. It broke out in the cantonments at Morar on 14 June among a contingent of the Bengal Army stationed there. After killing what officers and their families they could find, the troops remained at Morar and later formed part of the force that, under Tatya Tope, attacked Maj. Gen. Charles Windham at Kanpur.

The Gwalior fort, one of the largest and most imposing in India, is built on a precipitous flat-topped igneous rock rising three hundred feet above the dusty plain. The countryside as one approaches Gwalior is marked by rock outcroppings like the one on which the fort is situated. Some of these outcroppings themselves resemble forts from a distance. The fort is one and three-quarters miles long and varies from six hundred to twenty-eight hundred feet in width. Two entrances lead into the

Fig. 4. Gwalior fort. Photograph by Rituraj Dvivedi, Gwalior.

fort, the main entrance on the northeast being protected by five gateways. From the main gate one enters the palace through the elephant gate, a high stone structure with domed turrets on the exterior. Horizontal bands of carved moulding on the palace facade were once inlaid with enamelled tiles. Access to the other gate of the fort is up a long winding road, along which rock faces are carved with enormous Jain images.

The origins of the fort are obscure, but the first inscription is in the sun temple inside the fort and is dated A.D. 525. Under the Gurjar Pratiharas the fort began to take its present form. In 1200 Kutb-ud-din Aibak, the Delhi sultan, conquered the fort, and the fort and palace as they stand today were completed by Man Singh Tomar in the mid-fifteenth century. Ibrahim Lodi captured the fort in 1523, and Babur took it in 1527 or 1528. Under both the Delhi sultans and the Mughal emperors it was used as a prison. The Sikh guru Hargovind Singh was imprisoned here by Emperor Jahangir. The fort was also captured by Sher Shah, the invader who drove the Mughal emperor Humayun from India in the sixteenth century. In 1784 the Maratha warrior Madhav Rao Scindia captured the fort and founded his dynasty in Gwalior.

Neither the maharaja nor his diwan knew of the secret visit of Tatya

Tope. Nor were they aware of the malaise among the troops at Gwalior. Moreover, Dinkar Rao had foolishly assured the maharaja that he could disperse the rebels "by a single round from his gun." The maharaja's bodyguard, however, warned him that Dinkar Rao's advice was absurd. Without consulting his complacent diwan, Jayaji Rao on 31 May issued orders for his troops to assemble at dawn the next morning. Despite the uncertain allegiance of his army, then, the maharaja marched his seven thousand infantry, fifteen hundred cavalry, and eight guns to a position two miles east of the Morar cantonments, where the rebel forces were positioned. When the insurgent cavalry rode toward Scindia's army they shouted *"Deen!"* ("Religion!"), and Scindia's troops gave an answering yell. This meant that the maharaja's army was not going to resist. There was no fight, except for brief skirmishing by the maharaja's still-loyal personal bodyguard. Scindia's troops joined the insurgents, and they congratulated each other and celebrated by eating watermelons in the bed of the Morar River.[10]

Faced with wholesale disaffection of the army, the young maharaja made for the Phoolbagh sector, where he changed his clothes, remounted, and rode hard for Agra and British protection. The diwan, dismayed at what had transpired, quickly rode after his maharaja with a few cavalry from the bodyguard. On 3 June Jayaji Rao reached Agra and the safety of the British garrison.[11]

The Rani of Jhansi, Rao Sahib, and Tatya Tope entered Gwalior in triumph. Nana Sahib was proclaimed peshwa of the Maratha Confederacy, and the peshwa's flag was flown from the fort. The Scindia treasurer, Amar Chand Banthia, opened the treasury and told the rebels to take what they wanted. This tactic saved Gwalior from being looted, but Banthia himself was hanged by the British in 1862. Scindia's troops were given five months' pay, and cash was distributed among the insurgent army. Jails were opened and prisoners released, but Scindia's servants were confirmed in their authority and positions. Rao Sahib wrote the dowager mother, Baiza Bai, in Nurwar, where she had fled, and urged her to return. It was not his goal to take Gwalior, he said, but "only to have a meeting and go on." He hoped that the Baiza Bai would return and take charge of affairs and in so doing prevent the departure of the maharaja.[12]

On 3 June Rao Sahib held a grand durbar and feast in the Gwalior fort. A special tent was erected and local notables appeared with flags, festoons, and magnificent clothes. Rao Sahib wore ropes of pearls and diamonds from the Scindia storehouse. Fanfares of trumpets, shouts of joy, and Vedic prayers mingled together in a festive atmosphere. Brahmin priests were summoned to preside over the recitation of mantras.

One person was notably absent from the festivities. The Rani refused to take part. She continued to worry about Rose's army, and after the celebrations had continued for two days she admonished Rao Sahib for his foolishness in celebrating before victory was won. She left the fort in a fury, taking her pistols and sword, and entered the Phoolbagh sector, where she was warmly received. Her excitable temperament and sense of crisis clearly separated her from Rao Sahib and Tatya Tope. No doubt she felt the irony of her situation—a military officer unable to take command of the army because of her sex, yet more capable than those endowed by their sex with the authority of command. She must have felt a sense of desperation now that her beloved fort and city were lost and two of her women companions killed at Kalpi. She was also by now acutely aware of what capture by her opponents would mean. While celebrations continued inside the fort, the Rani spent her time inspecting troops. "She is continually on horseback, armed with sword and pistol, at the head of 300 Horse," reported one account.[13] She alone of the rebel leaders seems to have had a sense of urgency about the need to cope aggressively with the crisis. Gwalior historian Dvivedi says several of the Rani's generals were still with her at Gwalior, among them Raghunath Singh, Chunni, Jhadu, and Ram Chandra Deshmukh,[14] but these men do not figure in British accounts.

As Rose mapped strategy for his assault on what was yet another rebel stronghold, he contemplated his goal: "the Fort which is the largest, and one of the strongest in India, Scindia's Treasury, his jewels, and those of his family of fabulous value; the Arsenal filled with warlike stores of every description, and upwards of 60 pieces of siege and field artillery."[15] Rose was equally aware that its central geographic position gave Gwalior a strategic importance equal to that of Jhansi. It was embarrassing that Gwalior had fallen into rebel hands and at the worst time of year, on the eve of the great rains. Possession of this political and military plum "would give the rebels time to reorganize and march south to raise the Deccan," in favor of the peshwa's government.[16]

Rose decided to attack Gwalior on its weakest side and thereby cut off rebel escape. He hoped investment of the city would be followed by the capture of the fort, as at Jhansi and Kalpi. He had no map of Gwalior, but with careful reconnaissance learned that to attack Gwalior from the Morar cantonment to the east he would have to cross the plain between

Morar and Gwalior under fire from the fort as well as from camouflaged batteries in the houses and along the banks of the canal. There was also a dry river bed in front of the Phoolbagh palace close to the Lashkar (new city) and south of the fort. The rebels were in control of hills to the left of the canal, Rose learned from reconnaissance. He decided therefore to build a bridge across the Morar, cross the river under cover of night, and take the road to Gwalior from the south, cutting the two rebel positions off from Gwalior. The best point of attack would then be from the south, the Lashkar direction. He planned to establish his initial foothold and hospital in the Morar cantonment, on the road to Kalpi.[17] The houses and buildings in the Morar cantonment stood empty after the Rebellion. The rebels also knew of the weak point of Gwalior's defense to the southeast and realized they would have to concentrate a large force there, reinforced with stores against the British advance.

Rose was joined the morning of the sixteenth by Brig. Gen. Robert Napier, his successor, who had reached Bahadurpur five miles east of Morar. Rose wanted to capture Gwalior as soon as possible to minimize problems attendant on the monsoon. The rebels now had plenty of cash and ammunition by virtue of their capture of the fort, treasure, and town of Gwalior. They were no longer a force of stragglers in retreat and disarray. Yet Rose had a good road at his back, the Gwalior-Agra road, and he learned that the Chambal River was passable even during the rains. He determined not to camp but to attack immediately. This would give him the advantage of surprise and might also prevent the burning of the buildings in Morar by the rebels.

Rose ordered all units to move into position on the morning of the seventeenth: Brigadier Smith to invest the east, Major Orr to watch the road to the south of Gwalior, Colonel Riddell to attack from the northwest and west. Napier he left behind in the cantonment to watch for possible insurgent retreat in that direction. On the eighteenth Rose marched from the Morar cantonment toward Kotah-ki-Serai to attack Gwalior from that point, the southeast of the city. All his forces were positioned for attack on the nineteenth.[18]

The Rani Falls in Battle

Brigadier Smith and Major Orr (now Lieutenant Colonel) meanwhile rendezvoused at Antri and marched toward Kotah-ki-Serai, arriving there at seven-thirty the morning of the seventeenth. Smith found rebel cavalry and infantry occupying the hilly ground between Kotah-ki-Serai and Gwalior and rebel batteries placed across the Gwalior road. It was difficult to use his cavalry in the circumstances. Smith decided he had to clear the road or he would not be able to move on Gwalior according to plan. He therefore ordered a squadron of the Eighth Hussars to charge the rebels blocking his path.

This section of the approach to Gwalior was, in Rose's opinion, the most difficult sector to defend because of its vulnerability to attack. It was also the point from which the rebels anticipated an enemy assault. It is all the more surprising, then, that the sole obstacle in the path of Smith's advancing squadron was the Rani and some of her troops. The responsibility for the assignment to this difficult sector may have been Rao Sahib's. It is more likely, however, that Lakshmi herself deliberately chose this desperate sector for her last stand. However the decision was made, the Rani faced her attackers bravely, in full battle dress. She dashed into the action without hesitation, a few officers of her army still at her side. Indian versions have it that one of her court women, Mundar, followed her into battle.

As the Rani clashed with soldiers of the Eighth Hussars on the road, she was struck and wounded by one of them, "ignorant of her rank and sex." The wounds proved fatal; the Rani's heroic struggle was at an end. Although the exact manner of her death is uncertain, all accounts, including those by English historians, attest to her bravery and daring. This single act of valor would be indelibly imprinted on the hearts and minds of Indians for generations to come.

The battle raged on, but with Lakshmi dead, the spirit went out of the rebel fight. Smith, by his maneuver against the Rani, gained command of the road. Meanwhile, Rose moved on toward the enemy under cover of ravines and broken ground. Rose could see that insurgent guns on the hills were being reinforced. He felt the more guns the enemy placed on hill batteries, the more he could capture next morning in the general attack. Yet Rose was not completely confident. "Our position was not a good one. We had it is true the road through the pass, the hills on the right and the deep canal on the left of it. But the enemy held the hills commanding the advanced part of the road, and the canal. The enemy occupied also in force the slope of a hill, threatening, from the other side of the Canal, my rear and Camp."[19] Rose recognized that it was imperative to drive the enemy from this position; "I did so," he added in his report. Reaching this height, he could see the entire area spread before him. "The heights descended towards Gwalior in a succession of ranges, one lower than the other, the lowest and last commanding the parade ground, and a great part of the Lashkar, all of which I saw I could take from the lowest range almost undisturbed by the fire of the fort."[20] Rose saw the rebels moving from the hills in a long line "extending from the centre of the Lashkar to the northernmost extremity of the old city, under the Fort."

Rose resorted to his favorite left flanking maneuver. Riddell attacked the west of Gwalior, and Rose ordered Smith to make an oblique movement from the left of his right front across the canal and over the shoulder of the hill against the enemy's left flank. The rebels lit haystacks to halt the British advance and kept up a steady fire from the fort. Yet Rose's strategy succeeded as it had at Koonch and Kalpi; he caught his enemy with their strength concentrated in the opposite sector. Moreover, the speed of Rose's march from Kalpi to Gwalior had surprised his adversaries.

The Rani's warnings against premature celebrating in the Gwalior fort were borne out all too well. Although the rebel swordsmen fought in the trenches and nullahs and made good account of themselves in hand-to-hand combat, Rose's reliance on surprise and the left flank attack were decisive. Rose reported, "The enemy's cavalry and infantry retreated before us through the Town so rapidly that we could not even get sight of them, although we advanced by more streets than one with a view to cut them off."[21] Scindia's agent reported to Rose that the fort was evacuated, but as a unit from Rose's force advanced to the fort, it was fired on. Next morning the fort was captured by a unit of the Twenty-fifth Native Infantry under Lieutenant Rose, a cousin of the general, who was mortally wounded in the capture of the fort.

Rose had ordered all roads from Gwalior closely guarded, but the insurgents fleeing from the city found the northwest road to Dholpur open and escaped in that direction. Napier pursued them and killed many. Thus ended the last organized resistance of the Rebellion. "The political atmosphere of Gwalior has been completely purified," Rose wrote in his battle report from Gwalior. The insurgent army was no longer an army of combatants but a group of "disheartened fugitives . . . without artillery, warlike stores or reserves."[22]

Most important, noted Rose, the Rani of Jhansi had been killed. "The Rani of Jhansi, the Indian Joan of Arc, was killed in this charge, dressed in a red jacket, red trousers, and white puggery; she wore the celebrated pearl necklace of Scindia which she had taken from his treasury and heavy gold anklets."[23] This jewelry she distributed among her troops as she lay mortally wounded, popular sources assert. Rose noted that "the whole rebel army mourned her." She was, in Rose's famous words, the "best and bravest of the rebel leaders," a phrase that has never been forgotten in India. With the death of this "most dangerous of all rebel leaders" all organized resistance by the insurgents collapsed. In view of Rose's praise of the Rani, a comparison made by Sir John Smyth is revealing. "Sir Hugh and the Rani were two of a kind," writes Smyth. "Both understood what had to be done—and did it. The difference lay in the support they received from their people."[24]

With the death of the Rani in battle her legend was born. It was the praise of her valor that came immediately from the pens of General Rose and other British officers in India that generated the beginnings of the legend. The English forgot the Rani in later years, but Indians did not. They perpetuated her epic in folk arts, poetry, and ballads, where it lives still.

Where was Tatya Tope when the Rani fell in action? The charge of the Eighth Hussars at Kotah-ki-Serai gave Brigadier Smith command of the defile and hills east of the canal, but Tatya Tope had the hills to the west of the defile and canal, and on the ridge had placed a battery of nine-pounders. When Rose ordered his guns up a steep hill, Tatya Tope, emboldened, prepared to attack Rose's troops and drive them out of the defile and hills to the east. Rose's offensive against the ridge and gorge, however, foiled Tatya Tope and drove him south. Tatya Tope was expelled from his positions from Phoolbagh to the Lashkar, and two days later, on the twenty-first, Napier overtook and defeated him at Jora Alipur.[25]

But Tatya Tope escaped. He continued to lead guerrilla resistance against the English throughout the whole of Bundelkhand for over a year after Gwalior's capture. Without tents or provisions, and minus over twenty guns he lost at Gwalior, Tatya Tope continued to elude a ring of British generals and divisions that pursued him. He became a kind of Robin Hood figure, a legend in his own right. He led an army consisting of valayaties, Bundelas, Bheels, and dacoits. Mounted on camels and ponies they bivouacked in deeply wooded glens at night to cook their food and sleep where they dismounted. They separated into small groups when attacked, which facilitated their escape and enabled them to rendezvous later and fight yet again.

Following the defeat at Gwalior, Tatya Tope fled with Rao Sahib and the nawab of Banda northwest toward Udaipur. In November 1858 the nawab surrendered and Rao Sahib was also captured. Tatya Tope hid in the jungle but was arrested nearly a year later, on 8 April 1859, betrayed by one of his own comrades whose family had been taken hostage. He was tried by court martial at Sipri, charged with rebellion and waging war against the British. Ten days after his arrest he was hanged publicly. "No sooner were the irons removed from his hands, he ascended the gallows with a firm step and placed his neck in the noose with the greatest *sangfroid*,"[26] writes a biographer. According to legend in Sipri and Jhansi, it was not Tatya Tope who was hanged but an impersonator; Tatya Tope lived on in the hills in the garb of a sadhu.

Tatya Tope had been a special target of British military command in India since his campaign at Kanpur against General Windham in November 1857. He represented, too, a vestige of the power of the Maratha Confederacy, having grown up with Nana Sahib, whose chief of staff he was. Moreover, his army at Gwalior was known as the "Peshwa's Army."

The fate of Nana Sahib is less certain. It is commonly believed that he escaped into Nepal, where he died two years later. Numerous persons appeared from time to time claiming to be Nana Sahib, and the time and manner of his death remained a mystery to the British, perhaps also to Indians. He did not fight at Koonch, Kalpi, or Gwalior, that much is certain. According to one legend, Nana Sahib lived on in a temple near Kanauj or in a jungle in Gujarat.[27]

Birth of the Legend

The several existing accounts of the death of Lakshmibai disagree in details of her death. We know with some certainty that she died on 17 June outside the Gwalior fort as she defended the difficult sector between Kotah-ki-Serai and Phoolbagh. She was killed by units of the Eighth Hussars commanded by Brigadier Smith. Certain, too, from all accounts, is the courage with which she met her attackers. Charles Ball writes: "This extraordinary female, whose age did not exceed twenty years, was in the dress of a mounted officer, superintending the movements of the cavalry on the field, and sharing in all the dangers of the struggle when struck down."[28] Some accounts say she was shot down, others that she was wounded by a sabre, and some that she received both wounds.

Robert Hamilton, onetime friend and later antagonist of the Rani, reported that she and her Muslim attendant were each shot in the breast and wounded fatally. "The Ranee died almost before she was put in the Palkee and carried off to a Mundir on the other side of town."[29] Another British account reports that she was "shot in the back by a trooper of the 8th Hussars. She turned and fired back at the man who then ran her through with his sword."[30] The version that has survived in the legend is that she was fighting with a sword in each hand, the reins of her horse in her teeth, when killed.[31] Some British accounts suggest that just prior to her death she was "seated, drinking sherbet," when the alarm was given of the approach of the Eighth Hussars. "Forty or fifty of them came up, and the rebels fled, save about fifteen. The Rani's horse refused to leap a canal, when she received a shot in the side, and then a sabre cut on the head, but rode off. She soon fell dead."[32]

A question is thus posed about whether she was actually killed on the battlefield or was wounded and died later. An adventurous Englishwoman who had accompanied her husband in the field alleged that she talked with General Rose about the circumstances of the Rani's death. The Englishwoman claimed the general told her that "though mortally wounded she was not actually killed on the field but was carried off the ground, and ordered a funeral pile to be built, which she ascended and fired with her own hand while almost in the act of dying."[33]

In the Kalyan Singh ballad she was wounded by a bullet in her thigh, and the sword of a British soldier scraped off the right part of her face as well. The ballad relates that she entrusted her son to Ram Chandra Deshmukh, and to Jawahar Singh and Raghunath Singh she gave the charge of keeping the flame of revolt alive. The ballad adds that Raghunath Singh refused the gift of her pearl necklace given her by the peshwa and promised to continue to work for the cause without reward. The ballad relates that her body was guarded vigorously by Raghunath Singh and Gaus Khan, who between them fired several guns and rounds of ammunition to prevent molestation of the body by British soldiers. The ballad has it that the Rani's faithful servant Mundar, who never left her side in life, also was with her in death, killed in the same action. Lakshmi's body was cremated on a funeral pyre in the prescribed manner. Today an impressive statue and small temple mark the spot near Phoolbagh where the Rani's body was said to have been cremated.

In some versions of the legend the Rani's death occurred because her favorite horse had been killed and the substitute mount refused to leap a canal; she fell off in the attempt or was cut down by a Hussar as she urged her horse to cross the canal.

Lakshmibai's death in battle gave her instant martyrdom and has since inspired generations of poets, painters, and patriots in India. She died "in a blaze of glory, consecrating with her blood the cause she espoused."[34] Even among the English her valor elicited universal acclaim. What better death, after all, for a true soldier, than death in battle? John Sylvester, British surgeon with Rose's army, wrote: "Thus the brave woman cemented with her blood the cause she espoused. It is well that it was so, and that she did not survive to share the ignominious fate of Tatya Tope. The fact of her death was not known to us for some days, as she was attired as a cavalry soldier."[35]

For some writers in Victorian England the Rani's death in battle at the hands of a soldier, an English soldier, was difficult to rationalize. The Eighth Hussars, according to one account, "were a bit upset by the incident, for at that period women were held sacred by British soldiers, who not infrequently risked having their positions over-run in action, rather than continue firing when there was any chance of hitting women. The Rani in particular, was greatly admired by all ranks for her romantic gallantry, which equalled that commonly displayed by British women during the horrors of Cawnpore, Lucknow . . ." The same author quickly added a salve to the Victorian conscience: "Any British soldiers who had the misfortune to fall into the hands of the Rani would certainly, however, have quickly altered their opinion of her."[36] Yet even those English who regarded the Rani as "treacherous, savage, cruel and licentious" had to concede their admiration for "her bravery and military qualities. She alone, with Kunwar Singh, among the rebel leaders showed herself to possess that first attribute of a soldier—courage in battle."[37]

The exact details of the manner of her death, though they remain shrouded in some mystery, do not alter the fact of her death on the battlefield or diminish her stature in the eyes of posterity.

10

Growth of the Legend

Your name, Rani Lakshmibai,
is so sacred
that we invoke it
in the early hours
of dawn.

—*Prayer sung by the*
Nagpur Rashtra Sevika Samiti

The Legend is Born

What is it that gives mythmaking its power in India and makes the Rani legend in particular so potent? Mircea Eliade suggests that most modern and Western societies perceive time as linear and therefore produce history, whereas Hindu civilization perceives time as cyclical and therefore produces myth, not history. In traditional societies, says Eliade, myth serves multiple functions: it provides an escape from the historic moment and a means of reentry into primordial time; it imparts a sacramental aspect to human existence; it moreover provides a defense against the inevitability of death.[1]

Carl Jung also sees myth as providing value to premodern man. Myth and symbol are products of the unconscious psyche generated out of the tension between spirit and nature to create meaning. Myth and symbol provide identity with nature and archetypal symbols of the universal psyche. For Jung, the dreamer should "dream the dream onward" in a never-ending process in order to avoid loss of meaning.

We might argue that myth and legend are two distinct phenomena, myth evolving from imaginary gods and heroes and legend inspired by historical heroes, and that Indian mythmaking is not relevant to the Rani legend. Yet a civilization that has generated such a rich tradition of myth and epic, it must also be recognized, has a special penchant for producing legends as well from real heroes and heroines. In Indian popular culture, the place of real and epic heroes and gods is often blurred, making distinctions between myth and legend artificial.

Myth and legend in India are often more important than fact. Legends proliferate spontaneously because of their close connection with folk or peasant culture and their lack of dependence on literate traditions. The majority of the Indian population has relied on oral rather than written transmission of cultural norms and messages from one generation to the next. This factor lends added significance to the function of mythmaking in India. The classical literary tradition of India was at base religious rather than historical in its concerns, and it flourished in myth and epic. In this matrix the Rani legend found fertile ground.

If we postulate a typology for the growth of a legend from the career of a historic individual, it appears essential to the growth of the legend that it be incorporated into the folk or popular culture and ethos and ultimately absorbed into the collective memory of a nation. The process begins shortly after the death of the individual, often in a martyr's death. The shedding of blood is the initial catalyst in the process, blood itself being the archetypal, mythic matrix. In an early second stage the legend grows by becoming the inspiration for ballads, songs, and poems. In later stages the legend proliferates through drama, statuary, visual arts, and even cinema. All these stages and forms can be traced in the legend of the Rani.

This efflorescence of the Rani legend in the arts also followed an earlier stage: short-term defeat in the process of military pacification, which in the Rani's case meant her death at Gwalior and the final suppression of the Rebellion. Historian Eric Stokes has suggested that the Rani of Jhansi and Tatya Tope only became national leaders at the point when revolt was already half defeated.[2]

The legend of the Rani, like other legends, illustrates an important fact, again differentiating history from myth. Legends, unlike human beings, never die; they grow incrementally, in Jungian fashion. They continue to grow and to reappear periodically, sometimes invoked in time of crisis or national peril. An interesting example of this phenomenon is offered by novelist Salman Rushdie in *Midnight's Children*, where in the perilous year 1947 visions of the Rani's ghost appeared to persons in Gwalior, where she died.[3] In times of danger the image of the Rani's valor still works, as it did in 1858. Legends, then, have a history of their own, apart from the historical persons who inspired them. Thus we return to myth and history as two distinct representations of the course and significance of past events.

A martyr's death often marks the parturition of a legend and separates the historic person from the later legendary personage. Martyrs are the raw material of legends; in fact, martyrdom almost automatically guarantees the generation of a legend. Col. G. S. Dhillon, one of three Indian National Army officers tried by the British in the Red Fort trial at the end of World War II, once said, "Every time you fight for your rights a legend will grow."[4] But fighting, in this context, is not as efficacious as dying. In the Red Fort trial of the INA officers, the trial itself may have served the function of a kind of allegoric death in battle insofar as the INA legend was concerned. Death for a cause, either in battle or at the hands of an oppressor, is a catalyst for metaphoric purification. Anyone who sheds blood for a just cause proves for all time his or her mettle. The legend is born spontaneously and immediately. The examples in history are so abundant as to obviate enumeration. The obvious analogue to the Rani is Joan of Arc. While the blood of others may be considered polluting, as is the case in India and many other traditional societies, the shedding of one's own blood in a just cause and in a heroic manner is purifying.

Blood as purifying agent had validity for English as for Indian commentators on the martyrdom of the Rani. Alive, for the English, she was "the horrid Ranee," the "Jezebel of India," "the Indian Boadicea," and "perpetrator of the most heinous crimes." Dying valiantly in battle, however, she was purified almost overnight in British eyes, transformed into "the best and bravest of the rebels," in Rose's famous phrase. British recognition of her soldierly qualities was instantaneous and ungrudging and elevated her to a higher plane, which in India is the realm not only of heroes and heroines but of gods and goddesses as well. The Rani's valor, fierce determination, discipline, knowledge of weaponry and horsemanship, and excellent tactical instincts were all traits with a long and honored tradition in British military annals and ethos. Rose recognized them, and his battle account began the process of rehabilitation of the Rani. It was partly through the prism of English military romanticism, then, that the legend of the Rani had its inception. General Rose's comparison of the Rani to Joan of Arc in his battle report served a significant function. Other contemporary British commentators followed in a similar vein. A Bombay newspaper report on her death noted, "Her life has been a brief and eventful one, and gives the revolt its only romantic tinge . . . her courage shines pre-eminent, and can only be equalled, but not eclipsed by that of Joan of Arc."[5]

Apart from death in battle or at the hands of an oppressor for a just cause, another incubator of legends is death in mysterious circumstances. While the Rani's death at the hands of the Eighth Hussars at Gwalior on 17 June 1858 is documented, the precise circumstances and manner of her death are less certain, as we have seen. Which was the fatal wound, the gunshot or the sword's blow, and did she die immediately or somewhat later? Was she cremated only after she breathed her last? The spot where she was reputedly cremated is marked today by a magnificent bronze statue, judged by some to be the best of the Rani statues. Or did she in fact commit a kind of sati, that exaggeration of the upper-caste Hindu ideal of wifely fidelity? Did she light her own pyre and embrace the holocaust? There are those in Jhansi and Gwalior who allege that she committed suicide, though not in a traditional sati on her husband's funeral pyre, but rather by climbing on a hayrick and lighting it with her own hand. These questions cannot be resolved, but they do indicate that the important element of mystery surrounds the Rani's death.

The typology of the making of legends can be extended to a figure of more recent times. Subhas Chandra Bose died in equally mysterious circumstances in a plane crash in Taiwan in August 1945. Calcutta abounds with those who insist that he never died, that he lives on as a sannyasi, a holy man, in the hills of Assam or in some other spot, and that he will reappear at some future time, perhaps for World War III. The fact that this legend, if true, would render his revolutionary career meaningless does not deter its perpetrators.

One version of the Rani's last battle at Gwalior has it that she did not die, but her battle wounds were dressed and healed with herbal remedies by a priest in a temple near the spot where she was wounded. She recovered, went underground as a Hindu religious celibate, a brahmacharin, and continued to carry on her struggle against the British. She thus derived power against her enemies in the classical tradition of demons and gods who gained power through practicing austerities.

Another comparison may be relevant here. It is noteworthy that while the Rani and Subhas Chandra Bose have become legends, in a sense Mahatma Gandhi has not, despite his saintly qualities, political genius, and impact on modern history. Part of the reason lies in the fact that he concentrated always on means rather than ends, so that despite his death at a particular point in his career, part of his mission had already been achieved. In another sense, his goals have been achieved as well—in the incorporation of many of his ideas into, for example, programs for rural development, for harijans, for women. In other words, Gandhi has become institutionalized in India. The Rani has not, nor has Subhas Chandra Bose. Their goals still appeared elusive, their missions incomplete, when they died. Moreover, Gandhi was killed by an extremist from within his own Hindu tradition. Had he been killed by the British like the Rani, or even by one Englishman, the impact would have been incendiary, and, more than likely, a legend would have been born. Nor was there much mystery surrounding the assassination of Gandhi. At least there was no chance of mistaken identity, of someone else having been killed and Gandhi escaping and working underground. The essential element of mystery found in the deaths of the Rani and of Netaji was lacking. Finally, the Rani and Bose were both killed in action against the British colonial power in the cause of national liberation. This factor is critical.

Death in mysterious circumstances in other times and places has similarly stimulated the growth of legends. In the United States the deaths of John and Robert Kennedy are obvious examples. Though one may argue that these men were legends in their own time whose photographs were found in village huts as far away as Nepal, the manner of their deaths has promoted their legends. Despite the expenditure of hundreds of thousands of dollars to investigate the circumstances of the assassinations of these two men, it is unlikely that the world will learn the truth. So, too, the posthumous peregrinations of the body of Eva Peron have contributed to the perpetuation of her legend in Argentina. The spectacular suicide by hara kiri of the Japanese novelist Yukio Mishima in 1970 was an act of death purposely engineered to promote a legend. Mishima performed his suicide in a staged grand finale in the headquarters of the Ground Self Defense Forces. While the act itself was not specifically mysterious, Mishima's suicide motive was sufficiently complex to promote endless speculation, analysis, and discussion over a period of many years.

A significant dimension of all these legends is the problem of verification. At the same time, the legend of the Rani of Jhansi is also an example of historiographic anamnesis—the attempt to preserve the memory of past events, to repossess the past, and to discover solidarity with vanished people and events. Her legend is a reminder that the glorious past is partly recoverable.

Hindu Sources of the Legend

A potent legend may gain force because it rides on the backs of older myths or traditions that have prehistoric, protohistoric, and/or religious origins. The Rani legend gains particular power because it evokes multiple resonances in the Hindu tradition. The Rani danced on a Hindu templet of extraordinary richness and diversity. In India the abode of heroes and heroines is often indistinguishable from the plane of gods and goddesses; the Rani as legend follows the lives of the deities.

One metaphor of the Rani legend, for example, is found in the theme of Hanuman, the helpful monkey god in the great epic poem the *Ramayana*. Hanuman and his monkey army leaped across the ocean to Sri Lanka, where they did battle with the evil Ravana, rescued Sita, and restored her to her husband, Rama. This theme is deeply embedded in the Indian ethos and is replicated in villages all over India annually in the Ramlila celebration. Like Hanuman, the Rani is alleged to have made astonishing leaps—she is said to have jumped twice from fort walls, once at Jhansi and again at Gwalior. On the wall of the Jhansi fort a marker has been placed to commemorate the spot from which she allegedly jumped on horseback some forty feet to the ground. These leaps would have killed ordinary mortals and their horses. Saint Joan is also credited with a jump from a sixty-foot castle tower into a moat, where she is said to have landed unconscious but still alive. And Netaji Subhas Chandra Bose, the INA hero, made a historic sea journey by German and Japanese submarine from Germany to Singapore, continuing the metaphor of Hanuman's epic leap from India to Sri Lanka, complete with the water imagery.

Other aspects of Hindu tradition have nourished the Rani legend. She is often identified in poetry and lore with the goddess Durga, the female avenger who trampled underfoot the demon Mahisha. Durga required the combined weapons of all the gods in order to defeat Mahisha successfully, and she is often depicted wielding weapons in each of her eight hands. It was Durga, a female rather than a male deity, who finally destroyed the demon. In the Rani legend the demon is of course read as the British Raj. The Rani, it is believed, shared with Durga a dreadful, ferocious fury which led her to perform superhuman feats in her struggle against the demon. As demon-slayer the Rani surpasses human female and even male prototypes and partakes of the power of gods and heroes in the epics. In several poems and novels, she wields swords with both hands and holds the horse's reins in her teeth, a feat she is said to have practiced, however superhuman. Bravery, wielding swords, and the female avenger slaying the demon are all features that identify the Rani with Durga. The Rani is regarded as "bravest of the rebels" both by historians and in the folk culture. In the leitmotif of the battle of virtues and vices she engages in a universal drama.

Another divine identification is with the goddess Chandi. In Bengal, Chandi was predominant from early times. She was an intriguing deity, apparently part war goddess and part Great Mother. As an aspect of Durga, it was Devi Chandi who slayed the demon and thus restored the gods' dominions to them.[6] The analogy with the Rani's struggle against the Raj is palpable.

A striking aspect of the Rani's career and legend was her knightly semblance as leader of warriors in battle. In war she was described as brave to the point of fearlessness, infusing courage and faith in her followers. She rejected female attire for a martial presence and emerged from purdah to fight. Some of her contemporaries criticized her for not shaving her head and behaving like an orthodox Brahmin widow.

The Rani's wearing of male battle regalia is related to the theme of the Hindu deity as androgyne, a theme that has resonances for the Rani legend as well. The androgyne in Hinduism is a significant religious model, connoting wholeness rather than the decadence suggested in some Western traditions. Shiva's manifestation as androgyne is known to all Hindus, his female facet represented both in Parvati/Uma and in Durga/Kali. The Rani in male dress, armed and riding into battle on horseback, is a powerful military idiom. This martial aspect also suggests that in her the male facet at critical times took precedence over the female. In this respect her legend partakes of the androgynous archetype. In one ballad the male aspect of the Rani is celebrated.

The Rani of Jhansi was as brave as a man
She left her mark on the world's wide span,
The Rani of Jhansi was as brave as a man
The cannon roared over the City wall,
The streets were riddled with powder and ball
By this Rani of Jhansi, as brave as a man
The Jhansi Rani who fought like a man,

Lighted a haystack and into it sprang
So died this Rani, as brave as a man.[7]

Stories of sex change occur in the *Mahabharata*. One example is the case of the daughter of King Drupada. Another, nonliterary example is found in a cult which has existed in parts of India for centuries. The cult is a form of bhakti (devotion to a particular god) in which men take on the behavior of women. They even enter ritual menses each month, retiring for three days and on the fourth day taking a ritual bath. Rumor in Bundelkhand has it that the Rani's husband performed this ritual. Whether or not there is any truth to this story, the existence of the cult illustrates the point. A male votary becomes a female in this cult to worship the male god/lover.

Still another aspect of the Rani legend is that she deliberately chose death over life without independence. She opted to die in battle rather than be tried and hanged by the British authority which had dealt with her unjustly and had already prejudged her guilt. Beautiful heroes and heroines who die in their youth are beloved of the gods, the Greeks believed. Perfection is preserved in violent youthful death. In the Hindu model, one who, after fulfilling all obligations in life, willingly leaves life, one who chooses the moment and embraces death uttering the name of God has died according to *paramagati*. Such a person goes "to the great way."[8]

The Rani's birth, like her death, may be viewed from the Hindu perspective as particularly auspicious. She was, for one, born at Kashi, or Varanasi, in the very lap of Mother Ganga, at the most holy confluence of three great sacred river systems. Her childhood name, Manu, was taken from Manikarnika, one of the names of the Ganges. Even the planets were auspiciously and powerfully positioned at the time of her birth. The astrologers predicted that she would embody the qualities of all three major female deities: Lakshmi, goddess of prosperity and well-being; Durga, the slayer of demons; and Saraswati, goddess of learning. The connection with Saraswati takes on special significance in light of Lakshmi's literacy in Marathi, perhaps even in Persian, accomplishments unusual for a woman of her time. Her name, Lakshmi, which she took at marriage, automatically identified her with that goddess as well.

In her identification with these three prominent goddesses, the Rani legend harks back to epic and Puranic literature and to the major place these three deities assumed in this great body of sacred texts. Moreover, identification with these deities also connected her to the primal, divine cosmic force, Shakti. Further, the goddess conceived as Shakti in general corresponds to the Absolute, Brahman, ultimate reality manifest as the world. In the Puranas the superiority of Shakti culminated in her representation as ultimate reality.[9] The Goddess reached her apogee in the concept of the cosmic principle as source of all creation, a female principle, the Mother. Worship of this female principle came to be formalized in the Tantric cult on the one hand, and in the Shakti cult and manifestations as various mother goddesses on the other.

The Hindu pantheon is populated by many mother goddesses, by some enumerations as many as sixteen. The Brahmo Samaj leader in Bengal, Keshab Chandra Sen, in an article on "The Motherhood of God," suggested that the Mother was a more apt symbolic representation of God than the Father.[10] The power of the Goddess was such that even the gods were unable to undo what was done by the Goddess.

These two powerful Hindu archetypes—the Mother and Shakti—infuse the Rani legend. The Rani was mother and guardian of her husband's heir, Damodar Rao. The worship of the Mother, which can be traced to the ancient Indus Valley civilization, has recognized in historic times multiple avatars. The theme of the Mother is represented in many statues and paintings of the Rani on horseback, her small son tied on behind her. In her role as mother the Rani partakes of one of the most powerful female archetypes in Hindu culture. As mother/Mother, the Hindu woman has far greater potency than she has as wife/Sita. This is a power which cannot be defeated. Sita, on the other hand, represents absolute fidelity and submission of a wife to her husband. As wife, woman's power is made safe by placing her under the control of her husband. But as mother, woman's power is not under control and can thus be dangerous, especially to men. Mother goddesses in rural India guard villages and preside over success of crops, give protection against cholera and smallpox, and ensure childbirth and child health. But the Goddess is ambivalent, and if her protection is withdrawn, the Bad Mother, the destructive aspect of the Goddess, may prevail. Cholera, smallpox, and death in childbirth may then be visited on a village or an individual. Given the power of this complex mythology, it is no accident that nineteenth-century nationalist hymns celebrated the Mother and India as Motherland rather than Fatherland.

In another metaphor of the Rani legend, the Mother—India or the

Rani—had been raped by the all-male structure of the Raj. This gave her the power of Durga, the female avenger again. In another sense, too, she took on the power of Durga. This time the catalyst was her rejection by the Raj, not sexually but perhaps allegorically so in Dalhousie's refusal to respond to her memorials.

Powerful as the Mother is, perhaps the most potent female force of all in Hinduism is Shakti, the primal, cosmic female power of the universe. The worship of divine mothers was closely associated with Tantric forms of Shakti worship. Shaktism diverged from Shaivism and "developed as a separate cult and focal point for all mother goddess epiphanies."[11] Shaktism flourished in medieval India. Shakti relates also to the female principle of the universe, Prakriti, as the more visible, active, and immanent force. The male counterpart, Purusha, is purer and more spiritual, but also more inert and passive.

The Rani as legend thus partakes of the most powerful definitions of the feminine in the Hindu pantheon and cosmology. She is Shakti and Mother, *the* Goddess who cannot be controlled or defeated. She is, moreover, surely not the divine consort, not Krishna's Radha or Rama's Sita. These Hindu female roots have propelled the Rani legend forward in time and facilitated its florescence in the popular, folk, and even fine arts.

The Legend in the Popular Arts

The Rani legend developed and still flourishes in the area around Jhansi in the popular and folk arts that do not depend on literary tradition. The Rani's memory is preserved in oral literature—poetry, ballad, and song—passed from one generation to the next. Today some of this oral literature survives in written form, while the rest has either vanished or remains in the memory of poets to be retold whenever they gather. The legend of the Rani lives, too, in many paintings. Some are preserved in museums and others are in the possession of residents of Jhansi, Gwalior, Nagpur, and neighboring villages and towns. Images of the embattled Rani adorn walls of many homes and temples.

The heroic qualities of Lakshmibai have also been illustrated in several statues, some in bronze, others in less sophisticated media. Most famous and politically, if not artistically, significant is the statue in Jhansi created by Rudra Narain Singh. Rudra Narain was a freedom

Fig. 5. Plaster statue of the Rani by Rudra Narain Singh.

fighter and associate of Chandra Shekhar Azad, another U.P. revolutionary who made his home near Jhansi. Rudra Narain, a painter, for many years regretted that the people of Jhansi had not erected a statue in memory of the Rani. He began collecting small donations from his friends and spent his time making hundreds of sketches of horses. The final product, as was envisioned by this revolutionary sculptor, is plaster over a steel frame. This statue is more highly regarded by the people of Jhansi than is the professionally cast bronze statue of her that stands in a park in front of the fort. The magnificent bronze statue at Gwalior, on the spot where she was cremated, is judged to be the best of the Rani statues. Interestingly enough, in this statue, unlike some others, the Rani is seated astride the horse without her adopted son behind her. The sculptor no doubt accurately judged that she would have ridden into battle thus, alone. In addition to the statues at Jhansi, Gwalior, Poone, and Nagpur, miniature statues of her are sold in the markets in Jhansi and Nagpur and cherished by residents.

The Legend in Literature

Probably the first evocations of the Rani in the popular arts appeared in ballads and poetry written within a few years of the Great Rebellion. Since it was not possible to publish heroic poems and stories of the Rebellion in its aftermath, this literature was oral. Apart from the political atmosphere that fostered its growth, Bundelkhand otherwise has an especially rich oral heritage. Some rulers patronized the arts, including poetry. The maharajas at Jhansi and Orchha, for example, kept court bhats, or bards, in their employ. In Jhansi the Newalkar maharajas were known as patrons of poets, painters, dancers, musicians, and actors. Gangadhar Rao was particularly recognized as a connoisseur of Sanskrit drama, in which he acted himself. Poetry competitions were held between poets at various courts.

The best poets had many disciples. During the Rani's time three famous poets composed at Jhansi: Bhaggi Dauju "Shyam" of Mau Ranipur, "Hradayesh" Heeralal Vyas, and Pajnesh. Shyam was a Brahmin who saw the uprising at Jhansi but did not survive it. His poetry refers to the religious devotion of the people of Jhansi to the Rani and to her motherly concern for her soldiers.[12] Hradayesh was the court bard of Jhansi and also a soldier. Pajnesh was a contemporary and rival of Hradayesh and known primarily for his poems of love and romance.

Not all poets were Brahmins. Brahmin poets excelled in prosody and the literary aspects of poetry, but craftsmen also composed verse. Tailors, coppersmiths, jewelers, dyers, carpenters, cobblers, and weavers all contributed to vernacular poetry. Folk songs and poems about the Rani by contemporary bards were all sung in Bundeli and almost never published. These songs and poems were spread through Bundelkhand by traveling bhats who were paid for singing wherever they stopped. Poems were also perpetuated by small, sometimes secret meetings of poets who might add to or subtract from this oral literature, with the result that almost nothing of the original survives today.[13]

Two ballads written shortly after the Rebellion survive in part, one written by the above-mentioned poet-official of the Datia court, Kalyan Singh Kudara, and the other, a ballad on Lakshmibai by the poet Madnesh. Kalyan Singh's ballad, written about 1870, focuses on Nathe Khan's invasion of Jhansi from Orchha. Since he was in the employ of the pro-British Datia raja, the poet praised the raja and celebrated his refusal to join Nathe Khan's invasion of Jhansi. This narrative ballad contains the names of the Rani's generals and information on their origins, for the most part around Dinara. According to this ballad, when the Rani was asked to surrender during the battle at Jhansi, she sent in reply cartridges and gunpowder to signify her continued resistance. This ballad also refers to the betrayal of Dulhaju, an adviser of the Rani, who is said to have traitorously opened one of the city's gates to the British. The betrayal by Dulhaju is a prominent theme in the literature and lore of Jhansi. The ballad also intimates that the Rani wished to marry Nana Sahib.[14] Other local versions have it that Nana Sahib proposed to her but she refused because they were of different subcastes.

The other narrative poem was written by the poet Madnesh beginning in 1861 and was meant to be sung. The original manuscript was discovered by Jhansi writer Naturam Mahor and was subsequently the subject of a volume by his nephew, B. D. Mahor, himself a freedom fighter. This ballad covers the Rani's entire career, from a physical description and discussion of her character to a chronicle of the major events of her life. In this version, following the deaths of her son and husband she devotes herself entirely to prayer, devotions, and reading or listening to the recitation of the *Bhagavad Gita* and other religious texts. It was while reading the *Gita* that she internalized the ideal of duty, or dharma, and emerged with an active concern for the administration of Jhansi and welfare of its people. She went through state papers and listened to witnesses to enable her to make just decisions in cases brought before her. Her reputation for intelligence, justice, and compassion to all comes through clearly in this ballad. She took particular care of beggars, her servants, and wounded soldiers, and sponsored special events for women of her court and of Jhansi as a whole.[15]

A folk song of 1857 sings of the Rani drawing her strength from the land and people of Bundelkhand.

From clay and stones
She moulded her army,
From mere wood
She made swords,
And the mountain she transformed
Into a steed,
Thus she marched to Gwalior.[16]

This song is still sung in and around Jhansi. Many poems written since 1857 identify the Rani with the goddess of violence and war, variously Durga, Chandi, or Bhavani. Durga/Kali is probably the deity most commonly associated with the Rani. One poem invokes several deities and qualities of the Rani.

Though Lakshmi, you are Durga
Like the Ganga purify all evil,
Your memory inspires to valor
So pleasing to hear,
In war you are Bhairavi and Chamunda,
In justice most fair
To subjects, like a Mother
You deserve respect and honor,
You are Kali,
Forgiving and protector of kindred,
Death-axe to the British enemy.[17]

Here Lakshmi, Durga, Kali, Bhairavi, Chamunda, and the Mother are all combined in the Rani. Bhairavi alludes either to one of dozens of local forms of the Mother Goddess or to shamanesses of the Tantric school.[18] Chamundis are demigoddess helpers of war goddess Chandi, who need blood sacrifice to keep them from attacking people. They help the goddess to protect her people from evil spirits.[19]

Another poem sung by women in Nagpur evokes the Rani's martial qualities.

Praise be to Lakshmi
Avatar of War Goddess Chandi . . .
Leader on the battlefield
She was Lakshmi, War Goddess Chandi.[20]

While in the first stanza she is an avatar of Chandi, later in the poem she is the goddess herself.

A popular present-day poet of Jhansi, K. S. Avadesh, has written over twenty-five poems about the Rani in addition to a drama. One of his poems contains this verse.

Three Durgas, the Shakti power,
She was equal to millions of women.

In Avadesh's poetry the Rani transcends the limits of human experience.

> She was the very blade of the sword
> The sword among the sword-bearers.

One of Avadesh's poems sings of the Rani emerging from the soil and rivers of Bundelkhand, in this case the Pahuj River.

> She shone like the glittering waters of the Pahuj
> Flowing in strength like its water, Symbol of the light
> Reflected by the waters of the Pahuj.

Avadesh offers a paean to her heroic death for liberty.

> If you must bow
> Bow before the sword,
> Prefer beheading by the sword
> To bowing before the enemy.
> It is better to die for freedom
> Than to live in slavery.

And again, Avadesh writes of her heroic sacrifice and patriotism.

> It is my wish that if I
> Take another birth again
> I may have another chance
> To give my life for the country.[21]

Another poet invokes several aspects of Durga and identifies them with the Rani. This poem was recited to me while I waited for a bus at the Kalpi bus stand.

> Her movement, her activity and her glory,
> The three faces of Maharani Lakshmibai,
> She left the lotus seat and
> Mounted a horse to fight with sword
> The remarkable thing is this:
> She holds a sword in her hand and
> Fire issues from her eyes . . .

She fought at Kalpi
On the banks of the Yamuna
In a manner without parallel.
When Rani Lakshmibai sprang forth
With sword in hand
Then it was like death personified . . .
Enemies were dying, tongues out, bleeding.

Here the Kali/Durga imagery is paramount.

One line that appears in many poems and ballads on the Rani, as in the folk legend and even in documentation in English, is the statement: "I will never surrender my Jhansi." In one poem the poet sings, "I will give my life, but will never give up my Jhansi." This line appears again in the popular comic book on the Rani.

Some of the poetry sung in Nagpur by the women's service organization, the Rashtra Sevika Samiti, is clearly devotional and bespeaks the Rani's sanctity. For example:

Oh, my Indian brothers,
Tarry here a moment
At this holy place where lies
The flame of valor,
Pay homage to the Rani of Jhansi.

And the same poem ends with this stanza:

Patriots bow in respect and honor
Brooks and trees shed tears
Even stones open to proclaim
To generations to come
The ever-inspiring story written in blood.

And a prayer sung by a member of the same Nagpur group in Sanskrit invokes:

Your name, Rani Lakshmibai, is so sacred
We remember it in the early hours of dawn,
The name of a woman worthy of retelling,
The name of a woman worthy of being followed by all . . .

Your image shall be in our minds forever,
Your legend repeated everywhere
Your memory fresh in mind eternally
Your ideals practiced by all for all time to come.

Another interesting feature of the Rani legend that occurs in poetry and lore is the ancillary legend of Manvati. Manvati was a metalsmith's widow and the mother of a young son named Vir Singh. As a widow she was persecuted until the Rani took her under her wing and enrolled her in the women's unit. During the Nathe Khan invasion the chief gunner, Gulam Gaus Khan, was ordered to deploy the defenses. He replied that in order to fire his gun (called Bhavani Shankar) a sacrifice was needed. In many parts of India it is still said that the construction of a dam or other large enterprise requires the sacrifice of a small child, usually male, to ensure the success and safety of the project. The poet Avadesh sings:

Vir Singh came forward
And was sacrificed,
The battle ensued,
Manvati was also martyred,
The Rani of Jhansi was victorious.

Many residents of Jhansi say this legend is apochryphal, that there was no such woman as Manvati. The legend of the sacrifice of Manvati and her son nonetheless persists in poetry and lore around Jhansi.

The most famous modern poet of the Rani is Subhadra Kumari Chauhan, who wrote a long narrative poem that is included in many school texts and memorized by generations of students. The poet herself joined the noncooperation movement, led a procession bearing the Tri-Color Flag after it had been trampled by police, and was jailed in 1940 and again in 1942. She fought for rights for women and harijans, opposed the dowry, and was elected to the Bihar Legislative Assembly before being killed in an auto accident in 1948.[22] Subhadra Kumari Chauhan's poem concludes with an arresting paean to the Rani and associates her with Shiva.

Thou art thy own memorial
Thou has shown the way

And teacheth thou a lesson—
Of Freedom and Fight
Of Honor and Pride
Bundelas sang of the Rani
The fighter for Right,
Honor, Justice and Freedom.
Chivalrous Bundelas sang
Chanting songs of Lord Shiva,
The Rani, the damsel fought for Jhansi,
Recount her valor, people of India![23]

Apart from the oral and written poetry on the Rani, numerous novels and plays have also appeared. The first Indian work of fiction on the Rani was written in 1888 by the Bengali author Chandi Charan Sen, who specialized in patriotic themes and was at one time put under house arrest for his writing. Sen's novel opens with the death of Gangadhar Rao and thus does not deal with Lakshmi's relationship to the maharaja but with her relations with other women and officials at the Jhansi court. In this novel, as in most other fiction and ballads, she is betrayed to the English by a traitorous adviser. This same traitor, here called Ahmed Hussein, also betrays the English inside the Jhansi fort. After promising them safe conduct, he has them killed. The Rani in this novel and in nearly all other literature in Indian languages is unaware of the killing of the English until after the fact. In this novel she asks, "Were the women also killed?" and her diwan, Lakshman Rao, replies, "Yes, Rani Ma, all were killed."[24] She is portrayed as unhappy about the massacre and in some versions even criticizes her officers, exhorting them to fight the English government, not individual Englishmen.

The most famous work of fiction on the Rani is by Vrindan Lal Verma, late of Jhansi, whose grandfather was a contemporary of the Rani and passed on to his descendants local stories about her. In the Verma novel and in other writings, the legend of Jhelkari is closely intertwined with the Rani legend. Jhelkari was a woman of the weaver caste, born of a very poor family. Though uneducated, she was spirited and courageous and came to the special attention of the Rani because of a strong physical resemblance to her. She came to the palace with other Jhansi women one day during a spring festival, and the Rani, noticing her, invited her to join the women's regiment. The Rani intervened on Jhelkari's behalf when her caste was about to punish her for accidentally injuring a calf owned by a Brahmin. Here the Rani appears as an advocate of the downtrodden and lower castes. Legend and the novel also describe the opening of the Jhansi gates by the traitor Dulhaju, whereupon Jhelkari gave herself up to the British disguised as the Rani in order to give her a headstart in her flight from Jhansi.[25]

One novel written by an Englishman stands alone among English language writings in depicting the Rani as a heroine. It opens with a verse, here in part:

> But in the eternal sanctuary of her race
> The holy river, holy Mother Ganges, that coveted embrace.
> Doth hold her ashes, and for a monument to her name,
> Sufficeth it, that in the people's hearts, her fame
> Doth shine immortal. For she was deeply loved, this Queen.
> The beauteous, valiant Rani, India's great heroine.[26]

Besides being a rare example of literary celebration of the Rani's heroic qualities by an English author, the author was better informed about her career than were most English authors.

In another, more typical work by an Englishman, an 1895 drama in verse, she emerges as an enemy dealing death to the English.

> But now my thoughts must be filled with plots
> And stratagems and wiles, that I abhor . . .
> Nay, those [English] we've here already in our hands
> Shall have a shorter journey—to the grave.[27]

Yet even in this drama she is recognized as protector of Jhansi and of Hinduism.

> This Sepoy mutiny shall be my light!
> As yet it flickers faintly, but in time
> Shall as the glorious noonday sun shine forth.
> I shall be Queen of Jhansi again!
> No more shall cows be slaughtered. Siva's fanes
> Shall be restored and Brahmins shall be fed.[28]

In a 1933 English play by Philip Cox the Rani is portrayed as angry at all men, including her father. In a speech infused with feminist rhetoric Cox has her say:

> Mama Sahib [Moropant] is like all men—just thinking of what he can secure for himself and heedless of the desires or convenience of others. He sold me first to Raja Gangadhar; then he helped to sell me to the English; and now he wants to sell me to these Sepoys. But I will not be sold again. Maharajah Scindia is right. This revolt is no concern of ours. We have more at stake than anyone else and must remain neutral.[29]

It was this same play that excited the anger of the Tambe family and others in Nagpur because of Cox's insinuations about the character of the Rani. In one scene Cox has the Rani offer an English officer anything—by innuendo including herself—to save Jhansi. The play moreover impugns her revolutionary fervor. Cox wrote a letter of apology to the Nagpur newspaper *Hitvad*.

Far more scurrilous is the parody of literature of the empire by the English novelist George Macdonald Fraser, *Flashman in the Great Game*. This novel, probably more widely read in English today than any other book about the Rani, is demeaning to her character. It deals in pornographic detail with her alleged sexual exploits with the English first-person protagonist, a fictitious official who travels to Jhansi.[30] Not surprisingly, this novel aroused public anger in Jhansi, Gwalior, Nagpur, and other places where the Rani's memory is held sacred. Whatever the author intended, it is tempting to interpret the maligning of the Rani's character as an effort to expiate the guilt many English felt at having mistreated and killed this heroic woman. In a sense this present-day portrayal of the Rani is a counterpart of earlier English depictions of her as "Jezebel of India," or "Indian Boadicea." In both cases the English rationalization of having killed her is facilitated.

Another English novelist portrays the Rani as not only licentious but basically cruel as well. She says to the English officer: "Kneel! Abase yourselves before Her Excellency, the Ranee of Jhansi! Prepare to pay the blood-debt of your countrymen for the murder of her people." She then cracks her whip across the kneeling officer's neck. The author writes, "The sinister beauty of the cruel lynx-eyed face [was] unmistakably those of a finely bred Indian woman in her twenties.[31]

The Legend in the Visual Arts

There is no known portrait of the Rani painted from life. The paintings of her referred to as portraits were probably all painted after her death, although it is possible that some of the artists had seen her. This is said to be the case with the often-reproduced painting of her with sword and shield. The original, found in the home of a family at Indore, was a mounted figure, but the lower part of the painting was eaten away and has subsequently been copied without the horse. It is noteworthy that from the position of the lower portion of the body that is visible, the woman appears to have been riding sidesaddle, unusual among women wearing the Maharashtrian sari, nor is the Rani otherwise depicted riding in that manner. This portrait shows Western influence in the shading, modeling, and treatment of drapery, common features of late nineteenth-century paintings. The other major portrait of the Rani shows only the head with a decorative sari over the head and jewelry. This portrait is less characteristic and more a type than a painting recognizable as the Rani.

Another alleged portrait is reproduced in the *Far Pavilion Picture Book* edited by David Larkin. It depicts a woman holding a goblet. Art historians doubt the identification of the subject as the Rani of Jhansi, since she would not have been depicted in this unaristocratic (for a woman of her caste) and anti-heroic pose, that is, with a wine goblet.[32]

Another genre of painting on the Rani depicts her in battle, mounted and armed, sometimes facing red-coated English soldiers likewise armed. Perhaps the best known of these is the late nineteenth-century painting *Rani Lakshmibai in Action* in the Lucknow State Museum. She appears in this painting astride her horse, her son tied on behind her and a woman in attendance. The artist has shown familiarity not only with the costumes of the period and with the legend that a woman attendant died in action with her, but has caught also the spirit of the action of the battle. Another battle scene in the Gwalior Corporation Museum contains fewer figures, and they are arranged in more regular rows than in the Lucknow painting, somewhat reminiscent of ancient stylized cave paintings. A third battle scene is the partly decomposed mural painting in an inner room of the Tele-ka Mundir in Jhansi.

Paintings such as these would not have found favor with the British, but on the walls of a temple or private residence they were not subject to political control. They were, in effect, underground political art. Mural paintings, it may be noted, occur widely in Uttar Pradesh and Madhya Pradesh and reached a high level of sophistication, particularly in Rajasthan in the eighteenth and nineteenth centuries. The palaces at Datia and Orchha contain fine examples of mural paintings, although not as elaborate as those in Rajasthan.

In another mural painting, the Rani appears among scenes from the *Ramayana* and *Mahabharata* covering the long wall of an entire room in an upper-class Jhansi residence. Done at the turn of the century by a craftsman, the style is popular rather than folk. The brightly colored paintings show the Rani in two scenes. In one she is astride a horse, in battle, though the action is implied rather than explicit. She is accompanied by rows of armed foot soldiers, some with swords others with guns or cannon. Flowered borders enclose the scene. In the other scene she is shown seated in a palanquin, which would have been the normal mode of travel for an upper-class woman in purdah.

Many paintings in nineteenth-century Central Indian style are in the possession of individuals in and around Jhansi and Gwalior. Most of these show the Rani in heroic pose, on horseback and armed. She is shown riding astride, which was common among Maharashtrian women and was possible with the distinctive divided sari. In these portraits she is generally shown alone, but sometimes with one or more attendants. In one painting two woman attendants appear with her on foot, no doubt representing Sundar and Mundar. In this particular painting, in the possession of the author, the horse is poorly drawn, and one authority believes it to be a copy rather than a nineteenth-century original.[33] The hairdress of the women in this painting is Muslim in style, suggesting that the painter was a Muslim.

Another genre of popular painting in which the Rani is portrayed is the Kalighat style. Kalighat paintings were sold for a nominal sum to pilgrims at the Kali temple, Calcutta. They were simple, sometimes not more than sketches, though the painting of the Rani is somewhat more ornate, particularly her headdress. Often Kalighat paintings were done as subtle political satire ridiculing the British.

Jhansi's municipal buildings today contain several recent paintings of the Rani. Three large oil paintings hang in the Circuit House. In one the pose is similar to the statue at Gwalior: horse rearing, the Rani's sword held high in one hand. In another painting the horse is shown at full gallop against a background that glows red, suggesting the city in flames behind her. A third painting in the Circuit House shows her with her small son on a galloping white horse, her sword held up in one hand against a blue background.

Poster art of the Rani is also common in Jhansi, as are small statues of metal-colored composition. In most posters she is depicted in a red sari, riding a white horse with her son tied on behind her. Often the fort appears in the background. A painting in another municipal building in

Fig. 6. Kalighat-style painting. Original in the British Library, London, MS. ADD. OR. 1896.

Jhansi also portrays her with sword, shield, and red sari, similar to the poster style. On the walls of this same hall, portraits of Gangadhar Rao, Chandra Shekhar Azad, and Subhas Chandra Bose also hang. In one of the rooms of this building stands a life-size cardboard cutout of the Rani. In most other public buildings in Jhansi, for example banks, some such popular representations of the Rani are displayed.

All this popular art—paintings, posters, large and small statues—in public or private buildings serves to keep alive the image of the Rani as a heroine of unparalleled qualities. It honors her self-sacrifice for her country, which serves as a model for all Indians, men as well as women.

11

Nationalism and the Legend

> In the poetry of the resistance after 1857 the use of the Rani's name became the symbol for resistance.
>
> —*B. D. Mahor,* The Impact of 1857

Political Uses of the Legend

Apart from the spontaneous growth of the Rani legend through the popular, folk, and fine arts, the legend of the Rani grew through political reinterpretations and served the interests of the nationalist movement. In the first three decades of the twentieth century the Rani's image was particularly useful as a metaphor for resistance to the British, which could not be voiced openly. Today in post-independence India, Lakshmibai continues to be reinterpreted in new modalities.

The process of creating modern nation-states in the nineteenth century was closely connected with the growth of a sense of nationhood. To stimulate nationalism and facilitate the birth of new nations, national ideals and heroes served as useful symbols. In Mexico, for example, the national hero was the Aztec Tlatoani Cuahtemoc, who resisted the Spaniards' final assault on Tenochtitlan and was subsequently tortured and executed. In the nineteenth century and particularly after 1910 he came to symbolize Mexican nationalism.[1]

Another national hero who became a political symbol was Shaka Zulu, most popular king of the Zulu Empire. Shaka became part of the Zulu oral legend that developed when "almost every evening Zulu fathers spoke to their children of the traditions of the Zulu nation, which they in turn had learned from their fathers."[2]

And in late nineteenth-century Japan after the Meiji Restoration, the oligarchs used the centuries-old emperor institution as symbol and focus of unity in their efforts to forge a nation out of several dozen fiefal domains. A new loyalty to nation and emperor was thus created out of loyalties to separate daimyo lords. This new sense of nationhood was critical to the far-reaching reforms that modernized and strengthened Japan in a remarkably short span of time. The emperor continued to serve as a potent focus for patriotism, through which national mobilization was successfully achieved during World War II.

So, too, in nineteenth-century India early nationalism focused on religious revivalism and the use of symbols from the ancient sacred texts. The mainstream of nationalism politically, from the inception of the Indian National Congress in 1885 until independence, has followed the nonviolent path advocated by Mahatma Gandhi. A second stream, an alternative political vision, has favored and used violent and revolutionary means to effect the liberation of India and the end of colonial rule. Revolutionary nationalists have found models in the epic figure Arjuna, hero of the *Gita*, or the historic example of Shivaji, founder of the Maratha Confederacy.

In the early twentieth century Bal Gangadhar Tilak wrote of the beauty of the bomb and was himself "one of the most powerful political myths in India" for three decades before the rise of Gandhi.[3] In the Hindu Ganapati festival honoring the elephant god Ganesha, Tilak's portrait was carried beside Shivaji's, his deeds likened to heroic struggles in the epics. Tilak was adept, moreover, in tapping modern, traditional, and charismatic sources of authority, as did the Rani legend.

By the turn of the century revolutionary nationalism was beginning to appear in Bengal, followed by the Punjab, Uttar Pradesh, and Maharashtra. For these revolutionary nationalists, rather than for the leadership of the Congress mainstream, the Rani of Jhansi came to serve as a model for the ideal of self-sacrifice for the nation.

The Punjab and the United Provinces (present-day Uttar Pradesh) by the decade of the twenties became the centers of a revolutionary nationalist group called the Hindustan Republican Association, after 1927 the Hindustan Socialist Republican Association. Two Bengalis were actively involved in organizing the group, which advocated and used terrorist methods. Members of the group stopped a train proceeding to Lucknow with railway ticket proceeds and took the money to purchase arms from Germany. In the Kakori conspiracy trial several conspirators were sentenced to transportation for life and served prison terms of several years. Activists and terrorists of this group were implicated in several terrorist acts: an attempt on the viceroy's life in 1926, the Delhi Conspiracy, the

Assembly Bomb Incident in Parliament, and the shooting of police official Saunders at Lahore in 1928. A leading member was Chandra Shekhar Azad, who lived near Jhansi and was a close associate of Jhansi painter and nationalist Rudra Narain Singh, creator of the famous statue of the Rani. Members of the group in Jhansi were inspired by the statue and were said to have held their political gatherings around it.

Chandra Shekhar Azad was born into a poor Brahmin family in the United Provinces and remained a bachelor brahmachari during his short career. When he was arrested as a child for participating in the noncooperation movement, he told police his name was Azad (Freedom) and that his father's name was Swatantra (Liberty). He was thereafter known as Azad. He conspired in the attempt on the life of the viceroy, the Assembly Bomb Incident, the Delhi Conspiracy, and the shooting of Saunders in 1928. Surrounded by police in 1931 in a shootout, he turned his last remaining bullet on himself in a dramatic suicide and martyrdom. Azad's name became political magic not only in Jhansi but nationally as well. His home near Jhansi is marked for visitors.

In more recent years Uttar Pradesh, Madhya Pradesh, and Maharashtra have been a base of Mahasabha and Rashtriya Swayam Sevak Sangh (RSSS) operations. Both were Hindu communal parties that resorted to terrorism and to anti-Muslim violence. A member of the Hindu extremist RSSS group that conspired for the assassination of Mahatma Gandhi still lives in Gwalior. Many RSSS members emerged from poor Brahmin origins in this part of the country, as did Azad.

Resistance Literature

Since it was not possible to write favorably about the Rebellion after the event, metaphor, allusion, and allegory were used, and an underground literature was born. In the special rhetoric of this political literature an apparently pro-British writer would allude somewhere in an essay, poem, or novel to the Rani of Jhansi or Tatya Tope to signify the real sentiments of the author. The demon was read as the British Raj, and good kings referred to freedom fighters. Flowers or sweet flowers were also used to symbolize freedom fighters. The Rani in one drama is depicted as the goddess Lakshmi riding on a white owl (read the English). When the white owl leaves, taking the goddess with it, poverty and unhappiness follow the departure of Lakshmi, or that which she symbolizes, prosperity.[4]

B. D. Mahor, leading historian of the literature of 1857, credits the Rebellion with inspiring vernacular journalism in India. Following the Rebellion many newspapers flourished in Bengali, Marathi, Gujarati, Tamil, and other languages while English language newspapers were strictly censored. This situation was altered by promulgation of the 1878 Vernacular Press Act, which provided for censorship and prohibition of seditious literaure. In one drama this act was depicted allegorically as a demon cutting out the tongues of people with a huge knife or scissors. Another drama features two poets, one a thin emaciated bard named Bharat (India) and the other a fat well-fed one. The fat poet tells Bharat he should say kind things about the English.[5] This form of political satire was difficult for English authorities to control.

A group of writers organized and met secretly in Jhansi—authors of poetry, drama, and fiction. They were active in the decades of the 1870s and 1880s and published some of their writings themselves. They called themselves Bharatendu, and the name Bharat figured in titles of many of their writings. They became masters of metaphor and allegory in their political satires. Many of them wrote secretly about 1857 and portrayed the Rani as leader of the people. Bharatendu members also read *Ghadr*, the journal of the revolutionary Sikh party in San Francisco that was being translated into several Indian languages secretly.[6]

This resistance literature was primarily ballad and drama, prose being more difficult to publish. And as oral literature, poetry moreover could be sung or presented at writers' meetings without attracting British attention, even after enactment of the Vernacular Press Act of 1878 or the Press Act of 1910.

In 1929 the government gave some attention to the Rani when the Archeological Survey cleaned and marked her grave at Gwalior. Encouraged by this public recognition, the poet Krishna Baldev Verma published an article titled "Jhansi ki Rani Lakshmibai" in *Vishal Bharat* in the same year. The issue was instantly banned.[7]

Even during the height of Gandhi's noncooperation movement, the Rani was often cited as a model of patriotism, courage, and leadership, and was thereby placed beside Shivaji and the epic heroes Rama, Krishna, and Arjuna. She became valor's new epiphany. Poet Subhadra Kumari Chauhan urged that the movement begun by the Rani and others in 1857 should be completed by Gandhi and his followers.

During the years 1920–1935 small poets' groups mushroomed throughout the country. They read poems and ballads about past heroes and contemporary revolutionaries. They met surreptitiously at members' home or common meeting places. It became fashionable for students and other young people to participate. Through these underground literary groups the youth of Bundelkhand began to take pride in their birth in the same region that had nourished Rani Lakshmibai. They also began to acquire a taste for reciting banned literature. The songs and poems were often acted out, adding to the excitement of the recitation.[8]

In 1928 a regional political conference met in Jhansi in conjunction with the national Congress meeting. It was followed by a gathering of poets attended by Chandra Shekhar Azad, Naturam Mahor, and others of like persuasion. Azad was pleased with the acclaim the Rani received during the meeting, even from poets of the Gandhian mainstream.[9] Azad himself became so popular in Jhansi that a statue of him has recently been erected in the city. He is depicted in characteristic posture, twirling his moustache.

During the decade of the 1930s the Rani became a potent symbol and model for revolutionary nationalists. Nearly every poet in Bundelkhand wrote in praise of the Rani and her sacrifice for freedom. She was held up as an example for generations to come. Such sacrifice could only result in freedom for India, in these poems of resistance. This poetry was collected by Naturam Mahor, who justified the killing of the English at Jhansi as part of the war of independence.

The poet Ramakant Gokhale wrote a biography of the Rani in 1939. Like much of the political writing on the Rani, Gokhale urged his readers to read about the Rani and thus gain the courage to fight for freedom. He criticized those who fought over religion and exhorted them to recognize that they were all one people regardless of religion or caste. This theme of unity was prominent in the nationalist literature of this period. During 1940 and the war years, any mention of 1857 or of the Rani was prohibited. Some poets continued to publish and to meet underground in support of the "Quit India" political leadership who had been imprisoned. During this period, Jhansi poet Vrindan Lal Verma wrote a novel about the Rani. It was banned immediately. It featured dialogues among freedom fighters in British jails.[10]

The Rani was a useful symbol of unity for all classes and communities. While it might be argued that her legend appealed to the peasant masses primarily through oral and visual arts, in its nationalist evocations the legend had a potent impact on the educated elite as well. Her legend and image thus became genuinely national. The special care she is reputed to have shown the deprived classes—beggars, prostitutes, and widows—added to the nationwide appeal of her legend. Legend also makes the Rani a heroine for Indians of all religions. Several of the women and generals closest to her were said to have been Muslims. Moti Bai, the female dancer and gunner who died at Jhansi with Gaus Khan, and the faithful servant Mundar, who is said to have died with her mistress at Gwalior, were Muslims. This distinctive national appeal made the legend particularly useful to revolutionary nationalists. This same cross-communal appeal also characterizes the Bose legend.

When India attained independence it became possible for the first time for Indians to write freely about 1857. In 1946, Vrindan Lal Verma's previously banned novel on the Rani was finally published. In it Verma depicts 1857 as a planned event, an early stage of the freedom struggle, and gives credit to the Rani and others who sacrificed their lives in the fight for freedom. Verma also assesses what he regards as the popular character of the movement and its grass roots support. He credits the Rani with being the first woman in Indian history to encourage women to become a fighting force. In the novel some of her women friends and her son ask her what will happen if they lose the kingdom. She replies that they may lose their small kingdom, but in the long run they will gain their country's freedom. Verma attributes the killing of the English at Jhansi to the resentment caused by ill treatment of Jhansi residents at the hands of Superintendent Skene. This unflattering image of Skene also appears in the Sohrab Modi film.

Any attempt to trace the growth of the Rani legend or Rebellion historiography in neat chronological units founders on several obstacles. It may be true that in the decades immediately following the Rebellion many Indian writers stressed loyalty and therefore minimized the national character of the Rebellion, and that after 1890 a marked shift in Indian opinion occurred, with the expression of revolutionary sentiments that strengthened the first war of independence position.[11] Yet several factors and series of events weaken this scenario of Indian views of the Rebellion. These same factors and events also affected the growth of the Rani legend in nationalism.

For one thing, Bengal and Bengali intellectuals offer some exceptions. There was no public disturbance in Bengal in 1857. Moreover, Bengali intellectuals at the end of the century continued to stress their loyalty to the Raj. One Bengali, Surendra Nath Bannerji, protested the Vernacular Press Act of 1878 and said publicly that there was no way the British could question the loyalty of those who had made British rule possible. Another Bengali and early Congress leader, Bipin Chandra Pal, wrote in his autobiography, "The Sepoy Mutiny, particularly in Bengal, left the general population of the country absolutely cold."[12] This was so, Pal continued, because of the palpable material advantages that the East India Company administration had brought in terms of protection and peace.

Other problems also vitiate attempts to trace the Rani legend in accord with Rebellion historiography generally. In 1898, after the beginnings of militant nationalism, a political situation arose that influenced the way writers interpreted the Rani's 1857 role. Her adopted son, Damodar Rao, made an appeal to the government to raise his pension from Rs. 150 to Rs. 250 and also claimed the seven lakhs of rupees that the Rani had left him as a legacy. For Damodar Rao to pursue his case successfully he needed to depict his mother as a loyal and misunderstood subject. As evidence for this portrayal of his mother he cited the famous letter Colonel Martin had reputedly written him describing his mother as innocent of complicity in the uprising or massacre at Jhansi.

While Damodar Rao's appeal was pending, a historian named Vasant Rao was invited from Gwalior to deliver a lecture in a well-known series in Poone. He held that the Rani had risen directly in revolt against the British and that she had never been reconciled with them. He protested that the depositions made by Damodar Rao in court were damaging to the Rani's reputation. His remarks were published in the Marathi newspaper *Kesari*, whose editor was the militant nationalist Bal Gangadar Tilak.

Damodar Rao was alarmed at the publication of the remarks in *Kesari* and rushed to Poone to see the editors. Tilak and his co-editor Agarkar were both in jail at the time, and Damodar Rao was able to persuade the assistant editor to retract the objectionable statements. In support of his case Damodar Rao allegedly produced many letters and documents of Jhansi Residents and Collectors. The work of D. B. Parasnis and Vishnu Godse, both writing in Marathi in 1898, was influenced by their awareness of Damodar Rao's case and their desire not to damage it.

Godse's purported eyewitness account of the Rani's flight from Jhansi was published forty years after the event. It has been quoted by several other Indian authors. In his account Godse tells how he was hiding in the bushes near a well when he heard horses approaching. One of the riders who had come to the well for water was the Rani in flight from Jhansi. In his version Lakshmi says, "As a widow I was entitled only to a handful of rice. What business had I to get involved in this?"[13] Godse's depiction of the Rani as an orthodox widow, loyal but forced by circumstances into opposition to the British, was published in the atmosphere surrounding Damodar Rao's case in Poone in 1898.

Damodar Rao, to further buttress his position, deposed that on the day his mother took charge of the fort a declaration was made, which read in part, "The Raj is the Queen's." Damodar held that the queen in question was Victoria, whereas Vasant Rao insisted the statement read that the Raj was "Rani Lakshmibai's." English accounts of this same proclamation specify, as above-mentioned, that it stated, "The Raj is Rani Lakshmibai's." Damodar also testified that for ten years the Union Jack had been hoisted over the fort. Vasant Rao objected that the flag of Jhansi was a joint flag, half saffron and half Union Jack, which was adopted in the time of Bentinck to signify friendship, though not necessarily loyalty. The 1898 political milieu sharpened the focus of the controversy surrounding the Rani's role in the Rebellion. (The trend at the time of the centenary to interpret 1857 as the first phase of the war of independence and to celebrate the deeds of its heroes is discussed further in the historiographical essay appended to this text.)

The political use of the Rani legend occurred again during a recent election campaign in India. The Congress I party, in a campaign film, reportedly depicted Indira Gandhi as a reincarnation of the Rani, dressed like her, complete with sword and shield. This interpretation of Prime Minister Gandhi as a reborn Lakshmibai was said to have gained credibility because the two women had the same birthday, 19 November. And on a calendar published recently by a feminist group in Bombay, 19 November is marked as a day to remember. There are many other uses of the Rani's name throughout India today. In some parts of the country, including the capital city, for example, streets bear the name Rani Lakshmibai. Several women's colleges and universities similarly bear the name of the Rani.

The Rani of Jhansi Regiment

The use of the Rani's name as a symbol of revolutionary nationalism reached its apex during World War II with the formation of the Indian National Army. The INA was spearheaded after 1943 by Subhas Chandra Bose, who early in his career in Calcutta came under the wing of C. R. Das and was active in the leftist Forward Bloc. The young Bose made a spectacular rise to the presidency of the Congress at the session in 1939 and again in 1940, even after breaking with Gandhi and Nehru over the issue of the use of force. When Gandhi was saying "I smell violence in the air I breathe," Bose was seeing the chief danger not as violence but continued submission to the British. An early act of resistance was giving up his Civil Service posting. Escaping house arrest in Calcutta in 1940, he made his way underground, disguised as a Pathan, through Afghanistan to Nazi Germany, where he organized the Indian Legion out of POWs from North Africa. Becoming disillusioned with prospects of German aid for India against England, he was transferred by German and Japanese submarine to Southeast Asia, where he assumed leadership of a revived Indian National Army.

Once in Southeast Asia, Bose, using the name Netaji (Leader or Fuehrer), created a women's regiment within the INA and called it the Rani of Jhansi Regiment. In his choice of the name, Bose recognized a special kinship with the Rani and, more important, the potent symbolic value of the Rani's name and image nearly a century after her death. As the Rani had done at Jhansi, Netaji issued a special appeal for Indian women volunteers. The response was over fifteen hundred women and girls from throughout Southeast Asia, some as young as sixteen and seventeen. Selected as commander of the Rani of Jhansi Regiment was Lakshmi Swaminathan, a spirited medical doctor from Madras practicing in Singapore. The coincidence of the shared name Lakshmi, and the fact that Dr. Swaminathan was an ardent nationalist as well as a medical doctor has led many Indians in later years to refer to her as the Rani of Jhansi, and at times to confuse her with the original Rani. Lakshmi Swaminathan, now Captain Lakshmi, married Col. P. K. Sahgal, one of the three INA officers tried in the Red Fort trial at the end of the war. She has since become an active organizer in the Communist Party of India-Marxist, which helps to perpetuate her image as a spirited fighter and worthy namesake of Rani Lakshmibai.

For Netaji, as for other revolutionary nationalists, the Rani of Jhansi was the model to be emulated by men and especially by women in the struggle for liberation from colonial rule. The Rani of Jhansi Regiment was drilled at Singapore in military discipline and the use of rifles. Although the regiment was not deployed in combat together with the INA units that fought in desperate campaigns in Imphal and Burma, there was no question that they were psychologically prepared to do so and resented any suggestion that their value was for propaganda only. To anyone who has attended a reunion of the Rani of Jhansi Regiment, the élan of these women is apparent even today. It is said that on the last night in Bangkok before Bose's fatal trip on a Japanese plane bound for Taiwan, a play on the Rani of Jhansi written by P. N. Oak was performed for Bose.

Post-Independence Interpretations of the Legend

Artistic evocations of the Rani in the visual arts at times took on a political tone and were viewed with alarm by officials of the Raj. Throughout village India the Ramlila drama is annually celebrated. It portrays the life of Rama and his Hanuman supporters fighting the opposing evil forces of Ravana, abductor of Rama's wife, Sita. In 1911 British officers in U.P. noticed that in some places figurines or pictures of national heroes appeared during the Ramlila festivities. Among the heroes who surfaced was the Rani, together with more contemporary figures such as Aurobindo Ghosh, Tilak, and Lala Lajpat Rai. One British official viewed this phenomenon as "a more or less deliberate attempt to foster seditious and disloyal feelings by the display of figures or pictures representing the Rani of Jhansi." In one example, at Banda, a depiction of the Rani riding on horseback with a British soldier transfixed on her spear was particularly alarming to the chief secretary of the U.P. government.[14]

No doubt the English also would have been displeased, had they noticed, at the wall paintings in the Tele-ka Mundir, a temple in the old town of Jhansi. On the walls of an inner room of the temple are murals of a battle scene showing the Rani on horseback, sword raised, facing English soldiers. This same temple also features wall painting portraits of the Rani and her husband, the maharaja.

In the post-independence period the Rani legend remains alive on more than one level. In the popular folk culture it is perpetuated in poems and ballads, in paintings and statues, and today at the more sophisticated level of reinterpretation by the educated.

We have seen that one reason for the strength and persistence of the Rani legend over the past century and more is that it had multiple roots in the Hindu tradition. This diversity in the origins of the legend also contributes to its continued vitality. A French-American historian, Elie de Comminges, commenting on modern-day interpretations of Joan of Arc said: "So little is known about Joan that she can be all things to all men . . . You can read just about anything you like into her story."[15] Similarly, the Rani legend has accommodated a variety of interpretations and amplifications in present-day India. Part of the dynamism of the legend is attributable to its roots in epic more than in history.

In the Republic Day parade of January 1983 a dance inspired by the Rani was performed before the grandstand where Prime Minister Gandhi and visiting dignitaries from other countries were seated. Women dressed as the Rani in divided Maharashtrian saris, swords and shields in their hands, danced in mock combat with red-coated figures of soldiers for the international audience.

On 24 January 1983 a women's group in Calcutta, the Rashtra Sevika Samiti, held a meeting "to commemorate the anniversary of her sacrifice." Although this date was the anniversary neither of her birth nor death, a group of women gathered and read poems about the Rani. The chief guest at this function spoke about the Rani's achievements as an administrator.

Perhaps the most significant theme in post-independence interpretations of the Rani is the emphasis on her role in elevating the status of women. She has become an important feminist symbol, a model for all women. B. D. Mahor saw the Rani as effecting a change in the self-image of Indian women. After her death, Mahor noted, women for the first time began to regard themselves as equal and in some respects superior to men rather than as second-class citizens.[16] Several years ago an ethnic Indian woman leading a labor union protest in London stated in the press that her model was the Rani of Jhansi. And a small girl who shows spirit may be called a Rani of Jhansi by affectionate parents. But the same epithet may be used for a woman who is felt to be too assertive with her husband. Either usage implies that one modern image of the Rani is as a woman or girl of exceptional spirit.

Nearly all third or fourth grade students in Indian schools are taught a lesson on the Rani. At Saint Francis School in Jhansi a reader used for the fourth, fifth, and sixth classes devotes several pages to the Rani. The lesson begins with a description of Lakshmibai as "a very brave and fearless lady who fought against the British in 1857," and ends with the exhortation, "India needs ladies like Lakshmi Bai, so girls let's try to be like Chhabili."

The famous maharani of Jaipur in recent years became involved in a political campaign. For one of India's most glittering women to take a public stand attracted much notice. The maharani responded to the attention by saying: "Rajaji wrote an article in the party newspaper, which he edited, comparing me to the Rani of Jhansi. The Rani of Jhansi, a great Indian heroine, led her troops to battle against the British in the cause of freedom. All I had done was join a political party in a free and democratic country."[17]

A Bundeli folksong sung at the time of marriage enumerates the Rani's virtues and achievements. It tells how, rising from humble origins, she created a women's regiment, brought about changes for women, administered ably, showed concern for all subjects, helped wounded soldiers and families of soldiers who died in action, and skillfully led her army and state. The Rani is thus also a model for girls at marriage.

A women's group in Nagpur emphasizes Lakshmi's encouragement of and concern for the women of Jhansi, including prostitutes, whom she helped to rehabilitate. Moreover, she is regarded by the Brahmin women directors of this group as the model for women and guardian of Hindu women's virtue and honor. Those who evoke her image as guardian of the virtue of women often speak of her wish that her body be burnt immediately so that it could not be touched by any Englishman. In Nagpur the publication of the Philip Cox play was the occasion for the public burning of the author in effigy.

At a seminar on Bose and the Indian National Army in Calcutta during the 1970s, Captain Lakshmi Sahgal of the Rani of Jhansi Regiment proclaimed in ringing tones that the regiment had fought not only for the liberation of India from colonial rule but also for the liberation of Indian women from the tyranny of men. This present-day interpretation of the Rani as a feminist is a major innovation in her legend.

After the war and particularly at the time of the centenary of the Rebellion, the image and legend of the Rani as a symbol of freedom has flourished. In 1957, in particular, a spate of poems, ballads, and dramas appeared in Hindi and Bundeli. In much of this centenary literature the emphasis is on the Rani's defiance and sacrifice. Bundelkhand experienced a revival of a genre of peasant poetry after 1960. This literature is simple in form and close to the heart of the villager. In this literature good and bad deeds are always recompensed, and the Rani is synonymous always with virtue and the welfare of the country.

An intriguing sidelight in the post-independence literature on the Rani features several authors who professed to have evidence that it was not she who died at Gwalior but rather her friend and companion Mundar (sometimes it was Sundar). The Rani is supposed to have survived until 1920 or some other later time, living on as a sannyasin for many years, some say until age eighty-four. Those who were to have cremated her body only reported they had done so in order to save her, in this version. According to one of these writers, Nath Singh, the Rani once said that if she were defeated and forced into exile, she would "travel from village to village and city to city and spread the message of freedom to all people."[18] In a sense the Rani as legend has fulfilled this allegorical function.

The image and legend of the Rani are also purveyed officially in Jhansi today. In the fall of 1982 the first sound-and-light show was held in the Jhansi fort and celebrated her struggle. In mid-June a nine-day puja is held annually in Jhansi for women. On the final day of the puja speeches are made in which women are exhorted to emulate the Rani and to serve the nation. In one such speech it was pointed out that the reason the Rani kept part of her jewelry and did not shave her head after being widowed was that she was wedded to the nation and wished to continue to honor and serve it despite the maharaja's death. This novel view is popularly held by women in Maharashtra. In the June puja, Jhelkari is also remembered by members of the Jhelkari Samiti and others. Nagpur also holds an annual celebration on 17 June, anniversary of the Rani's death. A parade, garlanding of the Rani statue, and an evening meeting featuring speeches are held. In all these evocations the Rani's name and legend still serve to foster pride in Jhansi and in the nation.

Conclusion

The story of the Rani of Jhansi is that of a young woman raised not as a proper Brahmin girl but among the boys at the court of the last peshwa at Bithur. She learned not the domestic and feminine arts but riding, swordsmanship, and literacy in Persian. Her playmates were not other Brahmin girls but boys, some of whom grew into rebel leaders—Nana Sahib, Tatya Tope, and Rao Sahib. Through this extraordinary childhood she was groomed for the exceptional political and military role she played following the death of her maharaja husband. Her spirited protest of the resumption of Jhansi state is a matter of record, and there is no disputing the heroism of her death in battle or her struggle to maintain Newalkar rule in Jhansi. Blamed by the British for an uprising she most probably did not instigate and for a massacre she is not likely to have condoned, she was marked for trial and hanging, but instead chose to die in battle. She thus became an eternal martyr to the cause of independence, the first heroine of India's "first war of independence."

The picture that emerges is that of a young woman of unwavering strength and determination, a ruler with a sense of justice and compassion for her subjects, a widow with a care for all women, a Brahmin with a feeling for the deprived classes, and a patriot with a burning desire for independence from British rule in her state. Muslims, Pathans, and Hindus were numbered among her officials and friends; beggars, prostitutes, and widows were granted her largesse; the impoverished and deprived attracted her concern.

Since her death the legend of the Rani has had a history and dynamism of its own, apart from the life and death of the historic Rani. In its growth and continuity the legend has displayed an exceptional vitality, the kind of dynamism that infuses epics and makes an indelible imprint on the collective memory of a nation. The vitality of the Rani legend bespeaks its multiple sources in nearly all traditional Hindu definitions of the feminine as revealed in the Hindu pantheon and cosmology. The legend is rooted in the prehistoric Mother, the primal Shakti, and the female avenger Durga/Chandi/Bhavani. Only Sita, the submissive female prototype, is missing. Deriving from this broad spectrum of traditional sources, the Rani as legend emerged as a new definition of female heroism, with multiple psychological and oneiric nuances.

The legend grew through representation of the Rani in many popular and peasant art forms. The rich oral tradition of Bundelkhand, contemporary ballads, murals of battle scenes, and paintings of the Rani—all these early popular evocations went into the making of the legend. The legend maintains continuity and dynamism in the twentieth century through portrayal in paintings, life-size and miniature statues, and in cinema. In the elite literate tradition as well, the legend has proliferated in poetry, fiction, drama, and the literature of the resistance. As metaphor for resistance to colonial rule that could not be voiced openly, the image of the Rani served nationalists for over eighty years.

The symbol of the Rani as freedom fighter served the political vision of revolutionary nationalists who sought an alternative to the non-violent philosophy of the Gandhian mainstream. However radical this revolutionary political tradition may seem, its use of violent means had antecedents in epic heroes such as Arjuna, a historic precedent in Shivaji, and successors in leaders like Tilak and Bose.

Finally, in independent India, the legend maintains its vitality not only because of its genesis in a rich cultural heritage but also through fresh, innovative interpretations. In the reinterpreted legend the Rani assumes many modern visages, is described and reinvented by successive generations. She is the prototype of a woman of spirit, the champion of causes of the oppressed and deprived—widows, prostitutes, beggars, the laboring classes. She reappears in parades and in political campaign films where leaders of the stature of Prime Minister Indira Gandhi seek to be identified with her. She is the model for schoolgirls and brides, epitome of the virtue of all Hindu women. Today she is also the archetypal feminist, who elevated the status of women and raised the self-image of half the population. In all these evocations, representations, and reinterpretations the Rani legend lives on today in villages, in women's groups, at weddings, and among poets, writers, and artists, particularly in Bundelkhand. Her legend, like stories from the epics, is told and retold as if it happened yesterday.

Historiographical Essay

The study of the Rani is sacred.
—*A resident of Jhansi*

Few written sources exist about the Rani. In English there are three volumes of nonfiction, two published plays, two novels, and a few essays.[1] In Indian languages the output is somewhat greater: at least three biographies, several novels, some plays, and a great deal of poetry, though most poetry is unpublished.[2] Most of the sources that view the Rani from the Indian perspective exist in the vast oral literature of Bundelkhand.

Fortunately for our reconstruction of the life, if not the legend, of Lakshmibai, British Company and Raj officials were among the world's most assiduous record keepers. They catalogued and numbered in great detail every official act, from buying a bullock to chronicling the tactical encounters of a battle. So eager were they to relate and often to justify their military exploits and official acts, in fact, that the annals of the British Raj and East India Company are replete with hundreds of military memoirs of postings in India. The Rebellion in particular inspired a proliferation of these memoirs and accounts. These records are in London's India Office Library, the official repository of the voluminous archives of the Company and the Raj in India. They are also available to the determined researcher in the National Archives of the Government of India in New Delhi. Thus we are far better able to document the life and career of the Rani from the British perspective than we are from the Indian viewpoint. Yet documentation does not furnish the whole story of this national heroine.

In India, particularly in Jhansi, the study of the Rani is viewed as sacred.[3] Moreover, the people of Jhansi feel that none but Jhansi residents can really understand the Rani.[4] The tradition of the Rani has been perpetuated in Jhansi chiefly by two local authors: Vrindavan Lal Verma in a novel, *Rani Lakshmibai,* and B. D. Mahor in two books, one based on a ballad written shortly after the Rebellion and the other a study of the impact of 1857 on Indian literature.[5]

Of the nonfiction Indian works on the Rani the two best are those by D. B. Parasnis and by S. B. Hardikar, in Marathi and Hindi respectively. In attempting to chronicle her career from an Indian perspective, both have relied heavily on legend and local tradition rather than on archival sources. In addition to these two volumes there are several volumes of fiction and drama in Indian languages. The legend of the Rani also has its place in the general corpus of Indian writings on the Rebellion, most of which at least allude to her. Many devote a chapter to her story. But it is the unpublished oral literature that in various ways has done the most to feed the growth of the legend and in turn has stimulated the development of nationalism during the past century and more.

The centenary year of the Rebellion was a tremendous stimulus for a spate of books on the subject, some of them studies commissioned by the government of India.[6] The standard Indian view at the time of the centenary was that the Rebellion was the first stage of the war of independence. English historians, on the other hand, have viewed it by and large as primarily a military revolt of Sepoys, a mutiny inspired by causes specific to the army.

More recently, however, Indian historians have tended not to adhere to one monolithic school of historiography on the Rebellion. The point at issue is precisely the one that generally divided Indian and British historians in the past: Was it solely a military revolt or was it a first phase in a national war of independence? Or was it neither, or both? A leading exponent of the second view is S. B. Chaudhuri, who contends that generalized fears of destruction of caste and religion led the civil population and feudal aristocracy in Central India to join cause with the Sepoys. When this happened the character of the insurrection changed from a military rising into a popular rebellion. In Chaudhuri's view, "There is not a single native of India who does not feel the full weight of the grievances imposed upon him by the very existence of the British rule in India."[7]

One of the most influential Indian advocates of the national war of independence theory is V. D. Savarkar. Writing first in 1909 and republished for the centenary, the author describes it as a glorious war of independence, fought by passionate heroic patriots. Savarkar represents today one extreme of the spectrum of Indian historical opinion on the subject.[8]

At least one English writer agrees with this reading of the Rebellion as a national revolution. W. H. Fitchett—although not of this persuasion himself—quotes a certain Justin McCarthy as saying, "It was 'a national and religious war,' a rising of the many races of India against the too-oppressive Saxon. The native princes were in it as well as the native soldiers . . . It was a revolution, like that in France at the turn of the eighteenth century."[9]

Other English writers have contributed to the view that an explosive potential had simmered long among the populace. In the words of one, "Among the Indian people, and especially the Mussulmans, the Brahmins, the Rajputs, and the armed classes in the North-West, there have always been *tens of thousands of latent rebels* . . . needing only the carefully applied spark to ignite the whole into combustion and explosion."[10]

A cogent catalyst in the transformation of this sentiment into a national movement was religion, which Indians felt British policies and presence threatened. They feared forcible conversion to Christianity. Religion became a rallying cry issued in the names of the Delhi emperor, the "King of Oudh," and others. Chaudhuri invokes several English authors in support of his thesis that widespread discontent among many segments of the populace enabled them to combine forces in an attempt to drive the English aliens from the shores of the subcontinent.[11]

That the rebels did not communicate effectively or form a nationwide organization is not taken as evidence contradicting the thesis in this view, since all lines of communication had been cut at the outbreak of the emeute. Whether or not the "night runners" who carried chapattis from village to village were indicative of widespread organization cannot be determined, since there is no conclusive evidence of what the chapattis signified.[12]

Variants on the national war of independence theory point to a wide variety of causes that contributed to popular malaise. Cited are Dalhousie's annexations, dispossession of landholding classes, suppression of social practices such as sati and thugi, fears of forcible conversion to Christianity or the remarriage of widows, rumors that ground bones were mixed with flour, and the causes that distressed the Sepoys. An interesting corollary to the thesis of the populist character of the uprising has it that only by a narrow margin did the British manage to retain India under these circumstances. One of the saving graces was seen to be the loyalty to the British of certain segments of the population and of particular princely states, including the Scindia family ruling in Gwalior. "Why, if Lord Ellenborough had treated Gwalior in the same way [as Dalhousie treated Oudh, Satara, Nagpur, Jhansi, etc.], at this moment we should probably have lost India, nay, perhaps have had all our throats cut," in the words of one observer.[13]

One Indian historian points to the Rebellion's popular character on a regional level. He asserts that most Sepoys derived from peasant origins and spent their leaves in their villages helping with agricultural work. Because of the village ties of the Sepoy, the Rebellion became a popular movement in some regions, though not nationally.[14]

Freedom of the press had been accorded by Governor-General Charles Metcalfe in 1835 and was perceived as further preparing the ground for rebellion among yet another sector of the populace, the intellectuals. This freedom enabled articulate Indians for the next two decades to voice demands for political rights and to express their dissatisfaction with missionary activities and with English criticism of Indian social and religious practices.[15]

Charles Ball was, in the view of S. B. Chaudhuri, one of the earliest English writers to explore the popular content of the Rebellion, maintaining that the Sepoys took the lead in the field mainly because they were organized and armed while the rest of the populace was not. In his letters from Nagpur during the Rebellion, Ball was a strong exponent of the national character of the revolt, supported widely, as he saw it, by disadvantaged villagers.[16]

Another provocative theory is that the Rebellion was the product of a Muslim conspiracy designed to regain the lost supremacy of Islam and the Mughal Empire in India. Since a Muslim, Mughal emperor Bahadur Shah, still sat on the throne in Delhi, however tenuously, this theory enjoyed some credence in English circles. Yet another view is the Marxist one that it was Manchester cotton and Western capitalism that were the culprits.[17]

Beyond these was the more general theory advanced by contemporary historian Sir John William Kaye. He asserted that the English national character—its assertion and "noble egotism"—lay at the base both of the outbreak and of its suppression.[18] The complement of this view was that expressed by Surendranath Sen, who contended that, beyond the issue of the greased cartridges of the new Enfield rifles, the Rebellion was the result of, "spoliation of our people, degradation of our princes, and worst of all—inconceivable insults to our religion."[19]

Yet another approach to the character of the Rebellion posits a developmental-stage typology for nationalist movements, as suggested by the late Cambridge historian Eric Stokes. For Stokes, 1857 marked a "post-pacification revolt," falling between the "primary resistance" of the formal apparatus of traditional society and the "secondary resistance" through pacific secular and religious associations. In this paradigm, leaders of the revolt such as Tatya Tope and the Rani of Jhansi only emerged as national leaders "at the point when the revolt was already half-defeated." Stokes sees economic causes of the revolt as paramount, prompting a response that could be "plotted in the material terms of loss or gain of land control rights."[20]

A whole corpus of English literature on the Rebellion alludes also to relations between Dalhousie and Sir Charles Napier, commander in chief of the Bengal Army. This literature created a tradition in which Napier sought to alter the conditions of the disaffected Sepoys for the better but was charged by Dalhousie with exceeding his power and thereupon resigned. This view was the focus of the *Red Pamphlet*, a sensational account by G. B. Malleson, a historian who served in the Bengal Commissariat. Dalhousie emerges in this version, as in other works, as the villain, a man of little vision who, apart from causing the resignation of a great general, failed to remedy problems in the Bengal Army or elsewhere in India.[21] Dalhousie was also a target of major criticism by both English and Indian historians because of his doctrine of lapse, under which he refused to recognize Hindu adoptions and annexed many states, not only Jhansi, when their rulers died without natural heirs but adopted on their deathbeds. In this view Dalhousie's policies spread dissatisfaction widely among the ruling classes and their retainers in Central India and thus swelled the ranks of the discontented and added to the populist character of the revolt.

Responsibility for the state of the Bengal Army, which contributed directly to the Rebellion, is another question that has been addressed by officers of the army. One officer charged: "For twenty years past, the Europeans connected with Bengal have been sedulously occupied in concealing faults instead of attempting to remedy them. The causes of the defects were never fairly investigated while, for discussing them, I was threatened with expulsion from the service."[22]

The "British interpretation" of the so-called Sepoy Mutiny as a solely military matter has had numerous champions in England, particularly among officers of the army. One of them, Sir George Campbell, states in his memoirs, "Certainly the great Mutiny was a simple Mutiny, and a Mutiny only of the Bengal Army."[23] Dalhousie's policies, in this view as in others, created problems primarily with respect to the pay of the troops, one of the chief Sepoy grievances. Certainly there is ample evidence of causes of discontent among the Sepoys. Apart from the notorious greased cartridges, discriminatory pay and overseas postings were other important complaints of the troops. But there is a difference between discussing the sources of Sepoy malaise and asserting that these were the only causes of the insurrection.

On the Indian side the leading exponent of the military revolt thesis is the eminent senior historian R. C. Majumdar. Majumdar's position is that liberation from British rule was not the motive for either Sepoys or civilians to take up arms. Their reasons for acting, when they did act, were selfish. Majumdar, however, concludes in a later edition of his book on the Rebellion that, while it cannot be regarded as a national war of independence, neither can it be viewed simply as a Sepoy mutiny. In support of the second part of his modified thesis he examines local risings, which he finds were organized by local leaders to serve their own interests and sometimes became outbursts of mob violence in the wake of the breakdown of authority. Although Majumdar was commissioned by the government to edit a history of the freedom movement, pressure from government officials to purvey the government view of 1857 caused him to withdraw from the project and to publish his study independently.[24]

Following publication of the first edition of his book, Majumdar found himself virtually alone in India in his refutation of the national war of independence thesis. With his second edition and revision of the military revolt theory, he comes somewhat closer to what might be called an intermediary position. Majumdar sees in the cause of defeat of the Rebellion the same factors that lend credence to his thesis that it was not a national war of independence. Most significant, in his view, was lack of national feeling and solidarity. Not only did no important chiefs join the Rebellion, but the intellectual class remained aloof or befriended the British. There was, moreover, the mutual mistrust of ruling chiefs, the legacy of historic rivalries. Lack of a general plan or central organization behind the movement reflected this absence of national feeling in Majumdar's view.[25]

Majumdar further sees it as his duty to de-sanctify the heroes of 1857. Bahadur Shah he depicts as a traitor and Nana Sahib as a "vainglorious nonentity." Only the Rani, according to Majumdar, has any claim to a place among heroes. "For even according to my book she deserved the highest praise for her courage, bravery, and military skill."[26] This is Majumdar's highest praise.

Other Indian historians fall somewhere between the two extremes, adhering to the position that the Rebellion was more than a military revolt but less than the first phase of a national war of independence. Among these is Surendranath Sen, who contends that "outside Oudh and Shahabad there is no evidence of that general sympathy which would invest the Mutiny with the dignity of a national war. At the same time it would be wrong to dismiss it as a mere military rising."[27] More significantly, another perceptive and pursuasive Indian assessment of the Rebellion, is the view that later memories of the Rebellion, however distorted, stimulated a nationalism which in the long run did more harm to the British Raj than the actual Rebellion.[28] In this view, while the Rebellion itself may not have been an expression of genuine nationalism, the later memories of 1857 informed the genuine nationalist movement that developed between 1857 and the turn of the century.

The view of the events of 1857–1858 as a mutiny were greatly inspired by the military memoirs of Englishmen who naturally tended to focus on the heroic exploits and derring-do of British officers. These accounts gave full scope to the British romantic military imagination in India. To view the events of the Rebellion from a strictly military perspective was seen not as a distortion or oversimplification but rather as a recalling to memory for English readers of all the excitement, exhilaration, and camaraderie of camp life in the up-country stations in India. These military memoirs did for Victorian Englishmen what the cult of true womanhood did for Victorian women. They also tended to expiate the sense of guilt that haunted some English and commanded the attention of readers in England who were caught up in the horror, heroism, and vengeful spirit of the epic. While accounts of the "night of horror at Meerut," the siege of the Lucknow residency, and Nana Sahib's massacre of the English at Kanpur played on English emotions, battle reports of the general in the field at times lent a more sober note in relating detailed tactical problems faced by troops on both sides.

The Rani's role and significance is debated by English writers. Her death in battle at Gwalior is well documented from the English side in official reports found in the archives of the India Office Library and

British Museum in London and in the National Archives in New Delhi. The Rani had strong champions in England, among them in some respects her opponent Rose. Rose had the highest praise for her as a military commander, as did her later biographer Sir John Smyth.

English official accounts and military reports do not always settle debated points about the Rani's specific actions and intentions during the outbreak and massacre at Jhansi. Whether or not she was actively implicated, the assumption that she was nevertheless became official with English administrators, who planned to bring her to trial and punish her for her alleged offenses. Official India remained unconvinced of her professed innocence or her helplessness against the Sepoys as related in her letters following the Jhansi uprising. In view of the failure of officials to respond to her repeated communications after December 1857 or January 1858, it is more than likely that she had knowledge or premonition of her impending fate. This point is critical to an understanding of her transformation into a rebel and her decision to take up arms against the British in March of 1858.

Yet another genre of historical writing on the Rebellion in which the Rani figures prominently is fiction. Numerous accounts in fiction and nonfiction focus on the massacres at Kanpur and Jhansi. English fiction tends to portray Lakshmibai as either murderous and treacherous in her political dealings or as lascivious and unscrupulous in her sexual relations, generally with British officers. In some of these novels the Rani is the chief protagonist, or more precisely, antagonist.[29]

An especially scurrilous English treatment is found in George Macdonald Fraser's *Flashman in the Great Game,* wherein her alleged sexual exploits with the English official-protagonist are detailed. Just as the Victorian male could not cope with the notion that English troops had killed an Indian queen in battle and therefore portrayed her as cruel and murderous, so too, this more recent English author in his parody of the literature of the empire uses other, but equally disparaging, means of diminishing her. Other fictional writings, such as those by John Masters and M. M. Kaye, while not making Lakshmi a central figure, nevertheless depict her character in unflattering terms.[30]

A more positive image of the Rani occurs in an interesting, if little-known, fictional treatment written at the turn of the century. The author, Michael White, describes her as "the beauteous, valiant Rani, India's great heroine." In White's version she is courted endlessly by various suitors, apparently to no avail, with turns of phrase particularly

Victorian, though they issued from the mouths of Indian officials and princes. "Never have I hungered for aught else but thee, fair Rani," one especially persistent suitor says.[31] In this novel, as in her life, Lakshmibai is surrounded by Rao Sahib, Tatya Tope, and the raja of Banpur.

Although the Rani has been the subject of a few less than flattering English plays and novels, the bulk of literary portrayals of her have come from Indian authors relying heavily on legend. On the Indian side, her courage against her adversaries and her martyrdom in battle stimulated the growth of an epic and transformed her from a woman who lived and died into a legend that is immortal. There is no doubt that her heroism has made an indelible imprint on the Indian imagination. But the Rani of Jhansi has taken a significant part in the historiography of the Rebellion as well. While questions remain about aspects of her historical role, the actions she took in battle make her place in history secure.

Notes

In citing unpublished government documents and personal papers in the notes, the depositories have been identified by the following abbreviations:

BML British Museum Library, London.
IOL India Office Library, British Library, London.
NAI National Archives of India, New Delhi.
PRO Public Record Office, London

Chapter 1

1. D. L. Drake, comp., *Jhansi, a Gazeteer* (Allahabad: U.P. Govt. Press, 1909), p. 1. The *Gazeteer* has appeared in several editions and is the source for some of this geographic description. Part of it also derives from the author's personal observation.

2. Drake, *Gazeteer*, pp. 1–33.

3. S. N. Prasad, conversation with author, National Archives, New Delhi, Jan. 1979. See also Pogson, *A History of the Boondelas*, p. 103, and Holcomb, *Jhansi History*, pp. 2–7, for information about the history of the Bundelas and of Jhansi.

4. Information on local traditions about the fort and palace was provided in conversations with B. K. Misra and B. D. Gupta, both of Jhansi, and in an unpublished description by B. K. Misra. See also Holcomb, *Jhansi History*, pp. 48–49.

5. Sardesai, *New History of the Marathas* 3:242–243. Bhagwan Das Gupta, "Marathas in Bundelkhand (1731–1804)" (unpublished).

6. A. L. Srivastava, *Shuja-ud-daula*, pp. 124–125.

7. Holcomb, *Jhansi History*, pp. 1–4.

8. Sinha, *Rani Lakshmi Bai*, pp. 4–7. "Baee" or "Bai" is an honorific appended to women's names in Maharashtra, thus Lakshmibai, etc.

9. Sinha, *Rani Lakshmi Bai*, pp. 7–8.

10. *Selections from the Records of Government—Northwestern Provinces*, vol. 3, pts. 12–20 (Agra: Secundra Press, 1855), p. 425.

11. Most Indian sources report Lakshmi's birthdate as 19 Nov. 1835, as does Yamuna Sheorey of Nagpur, who claims to be the granddaughter of the Rani's half-brother, Chintaman Rao Tambe. This date is used by Hardikar, Parasnis, and the Jhansi novelist Verma. Astrologers in Varanasi assert she was born on 13 Nov. 1835. Tahmankar and Sinha, on the other hand, suggest she may have been born in 1827. Most of this account of the childhood and marriage of the Rani depends on Indian written sources and on the Sohrab Modi film (in Hindi) on the Rani. Since accounts of early events of her life are unsupported by any English documentation, the Rani's early life, as presented here, at times verges on legend. Mrs. Sheorey relates that Moropant, the Rani's father, had two children by a second wife he married in Jhansi after his daughter's marriage.

12. Tahmankar, *The Ranee of Jhansi*, pp. 22–23.

13. As Sinha points out, if Manu was born in Varanasi and moved to Bithur at the age of three or four with her father in 1832, she must have been born in 1827 rather than 1835 (*Rani Lakshmi Bai*, pp. 10–11).

14. This incident is portrayed in the Sohrab Modi film and in a popular comic book on the Rani; it is also told by the people of Jhansi.

15. This event is also celebrated in the Modi film.

16. While in the contemporary West the marriage of a fourteen-year-old girl to a forty-year-old man might be objectionable, there are also records of such marriages of employees of the East India Company in the eighteenth century. What was abhorrent to Brahmin sensibilities was for a girl to pass puberty and remain unmarried. Moreover, in Hindu belief one was predestined to marry the same individual in each birth, which precluded individual choice. A girl typically had (and still has in some rural areas) two ceremonies: a betrothal at age eight or nine, followed by the *gauna*, or consummation of the marriage, after reaching puberty. An upper-caste Hindu widower, furthermore, would not have had an opportunity to marry a widow closer to his own age, since widows of the higher castes did not remarry. Widow remarriage and divorce were more commonly practiced among the lower castes.

17. Indian sources disagree about her age and date of marriage as on her birthdate. A. S. Misra asserts Lakshmi remained in Bithur until the age of fourteen, when she married (*Nana Sahib*, p. 332). From the date of birth at 1835 it is likely that the first ceremony took place in 1842 and the *gauna* in 1849, followed by the birth of her son in 1851.

18. This story is also related in the comic book on the Rani.

19. This account of the wedding ceremony is popularized in the Modi film

and also related by the people of Jhansi, including priests at the temple where the wedding took place.

20. Hardikar, *Rani Laxmibai*, p. 6.

21. Malleson, *The Indian Mutiny of 1857*, p. 258.

22. Apparently this is an allusion to the outbreak of the Mutiny at Meerut on a Sunday morning in May 1857.

23. Tahmankar, *The Ranee of Jhansi*, p. 28.

24. Lang, *Wanderings in India*, pp. 93–94. A recent article indicates that Lang was an Australian who studied law in England and practiced in Calcutta, and that he also wrote two novels about English social life in India (see Bond, "In Search of John Lang").

25. E. G. Tambe, conversations with author, Nagpur, Mar. 1983; also see Holmes, *History of the Indian Mutiny*, p. 291.

Chapter 2

1. IOL, Foreign Political Consultations, 2 Dec. 1853, nos. 362/5.

2. Ibid.

3. Ibid., 31 Mar. 1854, nos. 153–183.

4. Maharaja Gangadhar Rao to Major Malcolm, 20 Nov. 1853, in ibid. Indian methods of reckoning relationship differ in some ways from Western methods and include many kin concepts without Western counterparts. "Cousin-brother," for example, may refer to a cousin who is regarded more as a brother. The term "cousin," in turn, is extended to those who bear no blood relationship to each other but are very close friends. The *gotra* was significant in adoption as in marriage among Brahmins.

5. IOL, Foreign Political Consultations, 31 Mar. 1854, nos. 153–183.

6. Minute by Governor-General, 27 Feb. 1854, pt. 12, ibid., no. 172.

7. NAI, Political Despatch to the Court of Directors, 4 Mar. 1854, no. 21.

8. Aitchison, *Collection of Treaties* 3:167.

9. Kaye, *Sepoy War* 3:120. PRO, Sessional Papers, 1–99, 27 Feb. 1854, p. 10.

10. Pemble, *The Raj*, p. 111.

11. Kaye, *Sepoy War* 3:360.

12. S. Sen, *Eighteen Fifty-Seven*, p. 38.

13. IOL, Dalhousie to Wood, 4 Mar. 1854.

14. Lee-Warner, *The Life of Dalhousie*, p. 178. See Baird, *Private Letters of Dalhousie*.

15. IOL, Foreign Political Consultations, 23 Dec. 1853, 31 Mar. 1854, nos. 153–183.

16. See discussion in Hunter, *Marquess of Dalhousie*.

17. Sleeman, *Iconoclastes*, pp. 33–35.

18. Bird, *The Indian Mutiny*, pp. 1–10.
19. Letter dated 28 Apr. 1854, NAI, Foreign Consultations, 12 May 1854, nos. 76–79.
20. Ibid.
21. Ibid.
22. IOL, Letter from Governor-General in Council, 30 May 1854, no. 95. NAI, Foreign Consultations, nos. 76–79. IOL, F/4/2606.
23. Letter dated 28 Apr. 1854, NAI, Foreign Consultations, 12 May 1854, nos. 76–79.
24. IOL, Letter from Governor-General in Council, 30 May 1854, no. 95. IOL, F/4/2606. NAI, Foreign Consultations, nos. 76–79.
25. IOL, Letter from Governor-General in Council, 7 Nov. 1854, no. 95. IOL, F/4/2606, NAI, Foreign Consultations.
26. IOL, Foreign Political Consultations, 31 Mar. 1854, nos. 153–183, 22 Nov. 1853.
27. Lang's description of the Rani has subsequently been widely quoted by English and Indian authors. See Lang, *Wanderings in India*, pp. 93–94.
28. IOL, Foreign Political Consultations, 31 Mar. 1854, nos. 153–183.
29. Ibid.
30. IOL, P/200/66.
31. IOL, Foreign Political Consultations, 31 Mar. 1854, nos. 153–183, no. 177 esp. useful. See also Aitchison, *Collection of Treaties* 3:164–174.
32. IOL, Foreign Political Consultations, 31 Mar. 1854, nos. 153–183, no. 176 esp. useful.
33. Ibid.
34. Ibid., 31 Mar. 1854, nos. 153–183, and 13 Jan. 1854, nos. 170–171.
35. PRO, Sessional Papers, 25 Nov. 1853, 1854–1855.
36. Ibid., 31 Dec. 1853, no. 34 of 1853.
37. NAI, Foreign Consultations, 12 May 1854, nos. 76–79; and IOL, F/4/2600; IOL, P/200/65, Ft. William, 23 June 1854.
38. NAI, Foreign Consultations, Apr. 1854; IOL, F/4/2600.
39. NAI, Foreign Consultations, Apr. 1854; IOL, F/4/2600.
40. NAI, Foreign Consultations, Apr. 1854; IOL, F/4/2600.
41. IOL, Z/E/2600.

Chapter 3

1. NAI, Foreign Dept. Supplements, Political Despatch from the Court of Directors, 10 Oct. 1855, no. 27.
2. IOL, P/220/38, 31 Mar. 1854, nos. 153–183.
3. IOL, Z/P/3727, 28 Apr. 1854; IOL, P/220/34, 27 May 1854.
4. IOL, P/220/38, 20 June 1854.

5. IOL, P/220/38; IOL, P/220/39.

6. IOL, Foreign Political Consultations, 31 Mar. 1854, nos. 153–183, no. 182 esp. useful.

7. Foreign letter from President in Council, 16 Mar. 1850, no. 20, IOL, Foreign Political Consultations. IOL, F/4/2618, no. 165–166, draft 22 of 1856.

8. IOL, Coldstream Papers, MSS Eur D706/1.

9. IOL, L/PS/6/77. IOL, Letter from Governor-General in Council, 3 May 1856; IOL, Hamilton's Report, 1854/1856, in Coldstream Papers; NAI, Foreign Consultations, 28 Dec. 1855, nos. 34–38; Hamilton to Secretary, Govt. of India, 29 May 1855, NAI, Foreign Consultations, 28 Dec. 1855.

10. NAI, Foreign Consultations, 28 Dec. 1855, nos. 34–38.

11. Ibid.

12. IOL, L/PS/6/77, no. 15. NAI, Political Proceedings, Aug.-Sept. 1855–1897.

13. IOL, P/200/64, 15 May 1854.

14. IOL, P/220/41, 9 Sept. 1854.

15. This was suggested by Rizvi and Bhargava in *Freedom Struggle in Uttar Pradesh* (2:iii-iv). See also IOL, Pinkney, *"Narrative."*

16. NAI, Political Consultations, 28 Feb. 1856, nos. 30–31.

Chapter 4

1. Malleson, *The Indian Mutiny of 1857*, pp. v, vi. Edwardes, *Battles of the Indian Mutiny*, p. 3.

2. Showers, *Missing Chapter*, p. 88.

3. Report from Robert Hamilton to Secretary, Govt. of India, 29 May 1855, NAI, Foreign Consultations, 28 Dec. 1855.

4. S. B. Chaudhuri, *Civil Rebellion*, pp. 214–215. IOL, Pinkney, "Narrative."

5. IOL, Sturt Memoirs.

6. IOL, Foreign Political Supplements, 30 Dec. 1859, no. 283. See also Edwardes, *Red Year*, p. 113, and Kaye, *Sepoy War* 3:362.

7. IOL, Pinkney, "Narrative," p. 912. Kaye, *Sepoy War* 3:363–368. IOL, "Narrative of the Mutiny"; IOL, L/MIL/3/628.

8. IOL, "Narrative of the Mutiny."

9. IOL, Pinkney, "Narrative," p. 911. India Army Headquarters, *Revolt in Central India*, p. 16.

10. India Army Headquarters, *Revolt in Central India*, p. 16. IOL, Pinkney, "Narrative," p. 911.

11. India Army Headquarters, *Revolt in Central India*, p. 18. IOL, Pinkney, "Narrative," p. 911.

12. IOL, "Narrative of the Mutiny."

13. Servant's eyewitness account, in IOL, Erskine Papers.

14. Forrest, *Selections* 4:x, xii.

15. India Army Headquarters, *Revolt in Central India*, p. 20. Some details of these events are also provided in an eyewitness account by a servant of Captain Gordon (included in IOL, Erskine Papers).

16. India Army Headquarters, *Revolt in Central India*, pp. 18–19.

17. Ibid.; IOL, Erskine Papers.

18. IOL, "Narrative of the Mutiny."

19. IOL, Erskine Papers.

20. Kaye, *Sepoy War* 3:365–368.

21. Deposition of Gordon's servant, in IOL, Erskine Papers.

22. Sir John Kaye, "Narratives, Address of the Native Army," June 1857, handwritten, included in IOL, Pinkney, "Narrative." See also IOL, Erskine Papers.

23. Today the plaque in memory of the sixty-six English murdered at Jhansi is in the foreigners' cemetery and is overgrown with weeds. It was removed after independence from the Jokhun Bagh area where the massacre took place. Plaques marking massacres at other stations have also been removed since independence, for example, at Kanpur, where the English were massacred as they attempted to escape after they were let out of their prison, reputedly at the order of Nana Sahib.

24. India Army Headquarters, *Revolt in Central India*, p. 21.

25. Ibid., p. 19.

26. IOL, Pinkney, "Narrative," pp. 914–915.

27. "100 or 50" was probably a mistranslation for 150 in Erskine's translation, as "or" in Hindi means "and." Although "100 or 50" makes little sense in English, most accounts repeat this phrase. Texts of the Rani's two letters are in IOL, Secret Consultations, 31 July 1857, nos. 353–355, and NAI, Secret Consultations, no. 354.

28. Ibid.

29. NAI, Secret Consultations, 2 July 1857.

30. Edmonstone, Secretary to Govt. of India, to Erskine, Commissioner, Saugor and Nerbudda Territory, 23 July 1857, no. 353, NAI, Secret Consultations.

31. IOL, "Mutiny and Rebellion at Jhansie"; IOL, L/MIL/3/630.

Chapter 5

1. IOL, Pinkney, "Narrative," pp. 915–921.

2. Ibid., p. 916. India Army Headquarters, *Revolt in Central India*, pp. 22–25.

3. IOL, Pinkney, "Narrative," pp. 915–918.

4. IOL, Sturt Memoirs.
5. IOL, "Narrative of the Mutiny," pp. 1–20.
6. NAI, Secret Consultations, 30 Oct. 1857, nos. 602–604.
7. Ibid., no. 545.
8. P. C. Joshi, *Rebellion in 1857, a Symposium*, p. 119.
9. This possibility is also suggested by Kincaid in *Lakshmibai*, pp. 10–11.
10. This is pointed out in Henry Scholberg's unpublished play, "Another Time, Another Country."
11. IOL, Pinkney, "Narrative," p. 910.
12. Hilton, *The Indian Mutiny, a Centenary History*, p. 12.
13. IOL, Pinkney, "Narrative," pp. 910–911.
14. IOL, Sturt Memoirs. Also Majumdar, *Sepoy Mutiny*, p. 282.
15. IOL, Coldstream Papers, MSS Eur D706/1.
16. Erskine, *The Bengal Mutiny*, p. 5.
17. NAI, Secret Consultations, 30 Oct. 1857, nos. 602–604.
18. Thompson, *Other Side of the Medal*, pp. 102–103. This conclusion is shared by Forrest and Malleson. See discussion in S. B. Chaudhuri, *English Writings on the Mutiny*, pp. 165–166, 183–184.
19. Browne, Deputy Commander, Agra Fort, to Thornhill, Secretary to Govt., Northwest Provinces, 19 Sept. 1857, in IOL, "Mutiny and Rebellion at Jhansie"; IOL, L/MIL/3/630.
20. IOL, Pinkney, "Narrative," pp. 912–914.
21. See Ball, *History of the Indian Mutiny*, 1:274–290.
22. This possibility is also suggested by Majumdar, *Sepoy Rebellion*, pp. 140–145.
23. Ibid.
24. S. Sen, *Eighteen Fifty-Seven*, pp. 401–402.
25. Savarkar, *Indian War of Independence*, p. 239.
26. Kaur, *Women in the Freedom Movement*, pp. 59–60.
27. IOL, Foreign Political Supplements, proceeding no. 280, 30 Dec. 1859.
28. E. G. Tambe, conversations with author, Nagpur, 7–9 Mar. 1983. In Jhansi it is said that Moropant was more concerned with his wealth than with British rule and became involved in events simply through force of circumstance.
29. Forrest, *Selections* 4:xi.
30. Kaye, *Sepoy War* 3:369.
31. Majumdar, *Sepoy Mutiny*, pp. 284–287.
32. Forrest, *Selections* 4:lxix. Majumdar, *Sepoy Mutiny*, pp. 289–291.

Chapter 6

1. Tahmankar, *The Ranee of Jhansi*, pp. 89–90.
2. This information on the generals and army of the Rani is derived from

extensive conversations with Gwalior historian Hari Har Nivas Dvivedi, who translated for the author an article he wrote on the subject. His article is based on a ballad on the battles of the Rani by a contemporary poet, Kalyan Singh Kudara, who was also an employee of the raja of Datia. Dvivedi also relied on childhood memories of stories told him by an old Pathan of Rahatgarh, Rahim Khan, who claimed his father had fought for the Rani. Dvivedi's concern for the history of the Rani's battles derives from these childhood associations and memories. Valuable conversations were also held with Arthur Hughes, co-author with Dvivedi of a history of Gwalior. The author is greatly indebted to both these historians for information on the history of Bundelkhand and of Gwalior in particular.

3. From Dvivedi's article on the Kalyan Singh ballad.

4. By putting a bangle on the wrist of a male friend the woman creates a ritual relationship with him. He becomes a brother to her and is obliged to carry out her requests and see to her needs in times of difficulty. This custom continues in India today.

5. Atkinson, *Account of the North-Western Provinces*, pp. 299–300. E. B. Joshi, *Uttar Pradesh District Gazeteers*, p. 59.

6. On 12 Feb. 1983 a large surrender ceremony was held in which Phoolan Devi, a notorious "dacoit queen," and her gang surrendered to the chief minister of M.P. near Gwalior.

7. Burne, *Clyde and Strathnairn*, p. 105.

8. Smyth, *Rebellious Rani*, pp. 26–30.

9. Rani to Hamilton, 1 Jan. 1858, NAI, Foreign Dept. Supplements, 30 Dec. 1859, no. 266.

10. Ibid., no. 268.

11. Hamilton to Edmonstone, Secretary to the Govt. of India, NAI, Secret Consultations, 30 Apr. 1858, nos. 144–147. Burne claims the Rani had thirty to forty guns (*Clyde and Strathnairn*, pp. 109–110).

12. NAI, Foreign Dept. Supplements, 30 Dec. 1859, no. 265.

13. Abstract of Intelligence, Datia, 13 Feb. 1857, in Rizvi and Bhargava, *Freedom Struggle* 3:224.

14. Rizvi and Bhargava, *Freedom Struggle* 3:292; Abstract of Intelligence, NAI, Secret Consultations, 23 Mar. 1858, nos. 146–147.

15. IOL, Foreign Political Supplements, 16 Mar. 1858, no. 1765, 30 Dec. 1859.

16. Abstract of Intelligence, NAI, Secret Consultations, 30 Apr. 1858, nos. 146–147; Rizvi and Bhargava, *Freedom Struggle* 3:292.

17. Abstract of Intelligence, NAI, Secret Consultations, 23 Mar. 1858, nos. 146–147.

18. IOL, Foreign Political Supplements, 30 Dec. 1859, no. 1765.

19. Kincaid, *Lakshmibai*, p. 102.

20. Abstract of Intelligence, NAI, Secret Consultations, 17 Mar. 1858, nos. 146–147.

21. Quoted in Rizvi and Bhargava, *Freedom Struggle* 3:225–227.

22. IOL, Elphinstone Papers.

23. BML, Rose Papers.

24. Abstract of Intelligence, NAI, Secret Consultations, 17 Mar. 1858, nos. 146–147. The number Tatya Tope actually led to Jhansi was closer to 20,000.

Chapter 7

1. Rose Letter, 14 Mar. 1858, BML, Rose Papers.

2. Smyth, *Rebellious Rani*, pp. 111–112. Malleson, *History of the Indian Mutiny*, vol. 3.

3. NAI, Foreign Consultations, 13 Aug. 1858, nos. 25/27.

4. BML, Rose Papers, Saugor, 22 Feb. 1858.

5. Smyth, *Rebellious Rani*, p. 105.

6. Rose to Whitlock, 18 Mar. 1858, BML, Rose Papers.

7. Rose report, NAI, Foreign Consultations, 13 Aug. 1858, nos. 25/27.

8. Forrest, *Indian Mutiny* 3:196.

9. Rose account in NAI, Foreign Consultations, 13 Aug. 1858, nos. 25/27; also in Forrest, *Selections* 4:40–43.

10. NAI, Foreign Consultations, 13 Aug. 1858, nos. 25/27. Forrest, *Indian Mutiny* 3:196. Malleson, *History of the Indian Mutiny* 3:159–160.

11. Forrest, *Selections* 4:44. NAI, Foreign Consultations, 13 Aug. 1858, nos. 25/27.

12. S. N. Prasad, leading military historian of India, in a conversation with the author stated that Indian forts had such formidable defenses that there was no way they could be taken by siege. The only method that had any success in the capture of a fort was by bribery, a method in fact often employed historically. Part of the Indian legend of the capture of Jhansi fort by the British includes a resort to this traditional method. It is said in Jhansi that Dulhaju, a gunner at the Orchha gate of the city, was bribed by the British and let them in through the gate.

13. Sylvester, *Campaign in Malwa and Central India*, p. 87.

14. Forrest, *Selections* 3:196.

15. Burne, *Clyde and Strathnairn*, p. 116.

16. Ibid., p. 118; and conversations with Vasant Varkhedkar of Nagpur, Mar. 1983. Varkhedkar wrote a play and novel on Tatya Tope and was a leading authority on the subject.

17. Rose Report to Colin Campbell, 6 Apr. 1858, BML, Rose Papers. Lowe,

Central India during the Rebellion, pp. 249–259. D. Pal, *Tatya Tope*, pp. 158–162.

18. Rizvi and Bhargava, *Freedom Struggle* 3:299–300.
19. Forrest, *Selections* 4:47/48.
20. Hibbert, *The Great Mutiny*, pp. 378–379.
21. Forrest, *Indian Mutiny* 3:216.
22. Sylvester, *Campaign in Malwa and Central India*, pp. 115–116.
23. NAI, Foreign Consultations, 13 Aug. 1858, no. 2517. Rose Report no. 66, BML, Rose Papers.
24. Lowe, *Central India during the Rebellion*, p. 261.
25. Burne, *Clyde and Strathnairn*, p. 123.
26. *Telegraph and Courier*, p. 73.
27. Lyster, *Memorials of an Ancient House*.
28. Kincaid, *Lakshmibai*, p. 102.
29. Smyth, *Rebellious Rani*, pp. 143–144.

Chapter 8

1. Hamilton to Edmonstone, Secretary to Govt., 5 June 1858, no. 148, and Edmonstone to Hamilton, 10 June 1858, no. 149, both in NAI, Foreign Consultations, 13 Aug. 1858.
2. NAI, Secret Consultations, 25 June 1858, nos. 82–83; ibid., 27 Apr. 1858.
3. Forrest, *Selections* 4:66.
4. Smyth, *Rebellious Rani*, p. 153; Sylvester, *Campaign in Malwa and Central India*, pp. 128–133.
5. Hilton, *The Indian Mutiny, a Centenary History*, pp. 186–188.
6. Sylvester, *Campaign in Malwa and Central India*, p. 133.
7. Forrest, *Selections* 4:70–71.
8. Burne, *Clyde and Strathnairn*, p. 130.
9. Forrest, *Selections* 4:83.
10. Ibid.
11. D. Pal, *Tatya Tope*, p. 179; Rizvi and Bhargava, *Freedom Struggle* 3:321.
12. Forrest, *Selections* 4:81.
13. Hibbert, *The Great Mutiny*, p. 383; Forrest, *Indian Mutiny* 3:239.
14. Forrest, *Selections* 4:85–86. Burne, *Clyde and Strathnairn*, pp. 130–133.
15. Forrest, *Indian Mutiny* 3:240–247.
16. Forrest, *Selections* 4:83.
17. Burne, *Clyde and Strathnairn*, pp. 133–138. Forrest, *Indian Mutiny* 3:247–249.

18. Sylvester, *Campaign in Malwa and Central India*, p. 164. Forrest, *Indian Mutiny* 3:249–251. Smyth, *Rebellious Rani*, pp. 170–171.

19. Burne, *Clyde and Strathnairn*, p. 138. Allahabad to E. A. Reade, 1858, and Edmonstone to Agra, 2 June 1858, Telegrams, originals in U.P. State Archives, Lucknow, Mutiny Records. According to V. C. Joshi, only one authentic letter from this find is extant, and there is no other genuine letter in the hand of the Rani still extant.

20. As I waited at the Kalpi bus stand for a bus to Jhansi a number of people gathered and eagerly recited poems about the Rani when they heard I was interested.

21. Burne, *Clyde and Strathnairn*, pp. 139–140.

Chapter 9

1. Quoted in Forrest, *Indian Mutiny* 3:254.
2. Hilton, *The Indian Mutiny, a Centenary History*, p. 189. Smyth, *Rebellious Rani*, p. 178.
3. BML, Rose Papers, Calpee, 25 May and 1 June 1858.
4. Ibid.
5. Ibid., 6 June 1858.
6. Ibid., 7 June 1858.
7. Ibid., 8 June 1858.
8. Ibid.
9. Raikes, *Notes on the Revolt*, pp. 164–165.
10. Smyth, *Rebellious Rani*, p. 179.
11. Ibid. Forrest, *Indian Mutiny* 3:256–266.
12. Forrest, *Indian Mutiny* 3:264–266.
13. Despatch from E. A. Reade, quoted in Rizvi and Bhargava, *Freedom Struggle* 3:431.
14. Hari Har Nivas Dvivedi, conversation with author, Gwalior, Feb. 1979. Jhansi sources have Gaus Khan killed at Jhansi.
15. BML, Rose Papers, 28 June 1858.
16. Ibid.
17. Rose Report to Chief of Staff of the Army in India, 13 Oct. 1858, Poonah, in Forrest, *Selections* 4:129–141.
18. BML, Rose Papers, 23 June 1858.
19. Ibid.
20. Ibid.
21. Forrest, *Selections* 4:148–149.
22. BML, Rose Papers, 23 June 1858.
23. Ibid., 28 June 1858.

24. Smyth, *Rebellious Rani*, p. 169.
25. D. Pal, *Tatya Tope*, pp. 189–191.
26. Sheorey, *Tatya Tope*, pp. 90–94.
27. D. Pal, *Tatya Tope*, pp. 197–198, 107–111. A. S. Misra, *Nana Sahib*, pp. 327–328, 481.
28. Ball, *History of the Indian Mutiny* 2:352.
29. IOL, Hamilton's Report, 27 Aug. 1858.
30. Quoted in Hibbert, *The Great Mutiny*, p. 385.
31. Dvivedi article (see chap. 6, n. 2); numerous oral and written poems throughout India; also Hibbert, *The Great Mutiny*, p. 385.
32. Macpherson, *Memorials of Service in India*, pp. 334–335. D. Pal, *Tatya Tope*, p. 189.
33. Duberly, *Campaigning Experiences*, pp. 144–145.
34. D. Pal, *Tatya Tope*, p. 189.
35. Sylvester, *Campaign in Malwa and Central India*, pp. 182–183.
36. Oatts, *Emperor's Chambermaids*, p. 247. Indian and English historians alike refer to English atrocities against Indian women and children, contrary to the romantic Victorian ethos and officer club tradition. Atrocities, it should be noted, were not an Indian or English monopoly during the Rebellion.
37. Sedgwick, *The Indian Mutiny of 1857*, p. 135.

Chapter 10

1. See discussion in Eliade, *Myth of the Eternal Return*, and his *Myths, Dreams and Mysteries*, pp. 34–37.
2. Eric Stokes, *The Peasant and the Raj*, p. 132.
3. Rushdie, *Midnight's Children*, p. 293.
4. Col. G. S. Dillhon, conversation with author, Jhansi, Spring 1979.
5. *Telegraph and Courier*, 3 July 1858, p. 113.
6. Roy, *The Roots of Bengali Culture*, p. 5.
7. *Hitvad* (Nagpur), 27 Nov. 1927.
8. T. N. Madan, "Death in the Family: An Essay on Hindu Attitudes to Dying" (Paper delivered at the conference on Order and Anomie in South Asian Society and Culture, Delhi, Dec. 1982). And see discussion in Murthy, *Samskara*.
9. Kumar, *Shakti Cult in Ancient India*, pp. 277–278.
10. Heimsath, *Indian Nationalism and Hindu Social Reform*, p. 95.
11. Roy, *The Roots of Bengali Culture*, pp. 4–5. Mahor, *Impact of the Freedom Struggle*, p. 74. Much of this data on Bundelkhand's oral literature is derived from a written statement provided the author by J. L. Kanchan, professor of Hindi studies at Bundelkhand College.

12. Mahor, *Impact of the Freedom Struggle*, p. 74. Much of this data on Bundelkhand's oral literature is from J. L. Kanchan.

13. Mahor, *Lakshmibai Raso* (The ballad of Lakshmibai), pp. 7–8. This ballad was written by the famous poet Madnesh about 1904. Since it could not be published during British rule, it was kept hidden. Dr. Mahor discovered it and edited and published it in 1969.

14. Mahor, *Lakshmibai Raso*, pp. 12–13; Mahor, *Impact of the Freedom Struggle*, p. 72.

15. Mahor, *Impact of the Freedom Struggle*, p. 72.

16. P. C. Joshi, "Folk Songs of 1857," in his *Rebellion in 1857, a Symposium*, p. 278.

17. Song sung for author by a Brahmin women's group, Nagpur, Mar. 1983.

18. Bhattacharya, *The Indian Mother Goddess*, pp. 63, 291.

19. Preston, *Cult of the Goddess*, p. 67.

20. See n. 17 above.

21. These excerpts are taken from peoms from Avadesh and recited by him for the author on several occasions in Jhansi, most recently in Mar. 1983. Translations are by Col. G. S. Dhillon.

22. S. P. Sen, *Dictionary of National Biography*, s.v. "Chauhan, Subhadra Kumari."

23. Translation by J. L. Kanchan.

24. C. C. Sen, *Rani of Jhansi*. Parts of the novel were translated for the author thanks to librarian R. Kumar at the National Library, Calcutta.

25. Mahor, *Impact of the Freedom Struggle*, p. 314; Bhavani Shankar, *Heroine Jhelkari of 1857 in Jhansi* (in Hindi) (Jhansi: Jhelkari Samiti 1964).

26. White, *Lachmi Bai*, pp. 1–2.

27. Rogers, *The Rani of Jhansi*, pp. 20–21.

28. Ibid.

29. Cox, *The Rani of Jhansi*.

30. See Fraser, *Flashman in the Great Game*. An article based on this novel is said to have appeared in *Playboy* magazine.

31. Selwyn, *Sergeant Verity*, p. 122.

32. This judgment was expressed to the author by Jaya Appasamy, the late art historian of the Lalit Kala Akademi, New Delhi, 1979.

33. Also the opinion of Jaya Appasamy.

Chapter 11

1. Leon-Portilla, *The Broken Spears*, pp. 115–144. Meyer and Sherman, *The Course of Mexican History*, pp. 120–137.

2. Ritter, *Shaka Zulu*, p. ix.

3. Cashman, *The Myth of Lokamanya*, p. 2.
4. Mahor, *Impact of the Freedom Struggle*, pp. 88, 433.
5. Ibid., pp. 80–92, 92–93.
6. The Ghadr party was a Sikh revolutionary group active in the United States and Canada, especially in the 1920s and 1930s.
7. Mahor, *Impact of the Freedom Struggle*, p. 239.
8. Ibid., p. 242.
9. Ibid., p. 245.
10. Ibid., pp. 242, 245–246.
11. Ibid., pp. 284–285.
12. B. Pal, *Beginnings of Freedom Movement*, p. 3. Banerjea, speech on Vernacular Press Act, Calcutta, 17 Apr. 1878, in his *Speeches and Writings*, p. 232. See also discussion in Roy, *The Roots of Bengali Culture*, pp. 80–81.
13. Vasant Rao Varkhedkar quoted Vishnu Godse's book, *My Travels* (in Hindi), in a conversation with the author in Nagpur, 6–7 Mar. 1983. He also provided at that time information on the case brought by Damodar Rao in Poone that culminated in 1898.
14. J. W. Hose, Secretary to the Govt. of U.P., to all commissioners of divisions and district officers in U.P., 5 July 1911, General Admin. Dept., Govt. of U.P., U.P. Archives, Lucknow.
15. Quoted in *Japan Times*, 18 Jan. 1980.
16. Dr. Mahor, in conversation in Jhansi with the author before his death.
17. Rau and Gayatri Devi, *The Princess Remembers*, p. 261.
18. Mahor, *Impact of the Freedom Struggle*, p. 386.

Historiographical Essay

1. English works of nonfiction include Sinha's *Rani Lakshmi Bai*, Smyth's *Rebellious Rani*, and Tahmankar's *Ranee of Jhansi*. The plays are: Cox, *The Rani of Jhansi*, and Rogers, *The Rani of Jhansi, or the Widowed Queen*. An essay also appeared in English: Kincaid, *Lakshmibai, Rani of Jhansi and other Essays*. Works of fiction in English are: White, *Lachmi Bai*, and Fraser, *Flashman in the Great Game*. (The above titles are listed in full in the bibliography.)
2. The principal works of nonfiction in Indian languages are: Hardikar, *Rani Laxmibai*, and Parasnis, *Jhansi Ki Rani Lakshmi Bai*. (See bibliography for complete listings.) There are several novels in Indian languages. The first was published in Calcutta in 1888 in Bengali by Chandi Charan Sen, *Jhansi Rani*. Another more recent novel also has been published in Bengali, Mahasveta Bhattacharya's *Jhansi Rani* (Calcutta, 1956). A drama has also been written in Bengali: Manilal Vandhopadhyay, *Jhansir Rani* (Calcutta: Sriguru Library,

1954). The most famous work of fiction is in Hindi, written by the late Jhansi author Vrindanlal Verma: *Jhansi ki Rani Lakshmibai*, 4th ed. (Jhansi: Mayur Prakashan, 1954). Verma has also written a drama, as has Jhansi poet Avadesh. Novels have also been written in Malayalam: Madhava Pannikar, *Jhansi Paniyute Atmakatha* (Trichur: Mangalodayam, 1957); and in Marathi: Prabhakara Sidore, *Jhansici Rani* (Poone: Rajahamsa Prakasana, 1954).

3. Phrase used by B. K. Misra of Jhansi in correspondence and conversation with the author.

4. This viewpoint was expressed in conversation by several residents of Jhansi.

5. Both Verma and Mahor are now dead, but the author had the privilege of meeting Mahor on two occasions and also met with Verma's second wife several times.

6. Such was the case, for example, with Surendranath Sen's *Eighteen Fifty-Seven*.

7. S. B. Chaudhuri, *Civil Rebellion*, p. 258.

8. See Savarkar, *Indian War of Independence*. The first edition appeared in 1909.

9. Fitchett, *Tale of the Great Mutiny*, p. 8.

10. Duff, *The Indian Rebellion*, p. 189.

11. S. B. Chaudhuri cites: F. Cooper, *The Crisis in the Punjab;* H. D. Robertson, *District Duties during the Revolt* (1859); M. Thornhill, *The Personal Adventures and Experiences of a Magistrate during the Indian Mutiny* (1883); and John Kaye, *A History of the Indian Mutiny* (Chaudhuri, *Civil Rebellion*, pp. 258–260).

12. See S. Sen, *Eighteen Fifty-Seven*, p. 398, and the novel by John Masters, *Nightrunners of Bengal*, for scholarly and popular accounts of the circulating chapatti phenomenon.

13. Norton, *Rebellion in India*, p. 136.

14. Chattopadhyaya, *The Sepoy Mutiny*, pp. i, ii.

15. K. L. Srivastava, "Influence of the Press."

16. See S. B. Chaudhuri, *English Writings on the Mutiny*, pp. 14–15. Chaudhuri's is one of the most valuable works on the historiography of the Rebellion. In it the author deals with various theories of the causes and character of the event. He discusses in some detail standard accounts in English such as those by Kaye, Holmes, Malleson, Majumdar, S. Sen, and Savarkar. See also his *Theories of the Indian Mutiny*. Also valuable is Janice M. Ladendorf's *Revolt in India: An Annotated Bibliography*.

17. S. B. Chaudhuri, *English Writings on the Mutiny*, pp. 18–19.

18. Ibid., p. 89.

19. S. Sen, *Eighteen Fifty-Seven*, p. 1.

20. Stokes, "Traditional Resistance Movements."

21. S. B. Chaudhuri, *English Writings on the Mutiny*, pp. 10–11.

22. Brig. Gen. John Jacob, *The Views and Opinions of Brigadier General John Jacob* (London: Smith, Elder, 1858), pp. 419.

23. Campbell, *Memoirs of my Indian Career* 1:212.

24. Majumdar, *Sepoy Mutiny*, pp. ii, iii.

25. Ibid., p. 474.

26. Ibid., pp. iv, v.

27. Ibid., p. 411.

28. Mukherjee and Mukherjee, *Growth of Nationalism in India*, p. 35. It is with this assessment that the author is most inclined to agree.

29. In this category should be included Gillean, or Maj. J. E. Maclean, *The Rani, a Legend of the Indian Mutiny* (London: Gustavus Cohen, 1887). See discussion in the well-documented study by Shailendra Dhari Singh, *Novels on the Indian Mutiny*, pp. 164–166.

30. See Fraser, *Flashman in the Great Game*, Masters, *Nightrunners of Bengal*, and M. M. Kaye, *Shadow of the Moon* (London: Longmans, Green, 1957).

31. White, *Lachmi Bai*, p. 267.

Glossary

bhat Subcaste of poets.
brahmachari (*fem.* **brahmacharin**) Religious celibate.
chapattis Unleavened wheat bread, a staple of the north.
chaukidar; chowkidar Night watchman.
dacoit Armed robber, murderer.
daroga Jail warden.
durbar Public audience by ruler.
gotra Lit., cowshed; exogamous subcaste of Brahmins.
jagir Grant of land in lieu of salary by Mughal emperor.
jagirdar Holder of land grant from Mughal emperor.
mahal Palace; private residence.
nawab Muslim noble controlling an area under Mughal emperor.
peshwa Brahmin prime minister of the Maratha Empire.
purdah; pardah Lit., curtain; seclusion or cloistering of women.
rissaldar; resaldar Cavalry commander.
sannyasi (*fem.* **sannyasin**) Hindu holy man; ascetic.
sati; suttee Ritual suicide on husband's funeral pyre of a high-caste Hindu widow.
siphai (*Eng.* **Sepoy**) Soldier.
sowar Cavalryman.
subahdar Governor in charge of a subah, or province, in the Mughal Empire.
tehsildar; tehseeldar Revenue collector.
thugi; thuggee Murder and robbery of travelers as a form of worship of the Hindu goddess Kali.
tulwar; talwar Sword.
valayati Pathan (Afghan) mercenary who fought in Indian armies.
zenana Harem; women's quarters.

Bibliography

Unpublished Government Documents and Personal Papers

British Museum Library (BML), London. Rose Papers. XLI, Add. MSS 42812, Nov. 1857–Oct. 1859.

India Office Library (IOL), British Library, London:

William Coldstream Papers. MSS Eur 701.

Dalhousie to Wood. MSS Eur F78/18/1A.

Mountstuart Elphinstone Papers. MSS Eur F87, box 6620.

W. C. Erskine Papers. MSS D597.

E/4/831, p. 642. Rani's memorial of Aug. 1855 (Political Dept.).

F/4/—. Boards Collections (Parliamentary Board of Control).

Foreign Political Consultations. 1853, 1854, 1859.

Foreign Political Supplements. 1859.

Hamilton's Report. MSS Eur 706/1.

L/MIL/3/—. Enclosures to military letters from Bengal and India.

L/PS/—. Mutiny Series (includes Hamilton's report).

Letters from the Governor-General in Council. 1854, 1855, 1856.

"Mutiny and Rebellion at Jhansie. Misc. Regarding the Mutiny and Rebellion at Jhansee." Collection no. 69 to military letter from Bengal no. 307, 3 Dec. 1857.

"Narrative of the Mutiny of the Force at Nowgong in Bundelcund." Collection no. 73 to military letter from Bengal no. 281, 2 Nov. 1857.

P/200/64-P/201/2, P/220/34-P/220/41. Foreign Political Consultations.

Capt. J. W. Pinkney. "Narrative of Events attending the outbreak of disturbances and the restoration of authority in the Division of Jhansie, 1857–1858." 20 Nov. 1858, pp. 909–933.

Secret Consultations. 1857, 1858. Foreign Dept. (Ft. William).
John Venables Sturt Memoirs. MSS Eur C195.
Z/E/—. Files contain data on the lapse of Jhansi, claims to the area, uprising at Jhansi.
Z/P/3727. Revenue Proceedings, Northwest Provinces.
National Archives of India (NAI), New Delhi:
Despatch to the Secret Committee. No. 37, 1857. Foreign Dept. (Ft. William).
Foreign Consultations. 1854, 1858. Foreign Dept. (Ft. William).
Foreign Dept. Supplements. 1859. Political Despatches from the Court of Directors, 1854, 1855. Foreign Dept. (Ft. William).
Intelligence Reports to G. F. Edmonstone, Secretary to the Govt. of India. Nos. 32–33, 21 Mar. 1858; Nos. 41–42, 26 Mar. 1858; Nos. 57, 154, 295, and 4345, 1858. Foreign Dept. (Ft. William).
Political Consultations. 1853, 1854, 1855, 1856. Foreign Dept. (Ft. William).
Political Despatches to the Court of Directors. 1854. Foreign Dept. (Ft. William).
Political Proceedings. 1854. Foreign Dept. (Ft. William).
Ranee of Jhansee to the Agent for the Governor-General for Central India. Translation of *khareeta*. 1 June 1859.
Secret Consultations. 1856, 1857, 1858. Foreign Dept. (Ft. William).
Supplements. Nos. 264, 266, 267, and 268, 1859. Foreign Dept. (Ft. William).
Public Record Office (PRO), London. Sessional Papers. House of Commons. Vols. 30–57, 1858, 1854, 1855.

Other Sources

Aitchison, Sir Charles Umpherston. *A Collection of Treaties, Engagements and Sunuds relating to India and Neighboring Countries.* 7 vols. Calcutta: Bengal Printing Co., 1862–1865.

Andriolo, Karin R. "Myth and History: General Model and Its Application to the Bible." *American Anthropologist* 83, no. 7 (1981): 261–275.

Argyll, Duke of. *India under Dalhousie and Canning.* London: Longmans, Green, 1865.

Atkinson, Edwin T. *Statistical, Descriptive, and Historical Account of the North-Western Provinces of India.* Vol. 1, *Bundelkhand.* Allahabad: Northwest Provinces Govt. Press, 1874.

Baird, J. G. A., ed. *Private Letters of the Marquess of Dalhousie.* Edinburgh: Blackwood, 1911.

Ball, Charles. *The History of the Indian Mutiny.* 2 vols. London: London Printing and Publishing Co., 1858–1859.

Banerjea, Surendranath. *Speeches and Writings of Hon. Surendranath Banerjea Selected by Himself.* Madras: Natesan, 1878.

Bell, Maj. Evans. *The Empire in India: Letters from Madras and other places.* London: Turner, 1864.

Bhattacharya, N. N. *The Indian Mother Goddess.* Columbia, Mo.: South Asia Books, 1977.

Bird, Maj. R. Wilberforce. *The Indian Mutiny; Two Lectures.* London: Bosworth and Harrison, 1858.

Bond, Ruskin. "In Search of John Lang." *Imprint*, Apr. 1983, p. 43.

Burne, Owen Tudor. *Clyde and Strathnairn.* Oxford: Clarendon Press, 1891.

Campbell, Sir George. *Memoirs of my Indian Career.* 2 vols. London: Macmillan, 1893.

Cashman, Richard. *The Myth of the Lokamanya: Tilak and Mass Politics in Maharashtra.* Berkeley and Los Angeles: Univ. of California Press, 1975.

Chattopadhyaya, Haraprasad. *The Sepoy Mutiny, 1857: A Social Study and Analysis.* Calcutta: Bookland, 1957.

Chaudhuri, Nirad C. *The Continent of Circe.* London: Chatto and Windus, 1965.

Chaudhuri, Sashi Bhusan. *Civil Rebellion in the Indian Mutiny.* Calcutta: World Press, 1957.

———. *English Historical Writings on the Indian Mutiny, 1857–1859.* Calcutta: World Press, 1979.

———. *Theories of the Indian Mutiny, 1857–1859.* Calcutta: World Press, 1965.

Chick, N. A., comp., and David Hutchinson, ed. *Annals of the Indian Rebellion 1857–1858, Containing Narratives of the Outbreaks and Eventful Occurrences and Stories of Personal Adventures.* London: Charles Knight, 1974.

Cox, Philip. *The Rani of Jhansi: A Historical Play in Four Acts.* London: Allen and Unwin, 1933.

Dangerfield, George. *Bengal Mutiny, the Story of the Sepoy Rebellion.* London: Hutchinson, 1953.

Duberly, Mrs. Henry. *Campaigning Experiences in Rajpootana and Central India during the Suppression of the Mutiny, 1857–1858.* London: Smith, Elder, 1859.

Duff, Rev. Alexander. *The Indian Rebellion: its Causes and Results in a series of letters.* London: James Nisbet, 1858.

Durand, Henry. *Central India in 1857, Being an answer to Sir John Kaye's Criticisms on the Conduct of the late Sir Henry Durand, whilst in charge of Central India during the Mutiny.* London: Ridgeway, 1876.

Edwardes, Michael. *Battles of the Indian Mutiny*. London: Pan Books, 1963.

———. *Red Year: The Indian Rebellion of 1857*. London: Hamish Hamilton, 1973.

———. *A Season in Hell: The Defense of the Lucknow Residency*. London: Hamish Hamilton, 1973.

Eliade, Mircea. *The Myth of the Eternal Return, or Cosmos and History*. Princeton: Princeton University Press, Bollingen Series 46, 1954; Princeton: Princeton University Press, 1974.

———. *Myths, Dreams, and Mysteries: The Encounter between Contemporary Faiths and Archaic Realities*. New York: Harper Torchbook, 1960.

Erskine, Walter Coningsey. *A Chapter of the Bengal Mutiny, as seen in Central India, by one who was there in 1857–1858*. London: Blackwood, 1861.

Fitchett, N. H. *The Tale of the Great Mutiny*. London: John Murray, 1939.

Forbes-Mitchell, William. *Reminiscences of the Great Mutiny 1857–1859*. London: Macmillan, 1904.

Forrest, George W. *A History of the Indian Mutiny*. 3 vols. Edinburgh: Blackwood, 1912.

———. *Selections from the Letters, Despatches and other State Papers preserved by the Military Department of the Government of India 1857–1858*. 4 vols. Calcutta: Superintendent, Govt. Printing, India, 1912.

Fraser, George Macdonald. *Flashman in the Great Game: From the Flashman Papers 1856–1858*. London: Barrie and Jenkins, 1975.

Gilliat, Edward. *Heroes of the Indian Mutiny*. London: Seeley, 1914.

Greenberger, Allen J. *The British Image of India: A Study in the Literature of Imperialism 1880–1960*. London: Oxford University Press, 1969.

Gupta, Bhagwan Das. *Life and Times of Maharaja Chhatrasal Bundela*. New Delhi: Radiant, 1980.

Gupta, Pratul Chandra. *Nana Sahib and the Rising at Cawnpore*. Oxford: Clarendon Press, 1963.

Gupta, Sankar Sen. *Women in Indian Folklore*. Calcutta: Indian Publications, 1969.

Hardikar, Sriniwas Balajee. *Rani Laxmibai*. Delhi: National Publishing House, 1968.

Harris, John. *The Indian Mutiny*. London: Hart-Davis, MacGibbon, 1973.

Hawley, John Stratton, and Donna Marie Wulff, eds. *The Divine Consort: Radha and the Goddesses of India*. Berkeley: Religious Studies, 1982.

Heimsath, Charles H. *Indian Nationalism and Hindu Social Reform*, Princeton: Princeton University Press, 1964.

Hibbert, Christopher. *The Great Mutiny: India, 1857*. London: Penguin, 1978.

Hilton, Maj. Gen. Richard. *The Indian Mutiny, a Centenary History*. London: Hollis and Carter, 1957.

Holcomb, J. F. *Jhansi History and the Rani of Jhansi*. Madras: M. E. Press, 1904.

Holmes, T. Rice. *A History of the Indian Mutiny and of the disturbances which accompanied among the civil population*. 2d ed. London: Allen, 1904.

Hope, John. *The House of Scindia: A Sketch*. London: Longmans, Green, 1863.

Hunter, William Wilson. *Marquess of Dalhousie*. Oxford: Clarendon Press, Rulers of India series, 1890.

India. Army Headquarters, Intelligence Branch. *The Revolt in Central India*. Simla: 1908.

———. Publications Division. Ministry of Information and Broadcasting. *1857, a Pictorial Presentation*. New Delhi: 1957.

Inge, Lt. Col. D. M. *A Subaltern's Diary*. London: Rait, Henderson, 1894.

Jackson, Charles. *A Vindication of the Marquis of Dalhousie's Indian Administration*. London: Smith, Elder, 1865.

Jagan. *Jhansi Bai to Jawaharji* (The woman of Jhansi and Jawaharlal). Madras: Poornima Publishers, 1957.

Joshi, Esha Basanti. *Uttar Pradesh District Gazeteers: Jhansi*. Lucknow: Govt. of U.P., 1965.

Joshi, P. C. *Rebellion in 1857, a Symposium*. New Delhi: People's Publishing House, 1957.

Kakar, Sudhir. *The Inner World*. Delhi: Oxford University Press, 1981.

Kaur, Manmohan. *Role of Women in the Freedom Movement*. Delhi: Sterling Publishers, 1968.

Kaye, Sir John William. *A History of the Sepoy War in India*. 3 vols. London: Longmans, Green, 1896.

Keene, H. G. *Sindhia, otherwise called Madhaji Patel*. Oxford: Clarendon Press, 1916.

Kincaid, Charles A. *Lakshmibai, Rani of Jhansi and other Essays*. London, n.d. Reprinted from *Journal of the Royal Asiatic Society*, Apr. 1943.

Kopf, David. *The Brahmo Samaj and the Shaping of the Modern Indian Mind*. Princeton: Princeton University Press, 1979.

Koshambi, D. D. *Myth and Reality: Studies in the Formation of Indian Culture*. Bombay: Popular Prakashan, 1962.

Krishnan, V. S., ed. *District Gazeteers: Gwalior*. Bhopal: M.P. Govt. Central Press, 1965.

Kumar, Pushpendra. *Shakti Cult in Ancient India*. Varanasi: Bharatiya Publishing House, 1974.

Ladendorf, Janice M. *The Revolt in India 1857–1858: An Annotated Bibliography of English Language Materials*. Zug, Switzerland: Inter Documentation, 1966.

Lang, John. *Wanderings in India and other Sketches of Life in Hindostan*. London: Routledge, Warne and Routledge, 1861.

Lee-Warner, Sir William. *The Life of the Marquis of Dalhousie*. 2 vols. London: Macmillan, 1904.

Leon-Portilla, Miguel, ed. *The Broken Spears: The Aztec Account of the Conquest of Mexico*. Boston: Beacon, 1962.

Llewellyn, Alexander. *The Siege of Delhi*. London: Macdonald and Jane's, 1977.

Lowe, Thomas. *Central India During the Rebellion of 1857 and 1858, a Narrative of Operations of the British Forces*. London: Longmans, Green, 1860.

Luard, Capt. C. E. *Eastern States (Bundelkhand) Gazeteer*. Vol. 6-A. Lucknow: Newul Kishore Press, 1907.

———. *Gwalior State Gazeteer*. Vol. 1. Calcutta: Superintendent, Govt. Printing, 1908.

Lyster, Anthony Lionel. *Memorials of an Ancient House*. MSS 6702–6772. London: National Army Museum Library, n.d.

Macpherson, Samuel Charters. *Memorials of Service in India*. London: Murray, 1865.

McMunn, Sir George. *The Indian Mutiny in Perspective*. London: C. Bell and Sons, 1931.

Mahor, Bhagwan Das. *The Impact of the 1857 Freedom Struggle on Hindi Literature* (in Hindi). Ajmer: Krishna Bros., 1976.

———, ed. and trans. *Lakshmibai Raso* (The ballad of Lakshmibai). Based on the ballad by Madnesh. Jhansi: Rajiv Press, 1969.

Majumdar, R. C. *The Sepoy Mutiny and Revolt of 1857*. 2d ed. Calcutta: Mukhopadhyay, 1963.

Malleson, George B. [Col. G. B.]. *The Indian Mutiny of 1857*. London: Seeley, 1906. (Also published in 3 vols. London: Allen & Unwin, 1878, 1880.)

———. *Kaye and Malleson's History of the Indian Mutiny of 1857–1858*. 3 vols. London: Longmans, Green, 1897.

———. *The Mutiny of the Bengal Army: An Historical Narrative by one who has served under Sir Charles Napier*. London: Bosworth and Harrison, 1857.

Masters, John. *Nightrunners of Bengal*. London: Penguin, 1951.

Maude, Col. E. *Oriental Campaigns and European Furloughs: The Autobiography of a Veteran of the Indian Mutiny*. London: Fisher Unwin, 1908.

Mehta, Ashoka. *1857, the Great Rebellion*. Bombay: Hind Kitabs, 1946.

Metcalf, Thomas R. *The Aftermath of Revolt, India 1857–1870*. Princeton: Princeton University Press, 1964.

Meyer, Michael C., and William L. Sherman. *The Course of Mexican History*. New York: Oxford University Press, 1979.

Misra, Anand Swarup. *Nana Sahib Peshwa and the Fight for Freedom*. Lucknow: Govt. of U.P. Information Dept., 1961.

Mistry, Homi D. *Rebels of Destiny*. Bombay: Hind Kitabs, 1959.

Montgomery, Robert. *Statistical Report of the District of Cawnpoor*. Calcutta: Sherriff Bengal Military Orphan Press, 1849.

Mukherjee, Haridas, and Uma Mukherjee. *The Growth of Nationalism in India*. Calcutta: Presidency Library, 1957.

Nevill, H. R. *Cawnpore, a Gazeteer*. Allahabad: U.P. Govt. Press, 1909.

Nigam, N. K. *Delhi in 1857*. Delhi: S. Chand, 1957.

Norton, John Bruce. *Rebellion in India: how to Prevent Another*. London: Richardson Bros., 1857.

Oatts, Lt. Col. L. B. *Emperor's Chambermaids: The Story of the Fourteenth/Twentieth King's Hussars*. London: Ward Lock, 1973.

O'Flaherty, Wendy Doniger. *Sexual Metaphors and Animal Symbols in Indian Mythology*. Delhi: Motilal Banarsidass, 1980.

———. *Women, Androgynes, and other Mythical Beasts*. Chicago: University of Chicago Press, 1980.

Paget, Mrs. Leopold, *Camp and Cantonment, A Journal of Life in India in 1857–1859*. London: Longmans, Green, 1865.

Pal, Bipinchandra. *Beginnings of Freedom Movement in Modern India*. Calcutta: Yugayatri Prakashak, 1959.

Pal, Dharm. *Tatya Tope: The Hero of India's First War of Independence*. New Delhi: Hindustan Times, 1957.

Parasnis, D. B. *Jhansi ki Rani Lakshmi Bai* (in Hindi, trans. from original Marathi). Allahabad: Sahatya Bhavan Pvt., 1964.

Pemble, John. *The Raj, the Indian Mutiny, and the Kingdom of Oudh 1801–1859*. Sussex: Harvester Press, 1977.

Pogson, Capt. W. R. *A History of the Boondelas*. 1828. Delhi: B. R. Publishing, 1974.

Preston, James J. *Cult of the Goddess: Social and Religious Change in a Hindu Temple*. Delhi: Vikas, 1980.

Raikes, Charles. *Notes on the Revolt of the North Western Province of India*. London: Longmans, Brown, Green, 1858.

Ramanujan, A. K. *Samskara, a Rite for a Dead Man*. Translated by U. R. Anantha Murthy. Delhi: Oxford University Press, 1976.

Ramprasad, N. S. *Jhansi Lakshmi Bai*. Bangalore: Bharata-Bharati Pushtaka Sampada, 1975.

Rau, Santha Rama, and Gayatri Devi. *The Princess Remembers: The Memoirs of the Maharani of Jaipur*. New Delhi: Vikas, 1982.

Rawlinson, H. G. *History of Eighth King George V's Own Light Cavalry*. Aldershot: Gale and Polden, 1948.

Ritter, F. A. *Shaka Zulu: The Rise of the Zulu Empire*. London: Longmans, Green, 1955.

Rizvi, S. A. D., and M. L. Bhargava. *Freedom Struggle in Uttar Pradesh*. 6 vols. Lucknow: Govt. Printing, 1959.

Rogers, Alexander. *The Rani of Jhansi, or The Widowed Queen: A Drama of the Indian Mutiny*. Westminster: Constable, 1895.

Roy, Samaren. *The Roots of Bengali Culture.* Calcutta: Firma KLM, 1981.
Rushdie, Salman. *Midnight's Children.* London: Picador Pan Books, 1981.
Russell, William. *My Indian Mutiny Diary.* London: Cassell, 1857.
Sardesai, G. S. *New History of the Marathas.* 3 vols. Bombay: Phoenix, 1958.
Sareen, Tilak Raj. "Gwalior under the Mutineers." *Journal of Indian History* 43 (1965): 625–632.
Savarkar, V. D. *The Indian War of Independence.* London, 1909; Bombay: Dhawah Popular, 1947.
Scholberg, Henry. "Another Time, Another Country." Ames Library, Minneapolis. Typescript.
Sedgwick, Capt. F. R. *The Indian Mutiny of 1857: A Sketch of the Principal Military Events.* London: Forster Groom, 1920.
Selwyn, Francis. *Sergeant Verity and the Imperial Diamond.* New York: Stein and Day, 1976.
Sen, Chandi Charan. *Rani of Jhansi: A Historical Romance* (1st ed. in Bengali, 1888). Calcutta: 1894.
Sen, S. P., ed. *Dictionary of National Biography.* Calcutta: Institute of Historical Studies, 1973.
Sen, Surendranath. *Eighteen Fifty-Seven.* New Delhi: Publications Division, Govt. of India Ministry of Information and Broadcasting, 1957.
Sharma, Jagdish Saran. *The National Dictionary of India.* New Delhi: Sterling Publishers, 1972.
Shashtko, Pyotr. *Nana Sahib: An Account of the People's Revolt in India, 1857–1859.* Punne: Shubhada-Saraswat, 1980.
Sheorey, Indumati. *Tatya Tope.* New Delhi: National Book Trust, 1973.
Showers, Lt. Gen. Charles Lionel. *A Missing Chapter of the Indian Mutiny.* London: Longmans, Green, 1888.
Shrivastav, P. N., ed. *Madhya Pradesh District Gazeteers: Datia.* Bhopal: Govt. Press, 1977.
Singh, Sailendra Dhari. *Novels on the Indian Mutiny.* New Delhi: Arnold-Heinemann, 1980.
Sinha, Shyam Narain. *Rani Lakshmi Bai of Jhansi.* Allahabad: Chugh, 1980.
Sitarama. *From Sepoy to Subadar, being the Life and Adventures of a Native Officer of the Bengal Army.* London: Victoria Press, 1873.
Sleeman, William. *Iconoclastes on the Princes and Territorial Chiefs of India.* Cheltenham, 1853.
Smyth, Sir John. *The Rebellious Rani.* London: Muller, 1966.
Srivastava, Ashirbadi Lal. *Shuja-ud-daula.* Vol. 1, 1754–1765. Agra: Agarwala, 1961.
Srivastava, K. L. "Influence of the Press on the Outbreak of the Mutiny Especially in Central India—Malwa." *Indian Historical Records Commission Proceedings* 19 (1943): 156–158.

Srivastava, Kushhalal. *The Revolt of 1857 in Central India and Malwa*. Bombay: Allied Publishers, 1966.

Stokes, Eric. *The Peasant and the Raj: Studies in Agrarian Society and Peasant Rebellion in Colonial India*. Delhi: Vikas, 1981.

———. "Traditional Resistance Movements and Afro-Asian Nationalism: The Context of the 1857 Mutiny Rebellion in India." *Past and Present*, no. 48 (1970), pp. 100–118.

Sylvester, Asst. Surgeon John Henry. *Recollections of the Campaign in Malwa and Central India under Major General Sir Hugh Rose*. Bombay: Smith, Taylor, 1860.

Tahmankar, D. V. *The Ranee of Jhansi*. Bombay: Jaico, 1960.

Taimuri, H. M. "Some Unpublished Documents on the Death of the Rani of Jhansi." *Indian Historical Records Commission Proceedings* 29, no. 2 (1953): 157–159.

Telegraph and Courier. Overland Summary (Bombay). Apr. 1853–July 1858.

Thompson, Edward. *The Other Side of the Medal*. London: Leonard and Virginia Woolf at the Hogarth Press, 1926.

Thornhill, Mark. *The Personal Adventures and Experiences of a Magistrate during the Rise, Progress and Suppression of the Indian Mutiny*. London: Murray, 1884.

Thornton, James Howard. *Memories of Seven Campaigns: A Record of Thirty-Five Years' Service in the Indian Medical Department in India, China, Egypt and the Sudan*. Westminster: Constable, 1895.

Trevelyan, Sir George. *Cawnpore*. London: Macmillan, 1894.

Warner, Marina. *Joan of Arc: The Image of Female Heroism*. New York: Knopf, 1981.

White, Michael. *Lachmi Bai, Rani of Jhansi: The Jeanne D'Arc of India*. New York: J. F. Taylor, 1901.

Index

About the Author

Joyce Lebra-Chapman holds a doctorate from Harvard University and is professor of Japanese and Indian history at the University of Colorado. She has taught and lectured throughout the world and has led three research teams to Japan, India, and Southeast Asia to study women in the work force. Professor Lebra-Chapman has published numerous articles and is the author or editor of eight books, including *Jungle Alliance: Japan and the Indian National Army, Chinese Women in Southeast Asia,* and *Women and Work in India.* Her study of the Rani of Jhansi is the outgrowth of her earlier research in military and women's history and her close association with the scholars, poets, and people of India.